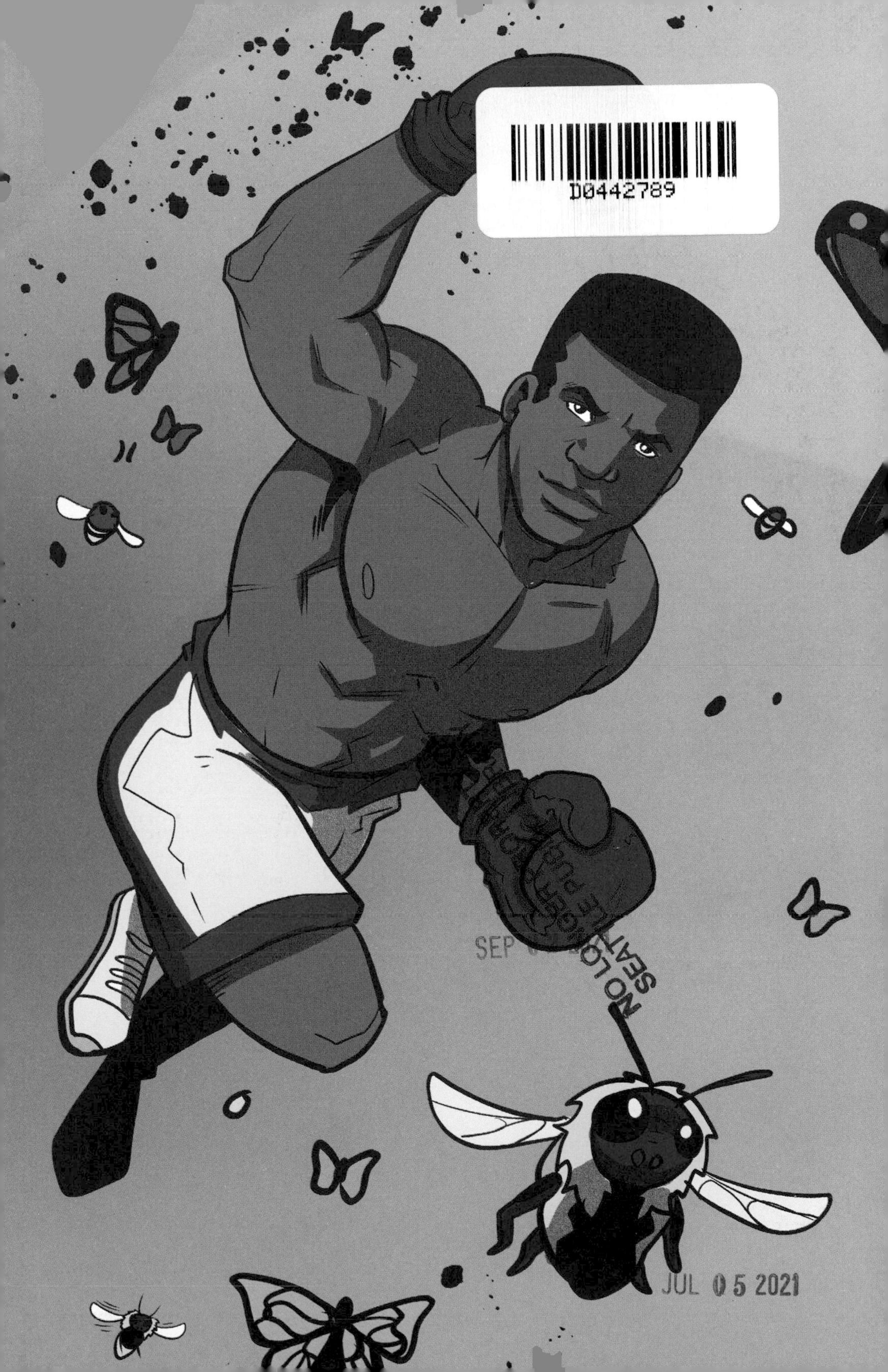

SHOW ME HISTORY! ™

MUHAMMAD ALI

The GREATEST of ALL TIME!

BY
JAMES BUCKLEY JR.

ILLUSTRATED BY
ANDY DUGGAN

LETTERING & DESIGN BY
SWELL TYPE

COVER ART BY
DERRICK DEVOE

PORTABLE
PRESS

SAN DIEGO, CALIFORNIA

Portable Press
An imprint of Printers Row Publishing Group
10350 Barnes Canyon Road, Suite 100, San Diego, CA 92121
www.portablepress.com • mail@portablepress.com

Song lyrics on page 17 from "A White Man's Heaven in the Black Man's Hell," Louis X, vocalist. Recorded 1960, Muhammad's Mosque No. 32.

Correspondence regarding the content of this book should be sent to Portable Press, Editorial Department, at the above address. Author and illustrator inquiries should be sent to Oomf, Inc., www.oomf.com.

Portable Press
Publisher: Peter Norton • Associate Publisher: Ana Parker
Developmental Editor: Vicki Jaeger
Editor: Stephanie Romero Gamboa
Production Team: Jonathan Lopes, Rusty von Dyl, Julie Greene

Produced by Oomf, Inc., www.Oomf.com
Director: Mark Shulman
Producer: James Buckley Jr.

Author: James Buckley Jr.
Illustrator: Andy Duggan
Colorist: Shane Corn
Lettering & Design by Swell Type: John Roshell and Forest Dempsey
Cover illustrator: Derrick DeVoe

Library of Congress Cataloging-in-Publication Data

Names: Buckley, James, Jr., 1963- author. | Duggan, Andy, illustrator. | Roshell, John, letterer, designer. | DeVoe, Derrick, cover artist. | Portable Press (San Diego, Calif.)
Title: Muhammad Ali : the greatest of all time! / by James Buckley Jr. ; illustrated by Andy Duggan ; lettering by John Roshell ; cover art by Derrick DeVoe.
Other titles: Show me history!
Description: San Diego, California : Printers Row Publishing Group | Portable Press, 2020. | Series: Show me history! | Audience: Ages 8 to 12 years | Audience: Grades 4-6 | Summary: "This graphic novel follows the life of Muhammad Ali as he became a world heavyweight boxing champion, activist, and philanthropist"-- Provided by publisher.
Identifiers: LCCN 2020000197 | ISBN 9781645174134 (Hardcover) | ISBN 9781645175247 (eBook)
Subjects: LCSH: Ali, Muhammad, 1942-2016--Juvenile literature. | African American boxers--Biography--Juvenile literature. | Boxers (Sports)--United States--Biography--Juvenile literature. | African American athletes--Biography--Juvenile literature. | Political activists--United States--Biography--Juvenile literature.
Classification: LCC GV1132.A44 B834 2020 | DDC 796.83092 [B]--dc23
LC record available at https://lccn.loc.gov/2020000197

Printed in China

24 23 22 21 20   1 2 3 4 5

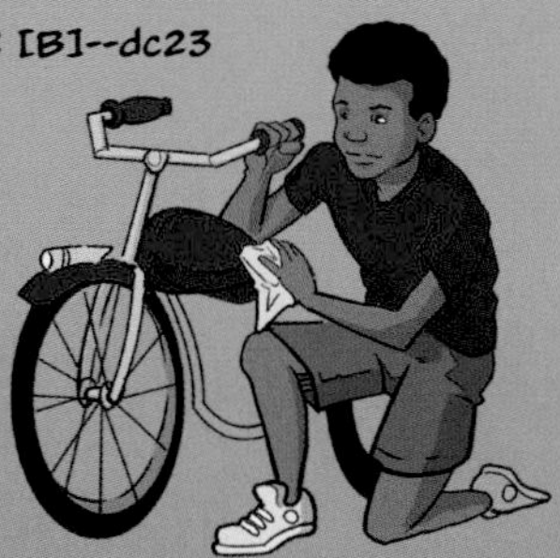

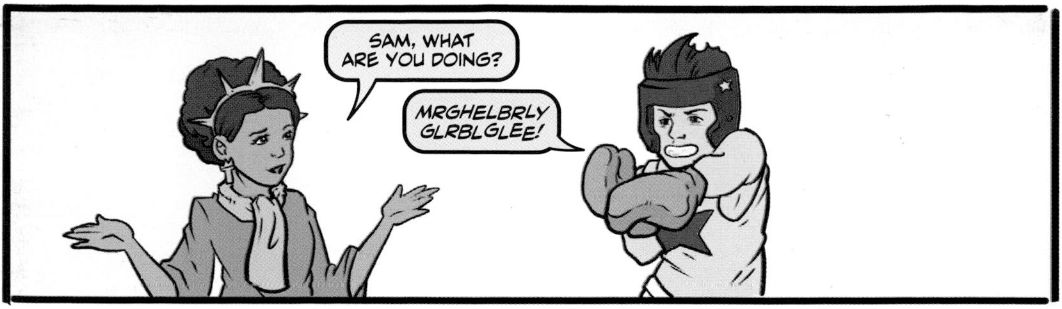
SAM, WHAT ARE YOU DOING?
MRGHELBRLY GLRBLGLEE!

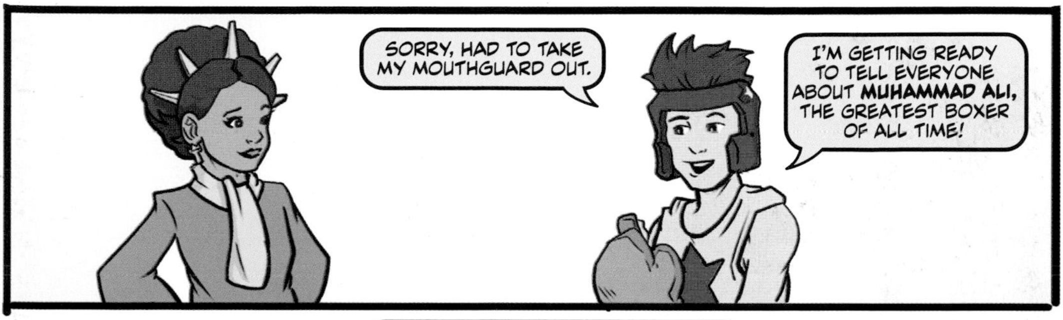
SORRY, HAD TO TAKE MY MOUTHGUARD OUT.
I'M GETTING READY TO TELL EVERYONE ABOUT **MUHAMMAD ALI,** THE GREATEST BOXER OF ALL TIME!

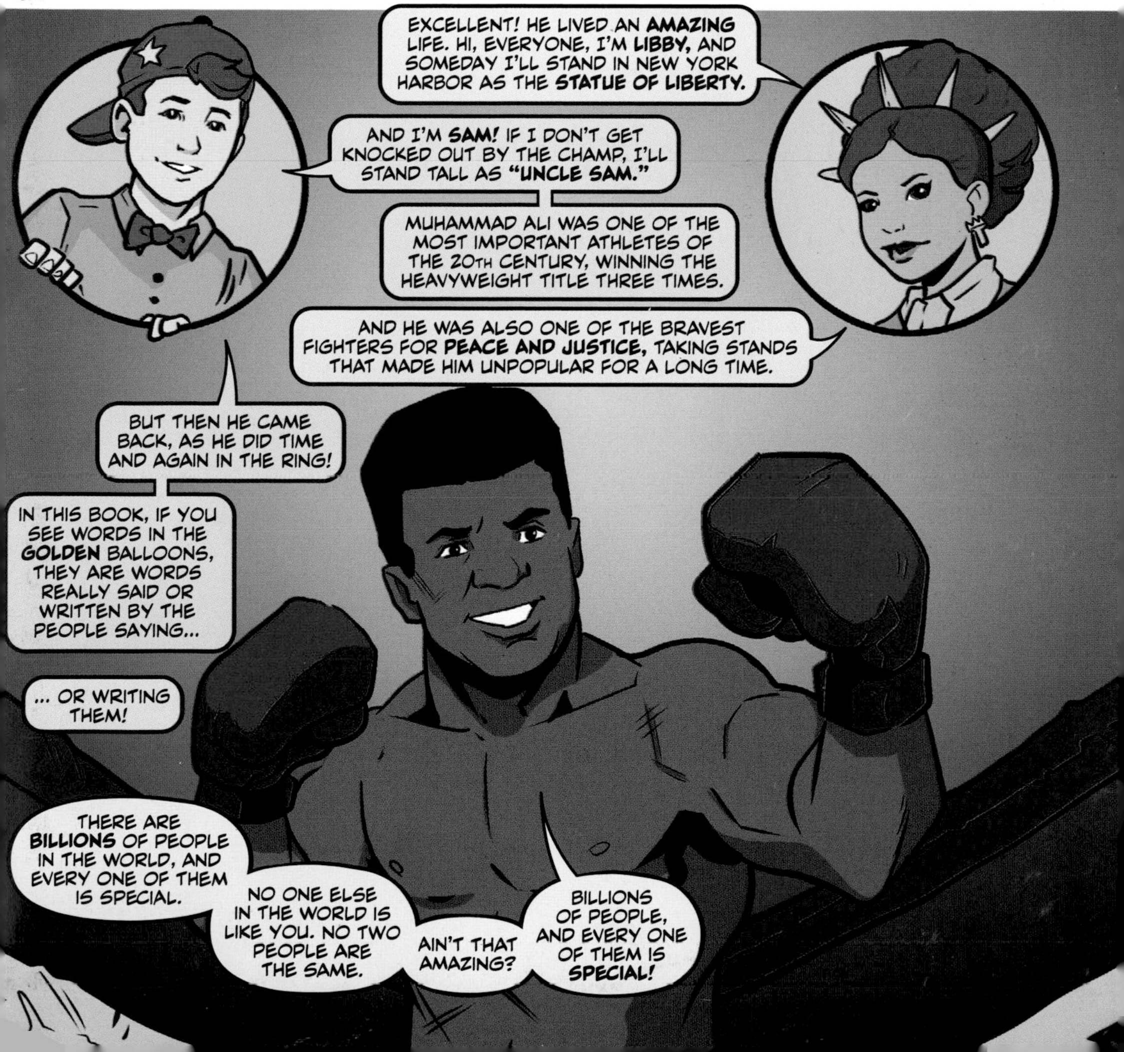
EXCELLENT! HE LIVED AN **AMAZING** LIFE. HI, EVERYONE, I'M **LIBBY,** AND SOMEDAY I'LL STAND IN NEW YORK HARBOR AS THE **STATUE OF LIBERTY.**
AND I'M **SAM!** IF I DON'T GET KNOCKED OUT BY THE CHAMP, I'LL STAND TALL AS **"UNCLE SAM."**
MUHAMMAD ALI WAS ONE OF THE MOST IMPORTANT ATHLETES OF THE 20TH CENTURY, WINNING THE HEAVYWEIGHT TITLE THREE TIMES.
AND HE WAS ALSO ONE OF THE BRAVEST FIGHTERS FOR **PEACE AND JUSTICE,** TAKING STANDS THAT MADE HIM UNPOPULAR FOR A LONG TIME.
BUT THEN HE CAME BACK, AS HE DID TIME AND AGAIN IN THE RING!
IN THIS BOOK, IF YOU SEE WORDS IN THE **GOLDEN** BALLOONS, THEY ARE WORDS REALLY SAID OR WRITTEN BY THE PEOPLE SAYING...
... OR WRITING THEM!
THERE ARE **BILLIONS** OF PEOPLE IN THE WORLD, AND EVERY ONE OF THEM IS SPECIAL.
NO ONE ELSE IN THE WORLD IS LIKE YOU. NO TWO PEOPLE ARE THE SAME.
AIN'T THAT AMAZING?
BILLIONS OF PEOPLE, AND EVERY ONE OF THEM IS **SPECIAL!**

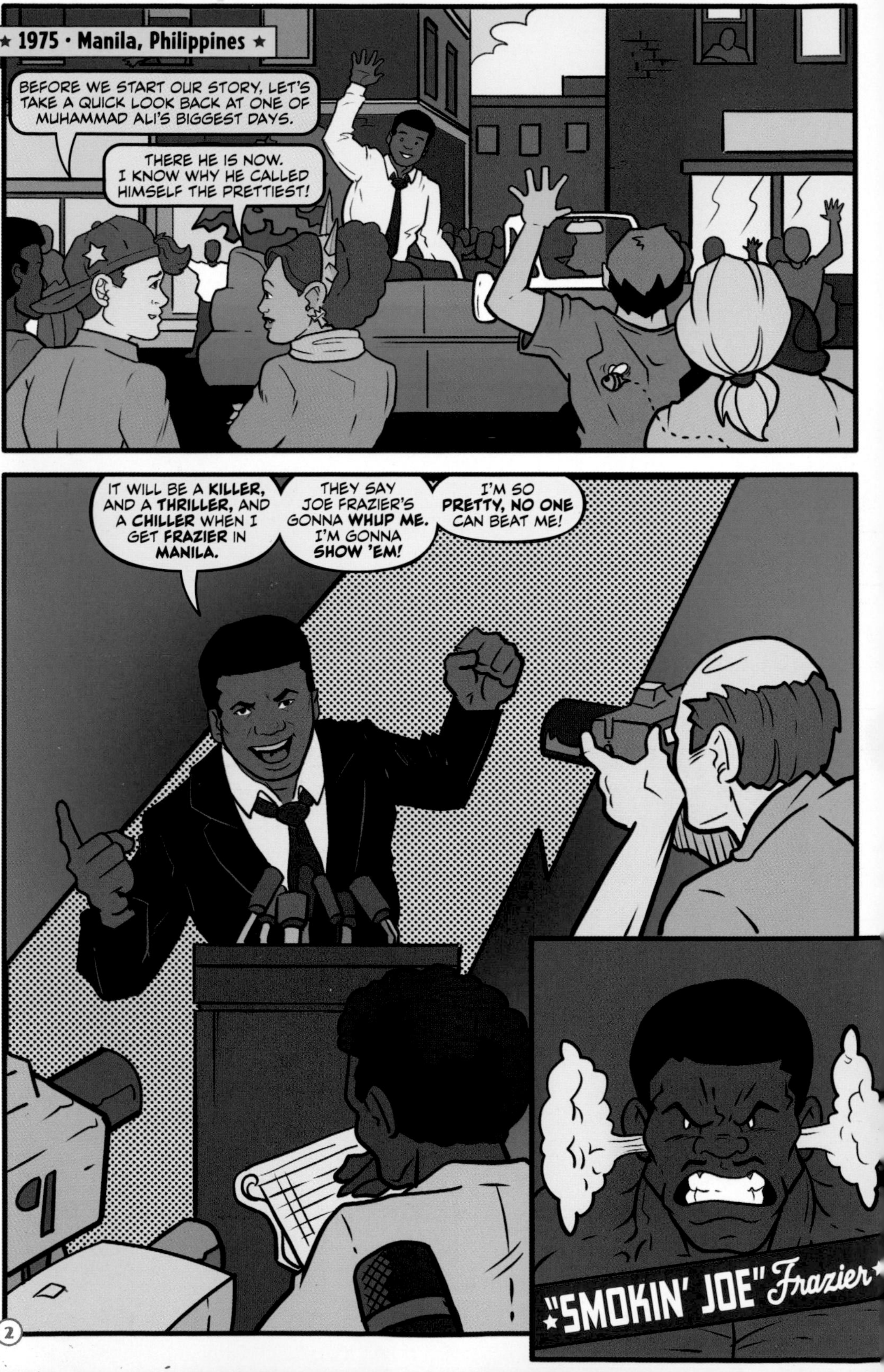
★ 1975 • Manila, Philippines ★
BEFORE WE START OUR STORY, LET'S TAKE A QUICK LOOK BACK AT ONE OF MUHAMMAD ALI'S BIGGEST DAYS.
THERE HE IS NOW. I KNOW WHY HE CALLED HIMSELF THE PRETTIEST!
IT WILL BE A KILLER, AND A THRILLER, AND A CHILLER WHEN I GET FRAZIER IN MANILA.
THEY SAY JOE FRAZIER'S GONNA WHUP ME. I'M GONNA SHOW 'EM!
I'M SO PRETTY, NO ONE CAN BEAT ME!
★ "SMOKIN' JOE" Frazier ★

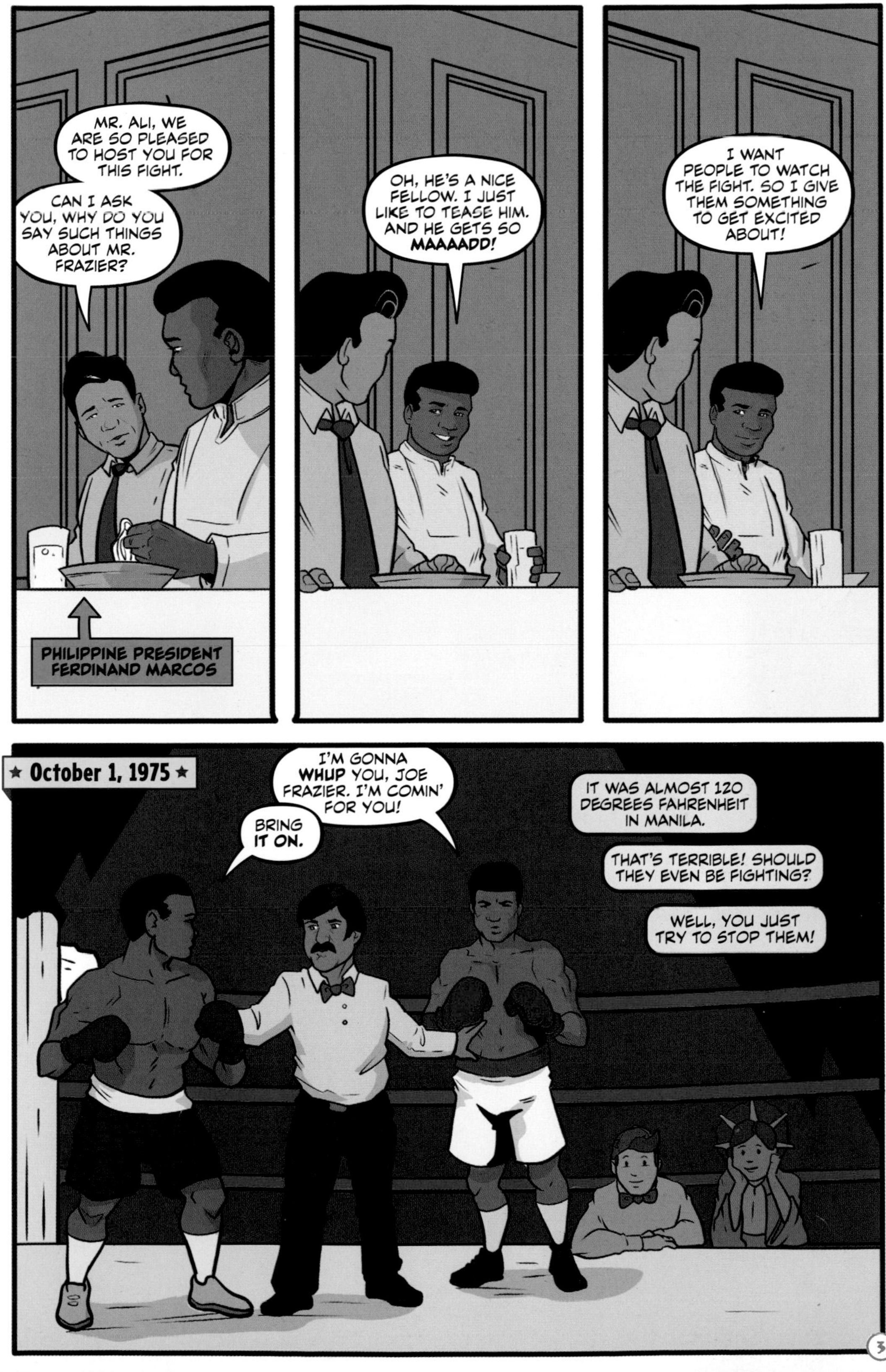

MR. ALI, WE ARE SO PLEASED TO HOST YOU FOR THIS FIGHT.
CAN I ASK YOU, WHY DO YOU SAY SUCH THINGS ABOUT MR. FRAZIER?
PHILIPPINE PRESIDENT FERDINAND MARCOS
OH, HE'S A NICE FELLOW. I JUST LIKE TO TEASE HIM. AND HE GETS SO MAAAADD!
I WANT PEOPLE TO WATCH THE FIGHT. SO I GIVE THEM SOMETHING TO GET EXCITED ABOUT!
October 1, 1975
I'M GONNA WHUP YOU, JOE FRAZIER. I'M COMIN' FOR YOU!
BRING IT ON.
IT WAS ALMOST 120 DEGREES FAHRENHEIT IN MANILA.
THAT'S TERRIBLE! SHOULD THEY EVEN BE FIGHTING?
WELL, YOU JUST TRY TO STOP THEM!

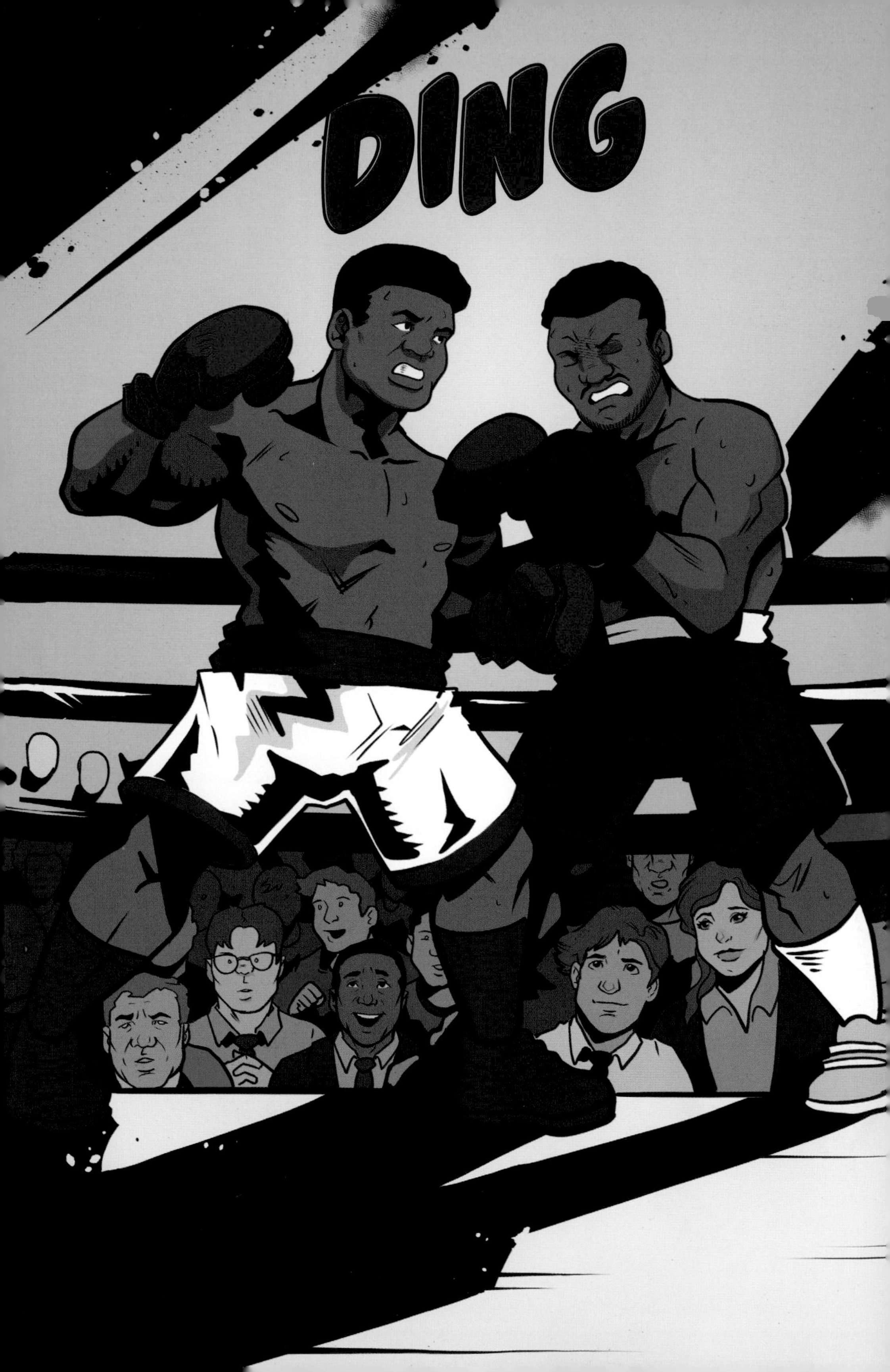
DING

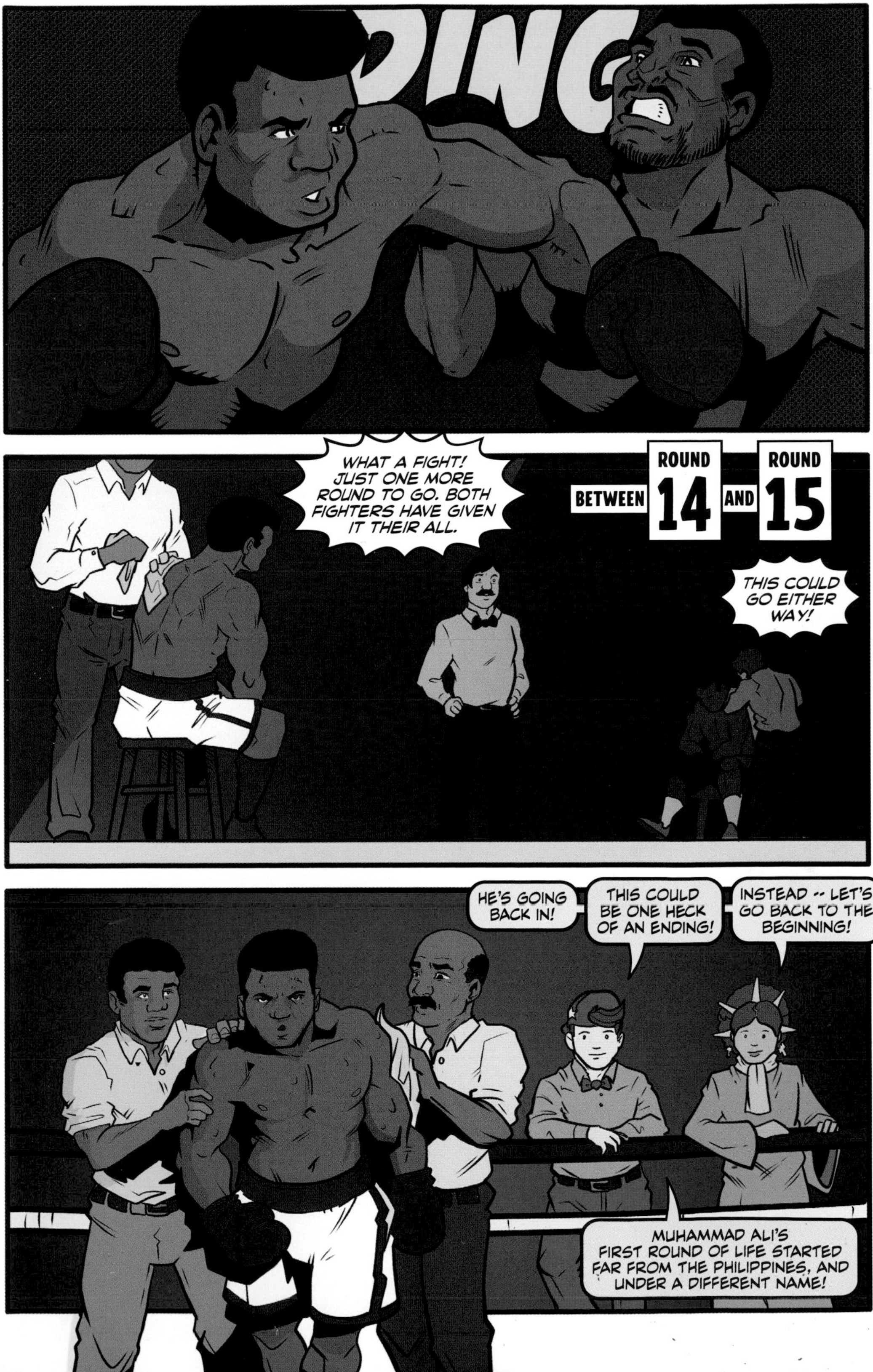
DING
WHAT A FIGHT! JUST ONE MORE ROUND TO GO. BOTH FIGHTERS HAVE GIVEN IT THEIR ALL.
BETWEEN ROUND 14 AND ROUND 15
THIS COULD GO EITHER WAY!
HE'S GOING BACK IN!
THIS COULD BE ONE HECK OF AN ENDING!
INSTEAD -- LET'S GO BACK TO THE BEGINNING!
MUHAMMAD ALI'S FIRST ROUND OF LIFE STARTED FAR FROM THE PHILIPPINES, AND UNDER A DIFFERENT NAME!

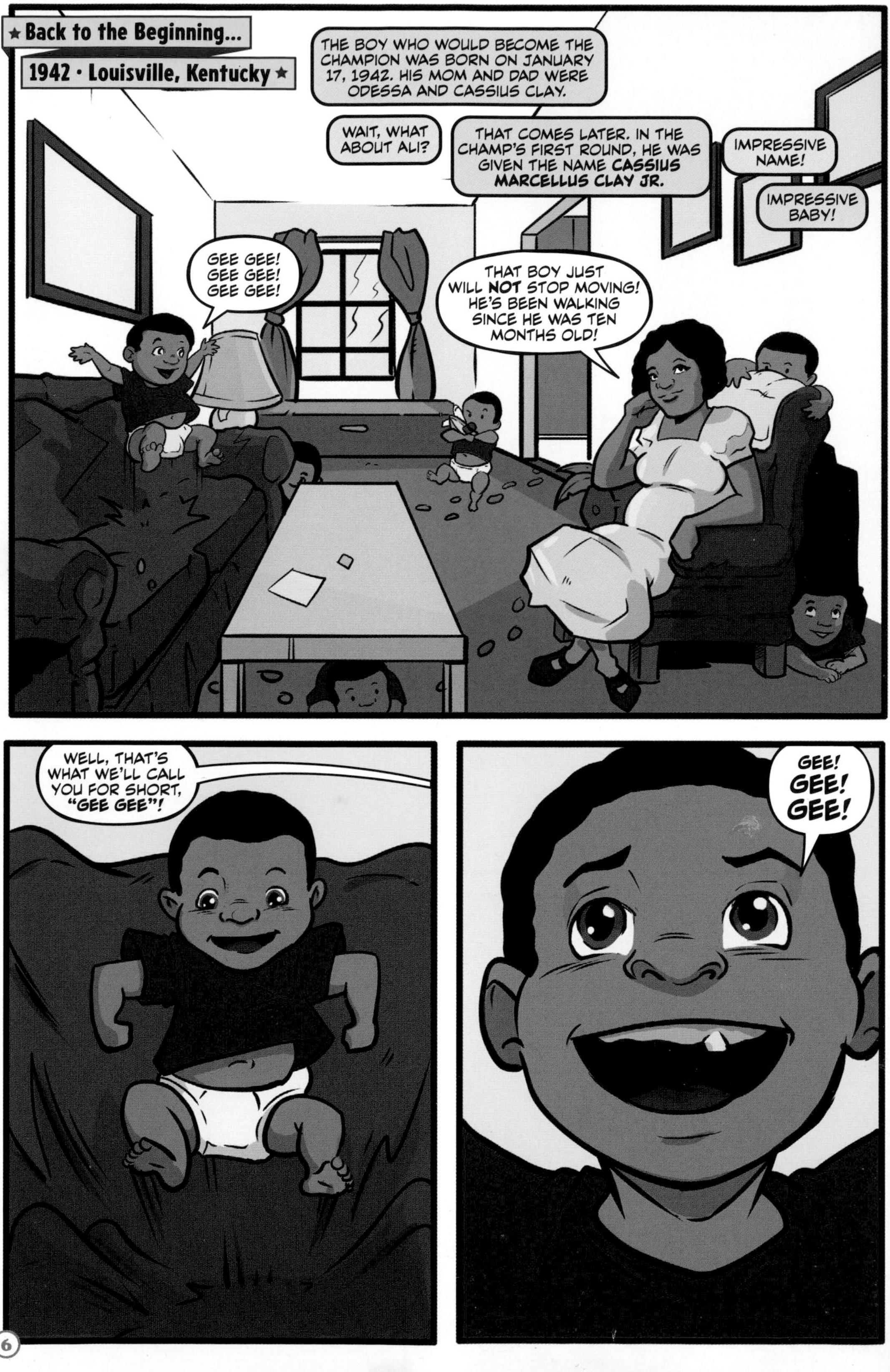
★ Back to the Beginning...
1942 • Louisville, Kentucky ★
THE BOY WHO WOULD BECOME THE CHAMPION WAS BORN ON JANUARY 17, 1942. HIS MOM AND DAD WERE ODESSA AND CASSIUS CLAY.
WAIT, WHAT ABOUT ALI?
THAT COMES LATER. IN THE CHAMP'S FIRST ROUND, HE WAS GIVEN THE NAME **CASSIUS MARCELLUS CLAY JR.**
IMPRESSIVE NAME!
IMPRESSIVE BABY!
GEE GEE! GEE GEE! GEE GEE!
THAT BOY JUST WILL **NOT** STOP MOVING! HE'S BEEN WALKING SINCE HE WAS TEN MONTHS OLD!
WELL, THAT'S WHAT WE'LL CALL YOU FOR SHORT, **"GEE GEE"**!
GEE! **GEE! GEE!**

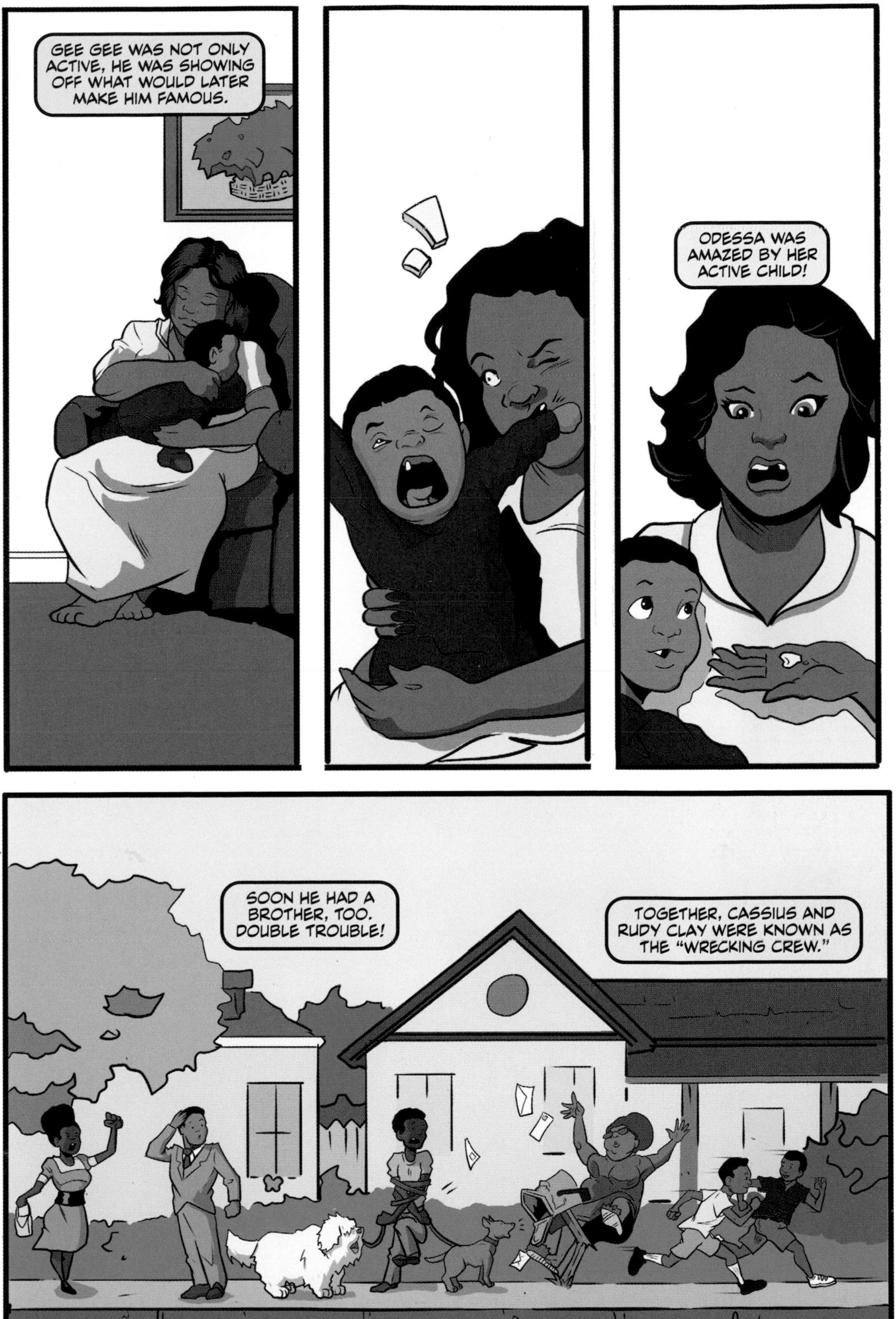
GEE GEE WAS NOT ONLY ACTIVE, HE WAS SHOWING OFF WHAT WOULD LATER MAKE HIM FAMOUS.
ODESSA WAS AMAZED BY HER ACTIVE CHILD!
SOON HE HAD A BROTHER, TOO. DOUBLE TROUBLE!
TOGETHER, CASSIUS AND RUDY CLAY WERE KNOWN AS THE "WRECKING CREW."

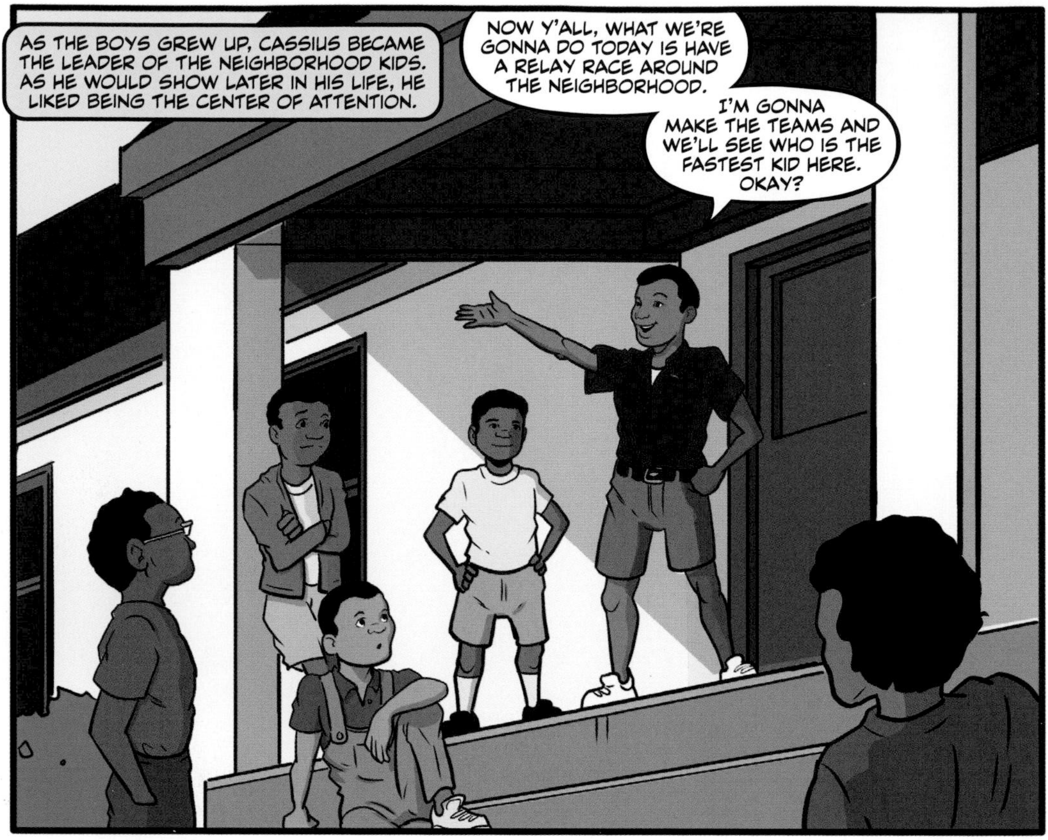
AS THE BOYS GREW UP, CASSIUS BECAME THE LEADER OF THE NEIGHBORHOOD KIDS. AS HE WOULD SHOW LATER IN HIS LIFE, HE LIKED BEING THE CENTER OF ATTENTION.
NOW Y'ALL, WHAT WE'RE GONNA DO TODAY IS HAVE A RELAY RACE AROUND THE NEIGHBORHOOD.
I'M GONNA MAKE THE TEAMS AND WE'LL SEE WHO IS THE FASTEST KID HERE. OKAY?

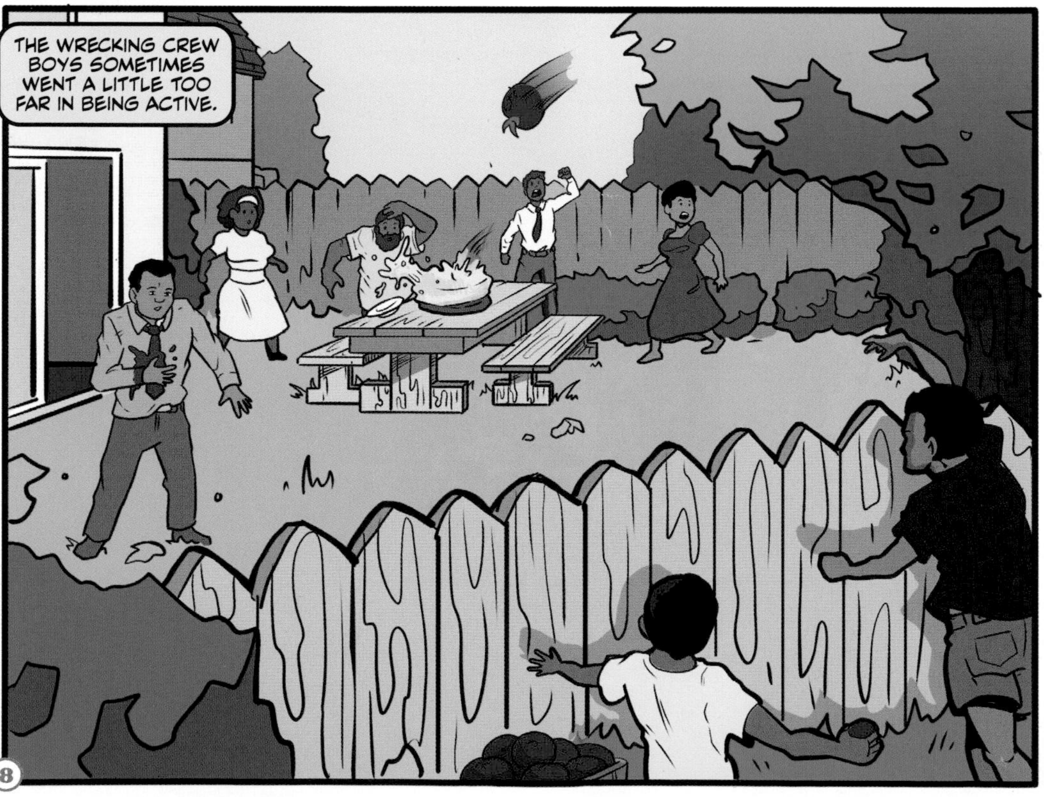
THE WRECKING CREW BOYS SOMETIMES WENT A LITTLE TOO FAR IN BEING ACTIVE.

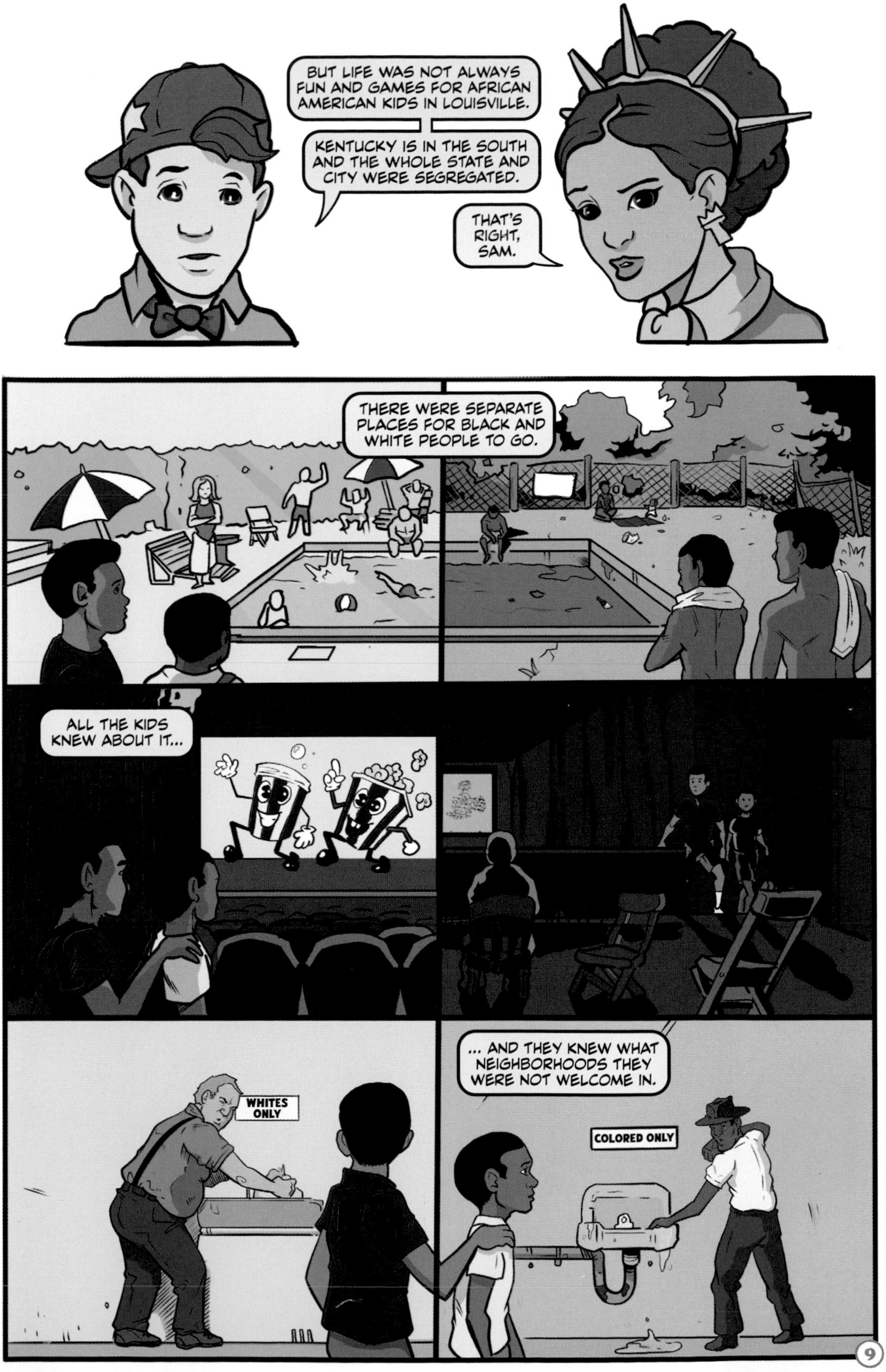
BUT LIFE WAS NOT ALWAYS FUN AND GAMES FOR AFRICAN AMERICAN KIDS IN LOUISVILLE.
KENTUCKY IS IN THE SOUTH AND THE WHOLE STATE AND CITY WERE SEGREGATED.
THAT'S RIGHT, SAM.
THERE WERE SEPARATE PLACES FOR BLACK AND WHITE PEOPLE TO GO.
ALL THE KIDS KNEW ABOUT IT...
WHITES ONLY
... AND THEY KNEW WHAT NEIGHBORHOODS THEY WERE NOT WELCOME IN.
COLORED ONLY

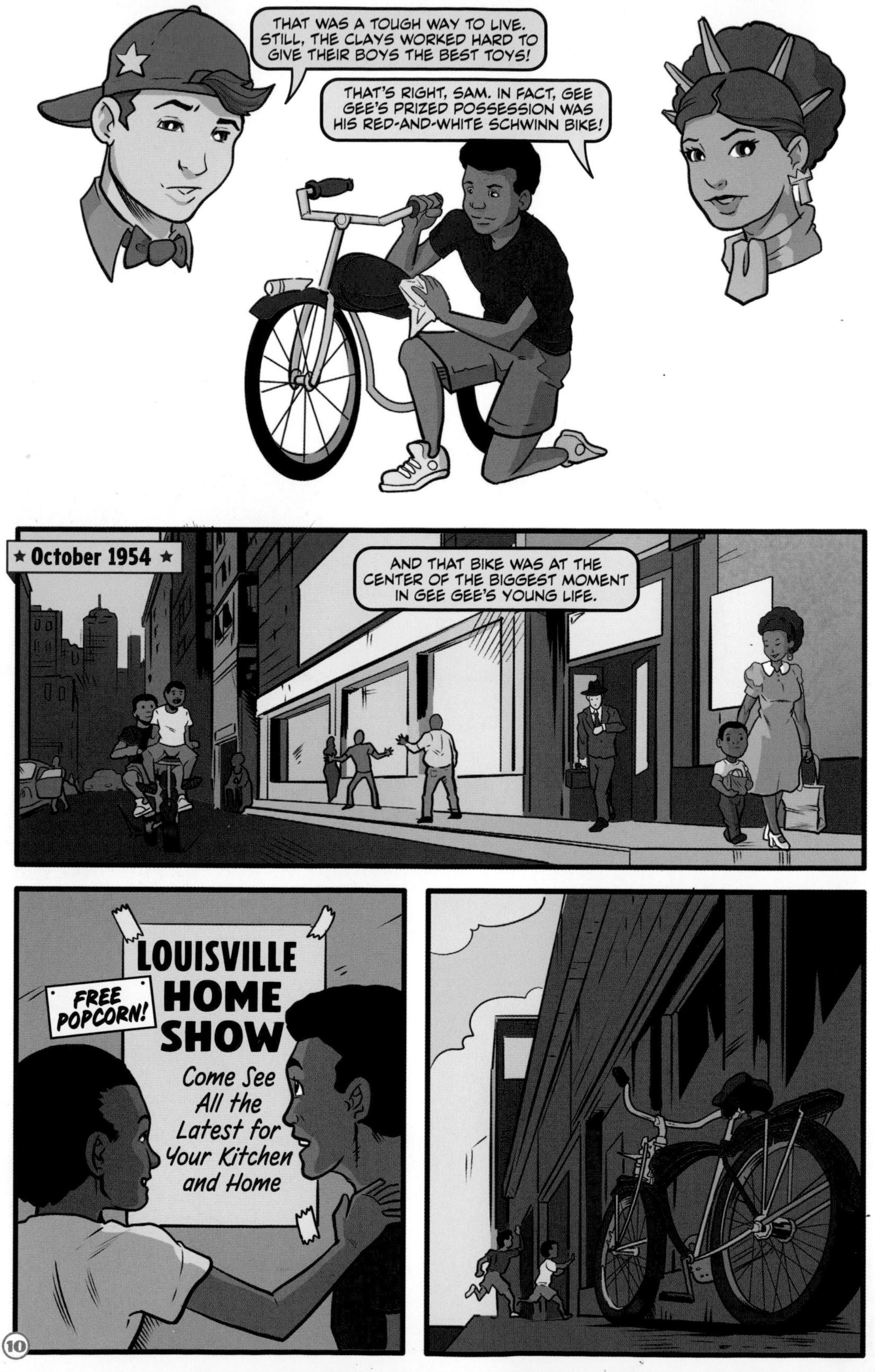
THAT WAS A TOUGH WAY TO LIVE. STILL, THE CLAYS WORKED HARD TO GIVE THEIR BOYS THE BEST TOYS!
THAT'S RIGHT, SAM. IN FACT, GEE GEE'S PRIZED POSSESSION WAS HIS RED-AND-WHITE SCHWINN BIKE!
October 1954
AND THAT BIKE WAS AT THE CENTER OF THE BIGGEST MOMENT IN GEE GEE'S YOUNG LIFE.
LOUISVILLE HOME SHOW
FREE POPCORN!
Come See All the Latest for Your Kitchen and Home

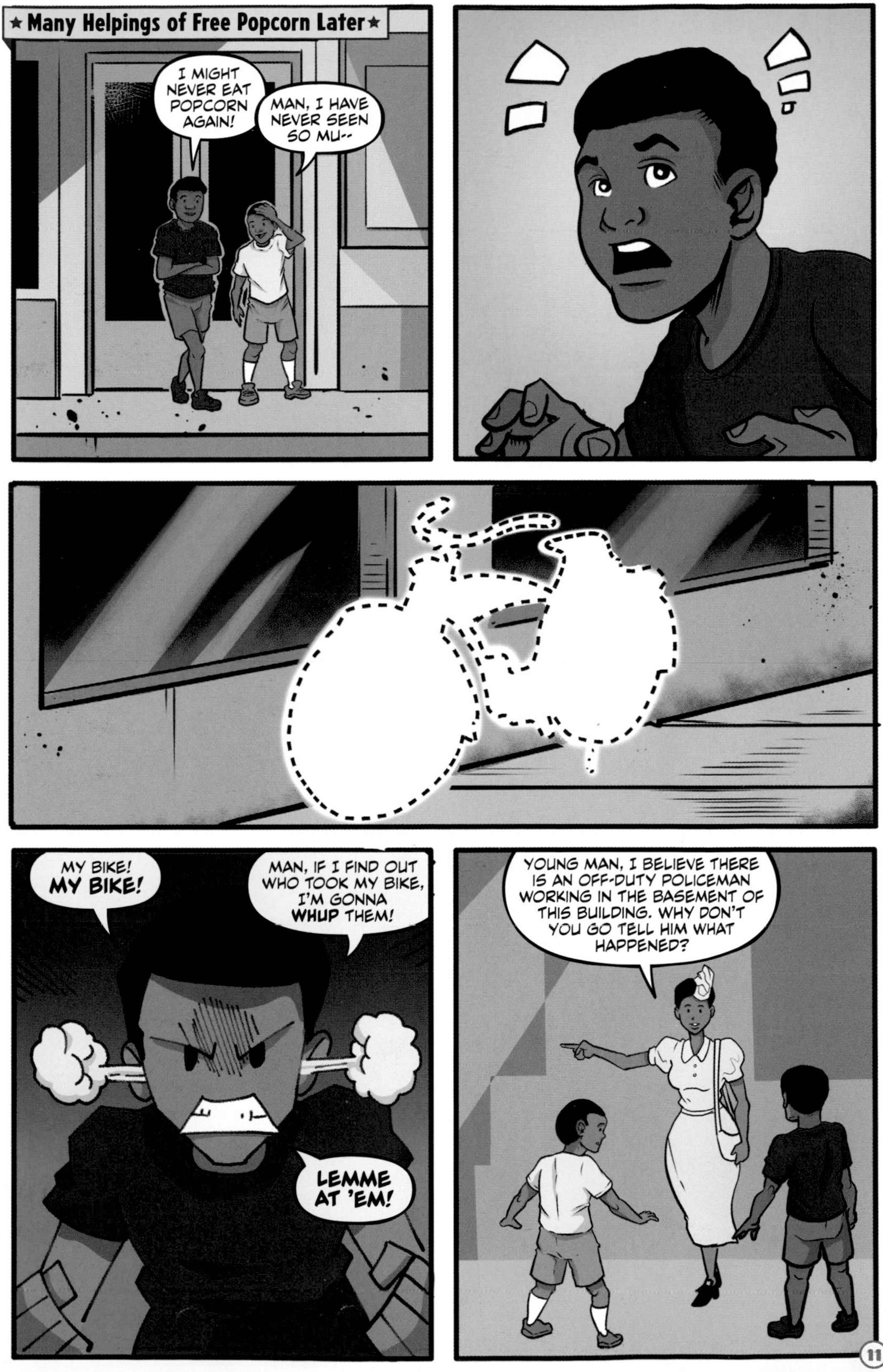

Many Helpings of Free Popcorn Later
I MIGHT NEVER EAT POPCORN AGAIN!
MAN, I HAVE NEVER SEEN SO MU--
MY BIKE! MY BIKE!
MAN, IF I FIND OUT WHO TOOK MY BIKE, I'M GONNA WHUP THEM!
LEMME AT 'EM!
YOUNG MAN, I BELIEVE THERE IS AN OFF-DUTY POLICEMAN WORKING IN THE BASEMENT OF THIS BUILDING. WHY DON'T YOU GO TELL HIM WHAT HAPPENED?

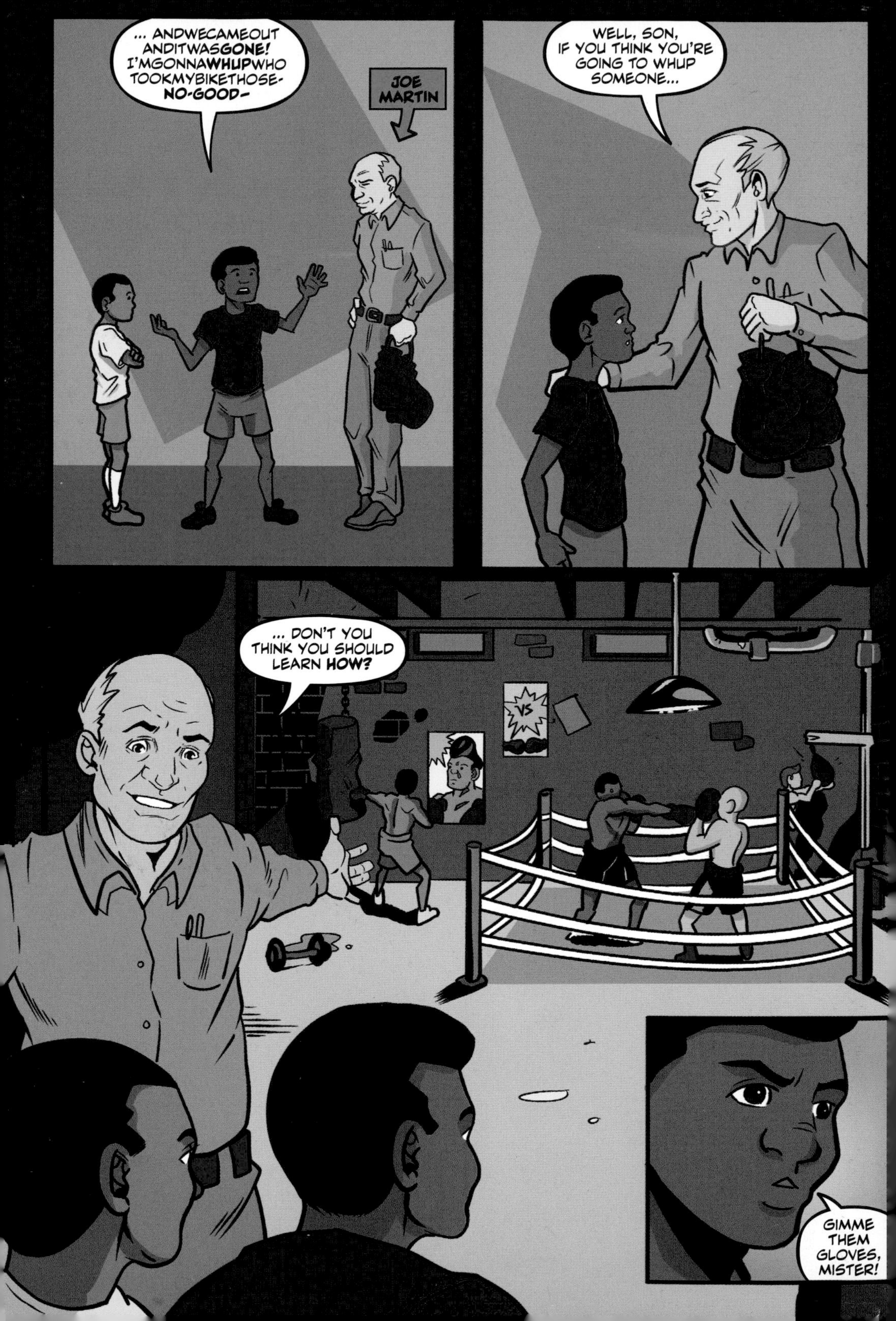
... ANDWECAMEOUT ANDITWASGONE! I'MGONNAWHUPWHO TOOKMYBIKETHOSE-NO-GOOD-
JOE MARTIN
WELL, SON, IF YOU THINK YOU'RE GOING TO WHUP SOMEONE...
... DON'T YOU THINK YOU SHOULD LEARN HOW?
VS
GIMME THEM GLOVES, MISTER!

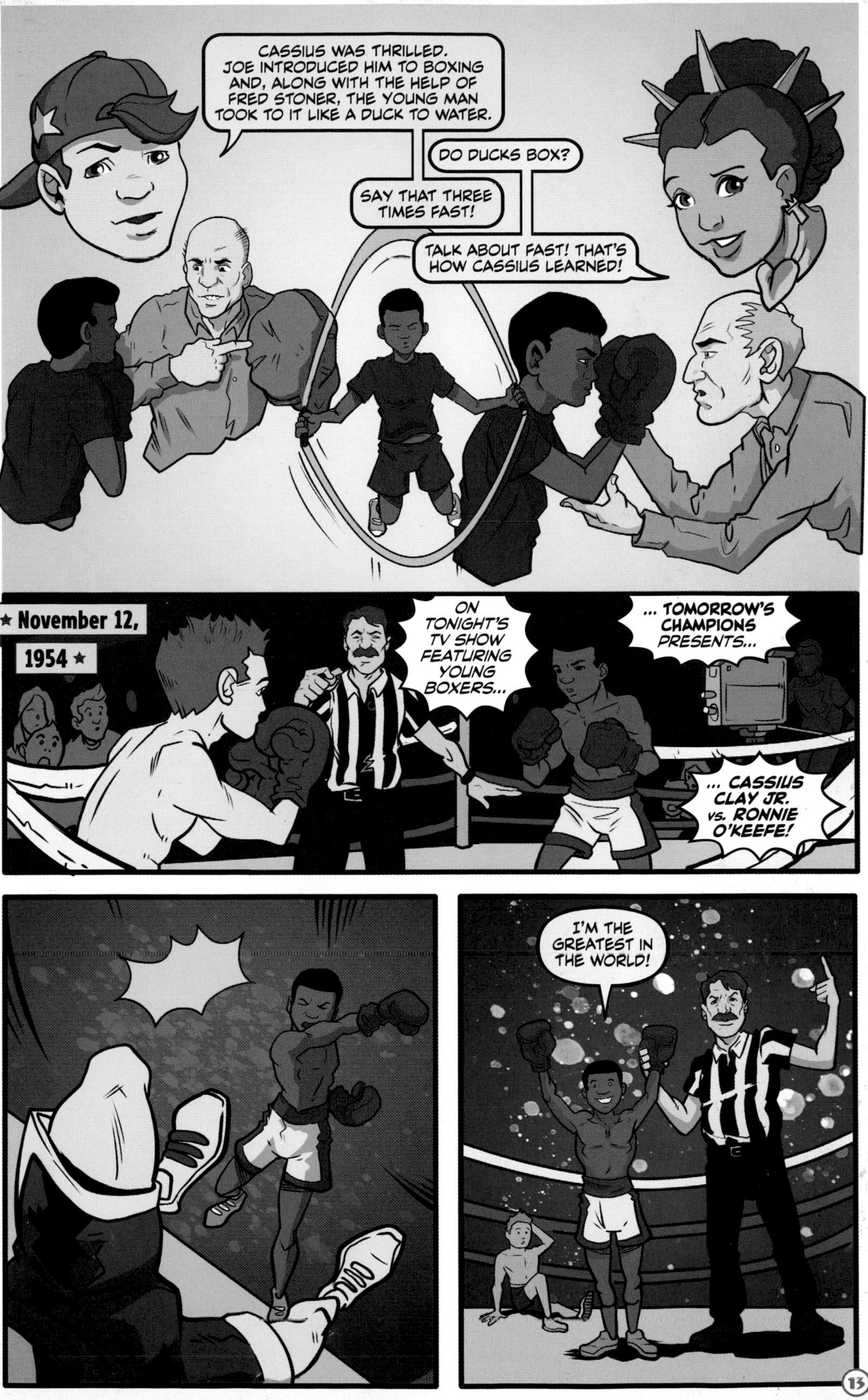
CASSIUS WAS THRILLED. JOE INTRODUCED HIM TO BOXING AND, ALONG WITH THE HELP OF FRED STONER, THE YOUNG MAN TOOK TO IT LIKE A DUCK TO WATER.
DO DUCKS BOX?
SAY THAT THREE TIMES FAST!
TALK ABOUT FAST! THAT'S HOW CASSIUS LEARNED!
★ November 12, 1954 ★
ON TONIGHT'S TV SHOW FEATURING YOUNG BOXERS...
... TOMORROW'S CHAMPIONS PRESENTS...
... CASSIUS CLAY JR. vs. RONNIE O'KEEFE!
I'M THE GREATEST IN THE WORLD!

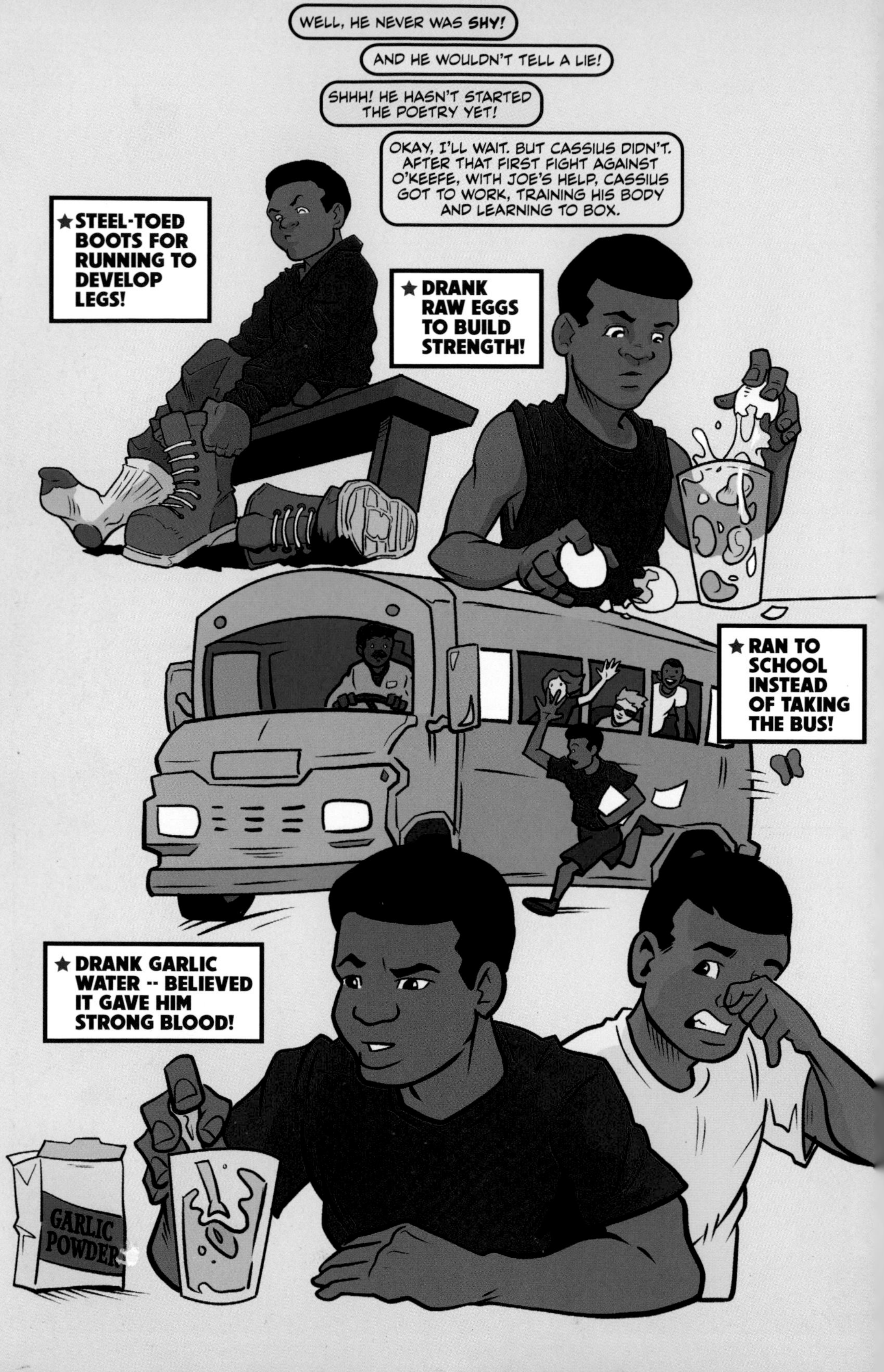
WELL, HE NEVER WAS SHY!
AND HE WOULDN'T TELL A LIE!
SHHH! HE HASN'T STARTED THE POETRY YET!
OKAY, I'LL WAIT. BUT CASSIUS DIDN'T. AFTER THAT FIRST FIGHT AGAINST O'KEEFE, WITH JOE'S HELP, CASSIUS GOT TO WORK, TRAINING HIS BODY AND LEARNING TO BOX.
★ STEEL-TOED BOOTS FOR RUNNING TO DEVELOP LEGS!
★ DRANK RAW EGGS TO BUILD STRENGTH!
★ RAN TO SCHOOL INSTEAD OF TAKING THE BUS!
★ DRANK GARLIC WATER -- BELIEVED IT GAVE HIM STRONG BLOOD!
GARLIC POWDER

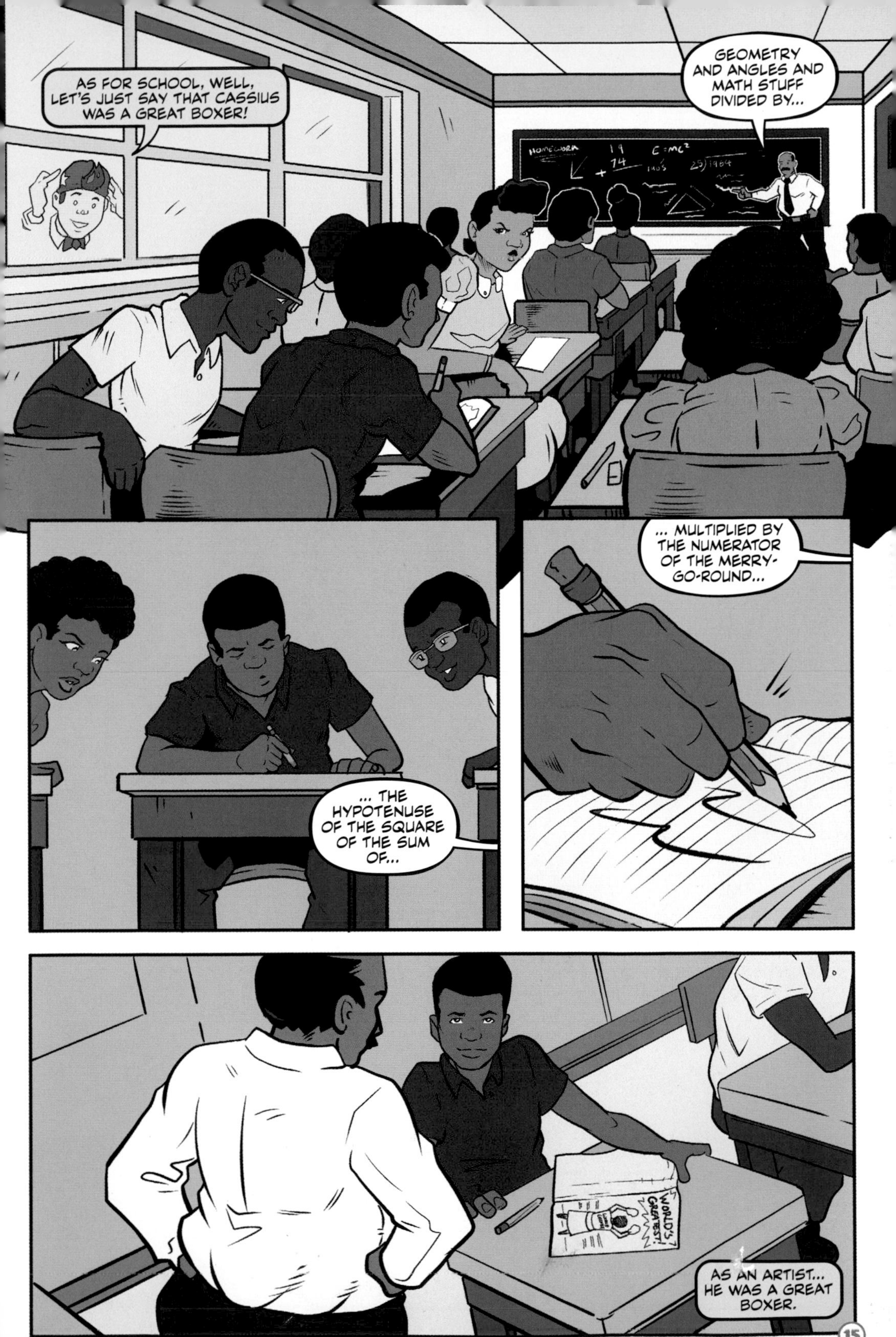

AS FOR SCHOOL, WELL, LET'S JUST SAY THAT CASSIUS WAS A GREAT BOXER!
GEOMETRY AND ANGLES AND MATH STUFF DIVIDED BY...
... THE HYPOTENUSE OF THE SQUARE OF THE SUM OF...
... MULTIPLIED BY THE NUMERATOR OF THE MERRY-GO-ROUND...
WORLD'S GREATEST!
AS AN ARTIST... HE WAS A GREAT BOXER.

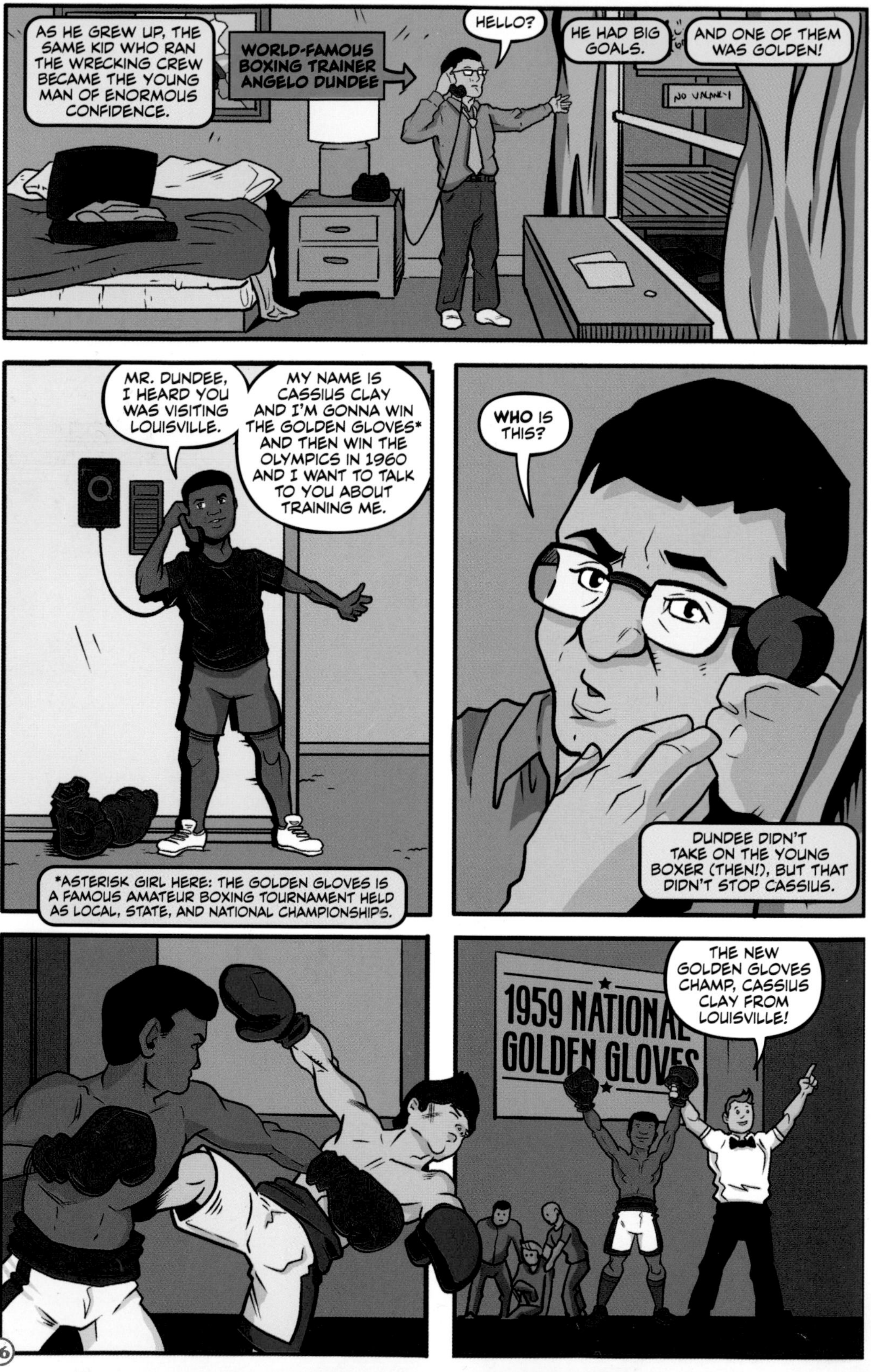
AS HE GREW UP, THE SAME KID WHO RAN THE WRECKING CREW BECAME THE YOUNG MAN OF ENORMOUS CONFIDENCE.
WORLD-FAMOUS BOXING TRAINER ANGELO DUNDEE
HELLO?
HE HAD BIG GOALS.
AND ONE OF THEM WAS GOLDEN!
MR. DUNDEE, I HEARD YOU WAS VISITING LOUISVILLE.
MY NAME IS CASSIUS CLAY AND I'M GONNA WIN THE GOLDEN GLOVES* AND THEN WIN THE OLYMPICS IN 1960 AND I WANT TO TALK TO YOU ABOUT TRAINING ME.
*ASTERISK GIRL HERE: THE GOLDEN GLOVES IS A FAMOUS AMATEUR BOXING TOURNAMENT HELD AS LOCAL, STATE, AND NATIONAL CHAMPIONSHIPS.
WHO IS THIS?
DUNDEE DIDN'T TAKE ON THE YOUNG BOXER (THEN!), BUT THAT DIDN'T STOP CASSIUS.
1959 NATIONAL GOLDEN GLOVES
THE NEW GOLDEN GLOVES CHAMP, CASSIUS CLAY FROM LOUISVILLE!

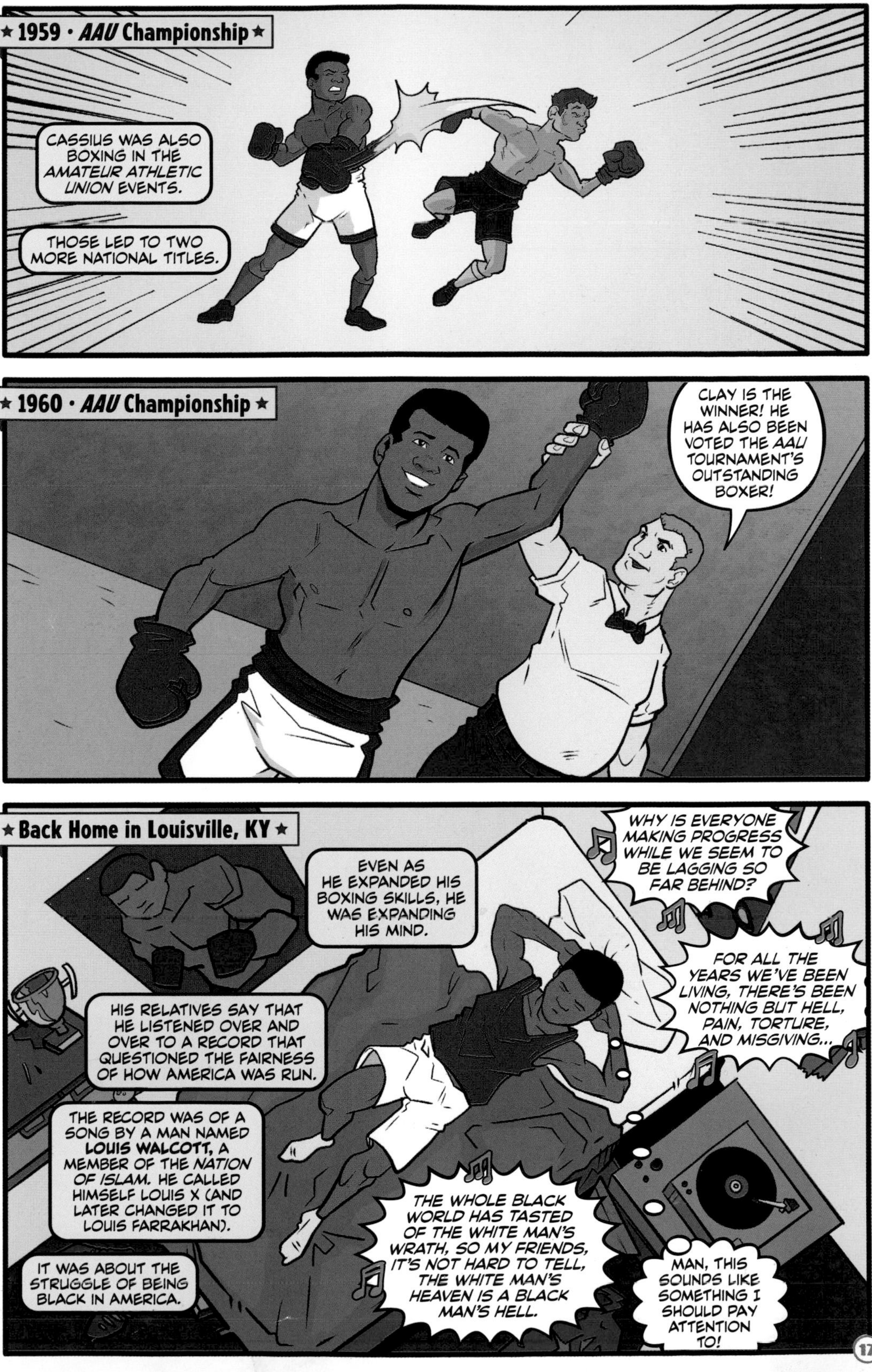
★ 1959 • AAU Championship ★
CASSIUS WAS ALSO BOXING IN THE AMATEUR ATHLETIC UNION EVENTS.
THOSE LED TO TWO MORE NATIONAL TITLES.
★ 1960 • AAU Championship ★
CLAY IS THE WINNER! HE HAS ALSO BEEN VOTED THE AAU TOURNAMENT'S OUTSTANDING BOXER!
★ Back Home in Louisville, KY ★
EVEN AS HE EXPANDED HIS BOXING SKILLS, HE WAS EXPANDING HIS MIND.
WHY IS EVERYONE MAKING PROGRESS WHILE WE SEEM TO BE LAGGING SO FAR BEHIND?
FOR ALL THE YEARS WE'VE BEEN LIVING, THERE'S BEEN NOTHING BUT HELL, PAIN, TORTURE, AND MISGIVING...
HIS RELATIVES SAY THAT HE LISTENED OVER AND OVER TO A RECORD THAT QUESTIONED THE FAIRNESS OF HOW AMERICA WAS RUN.
THE RECORD WAS OF A SONG BY A MAN NAMED LOUIS WALCOTT, A MEMBER OF THE NATION OF ISLAM. HE CALLED HIMSELF LOUIS X (AND LATER CHANGED IT TO LOUIS FARRAKHAN).
IT WAS ABOUT THE STRUGGLE OF BEING BLACK IN AMERICA.
THE WHOLE BLACK WORLD HAS TASTED OF THE WHITE MAN'S WRATH, SO MY FRIENDS, IT'S NOT HARD TO TELL, THE WHITE MAN'S HEAVEN IS A BLACK MAN'S HELL.
MAN, THIS SOUNDS LIKE SOMETHING I SHOULD PAY ATTENTION TO!

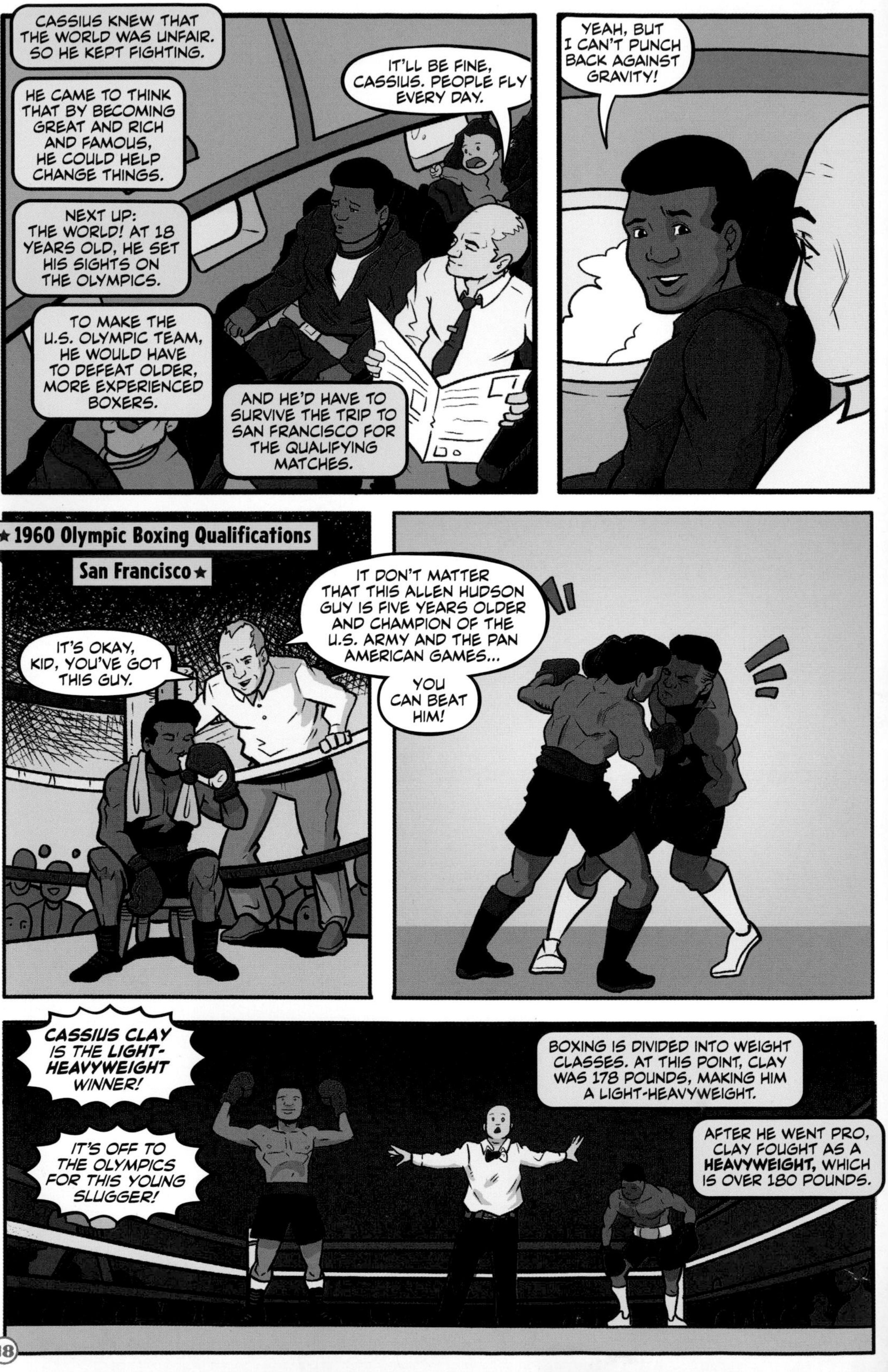

CASSIUS KNEW THAT THE WORLD WAS UNFAIR. SO HE KEPT FIGHTING.
HE CAME TO THINK THAT BY BECOMING GREAT AND RICH AND FAMOUS, HE COULD HELP CHANGE THINGS.
NEXT UP: THE WORLD! AT 18 YEARS OLD, HE SET HIS SIGHTS ON THE OLYMPICS.
TO MAKE THE U.S. OLYMPIC TEAM, HE WOULD HAVE TO DEFEAT OLDER, MORE EXPERIENCED BOXERS.
AND HE'D HAVE TO SURVIVE THE TRIP TO SAN FRANCISCO FOR THE QUALIFYING MATCHES.
IT'LL BE FINE, CASSIUS. PEOPLE FLY EVERY DAY.
YEAH, BUT I CAN'T PUNCH BACK AGAINST GRAVITY!
1960 Olympic Boxing Qualifications
San Francisco
IT'S OKAY, KID, YOU'VE GOT THIS GUY.
IT DON'T MATTER THAT THIS ALLEN HUDSON GUY IS FIVE YEARS OLDER AND CHAMPION OF THE U.S. ARMY AND THE PAN AMERICAN GAMES...
YOU CAN BEAT HIM!
CASSIUS CLAY IS THE LIGHT-HEAVYWEIGHT WINNER!
IT'S OFF TO THE OLYMPICS FOR THIS YOUNG SLUGGER!
BOXING IS DIVIDED INTO WEIGHT CLASSES. AT THIS POINT, CLAY WAS 178 POUNDS, MAKING HIM A LIGHT-HEAVYWEIGHT.
AFTER HE WENT PRO, CLAY FOUGHT AS A HEAVYWEIGHT, WHICH IS OVER 180 POUNDS.

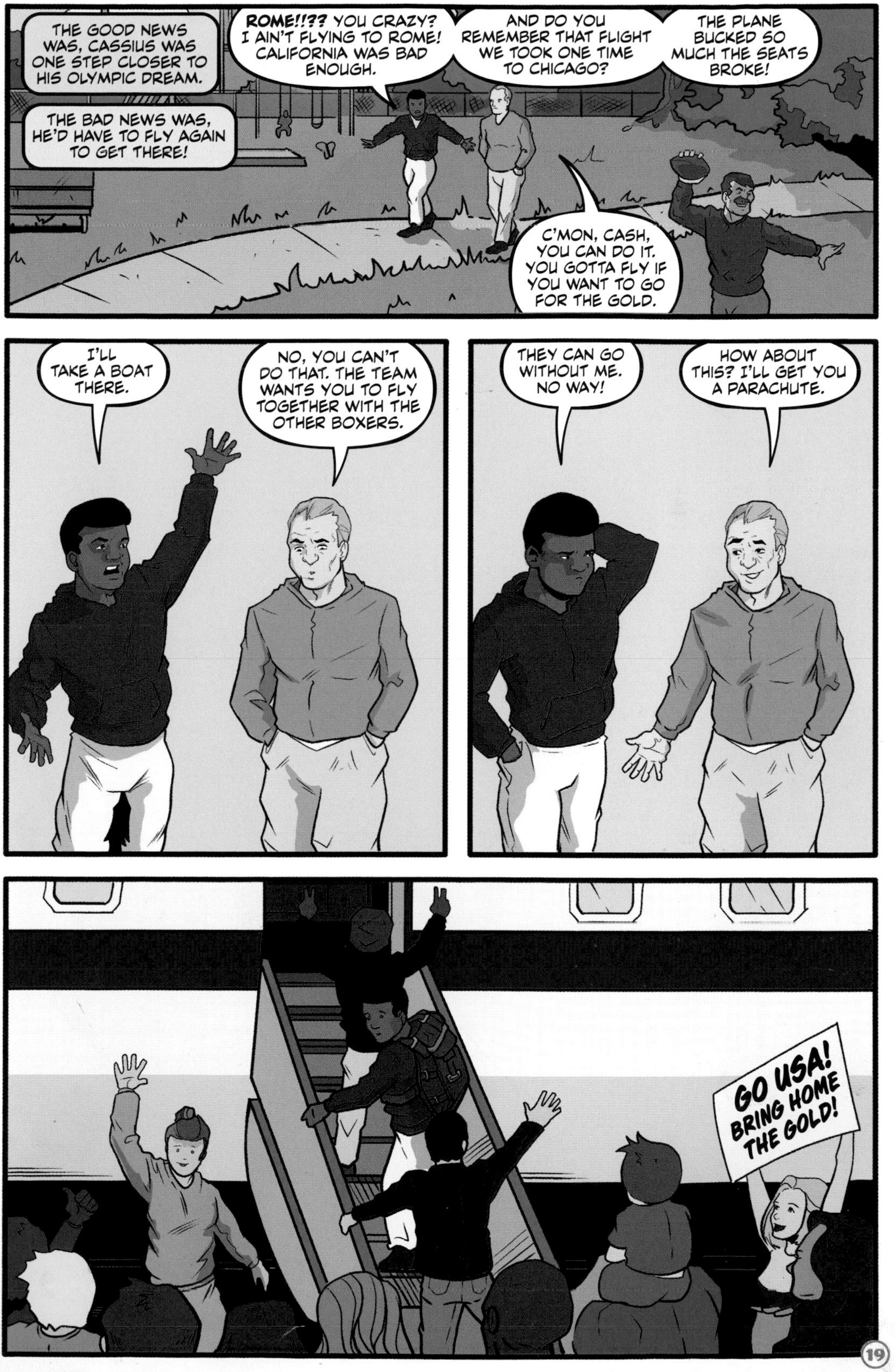
THE GOOD NEWS WAS, CASSIUS WAS ONE STEP CLOSER TO HIS OLYMPIC DREAM.
THE BAD NEWS WAS, HE'D HAVE TO FLY AGAIN TO GET THERE!
ROME!!?? YOU CRAZY? I AIN'T FLYING TO ROME! CALIFORNIA WAS BAD ENOUGH.
AND DO YOU REMEMBER THAT FLIGHT WE TOOK ONE TIME TO CHICAGO?
THE PLANE BUCKED SO MUCH THE SEATS BROKE!
C'MON, CASH, YOU CAN DO IT. YOU GOTTA FLY IF YOU WANT TO GO FOR THE GOLD.
I'LL TAKE A BOAT THERE.
NO, YOU CAN'T DO THAT. THE TEAM WANTS YOU TO FLY TOGETHER WITH THE OTHER BOXERS.
THEY CAN GO WITHOUT ME. NO WAY!
HOW ABOUT THIS? I'LL GET YOU A PARACHUTE.
GO USA! BRING HOME THE GOLD!

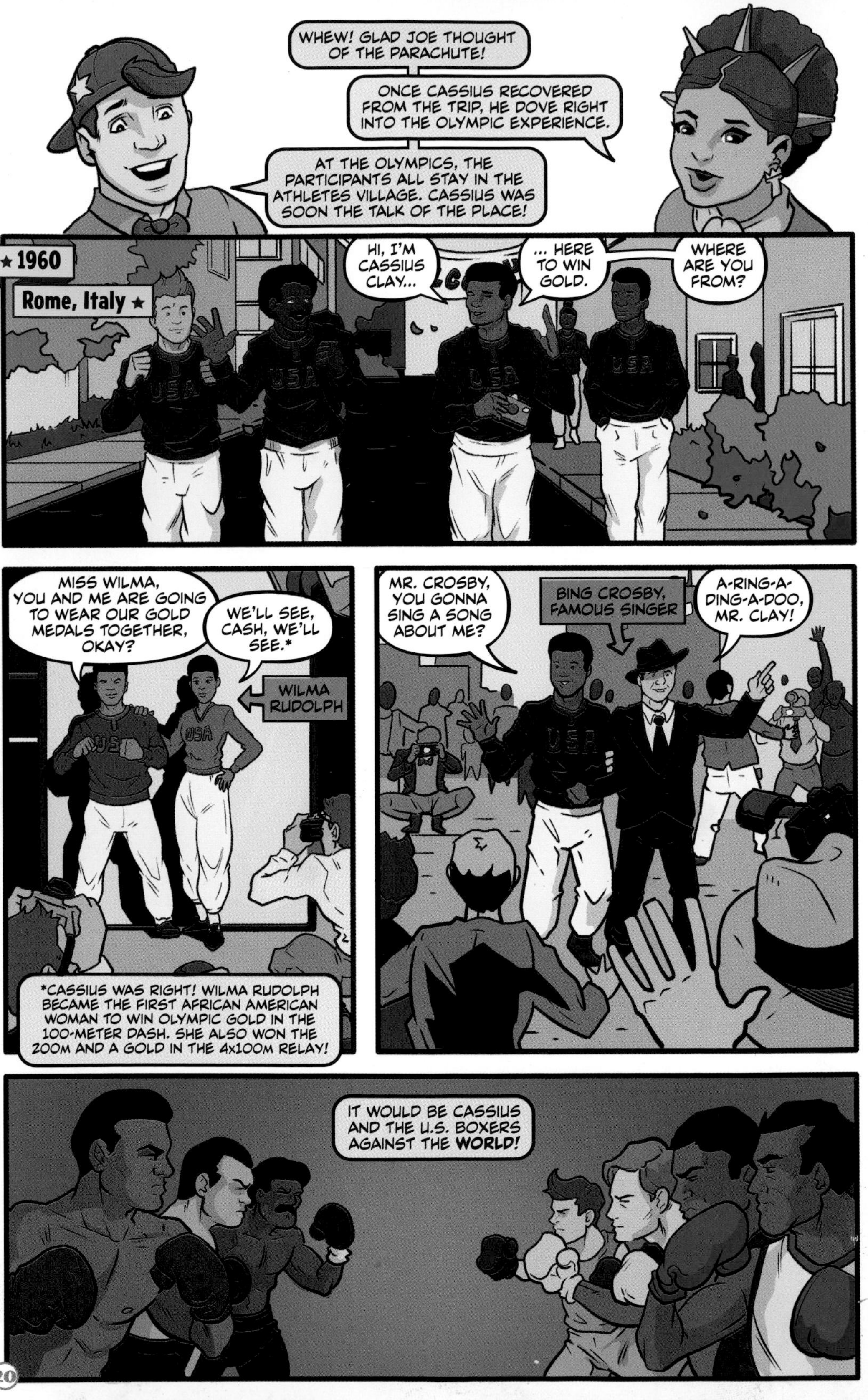
WHEW! GLAD JOE THOUGHT OF THE PARACHUTE!
ONCE CASSIUS RECOVERED FROM THE TRIP, HE DOVE RIGHT INTO THE OLYMPIC EXPERIENCE.
AT THE OLYMPICS, THE PARTICIPANTS ALL STAY IN THE ATHLETES VILLAGE. CASSIUS WAS SOON THE TALK OF THE PLACE!
1960
Rome, Italy
HI, I'M CASSIUS CLAY...
... HERE TO WIN GOLD.
WHERE ARE YOU FROM?
MISS WILMA, YOU AND ME ARE GOING TO WEAR OUR GOLD MEDALS TOGETHER, OKAY?
WE'LL SEE, CASH, WE'LL SEE.*
WILMA RUDOLPH
*CASSIUS WAS RIGHT! WILMA RUDOLPH BECAME THE FIRST AFRICAN AMERICAN WOMAN TO WIN OLYMPIC GOLD IN THE 100-METER DASH. SHE ALSO WON THE 200M AND A GOLD IN THE 4x100M RELAY!
MR. CROSBY, YOU GONNA SING A SONG ABOUT ME?
BING CROSBY, FAMOUS SINGER
A-RING-A-DING-A-DOO, MR. CLAY!
IT WOULD BE CASSIUS AND THE U.S. BOXERS AGAINST THE **WORLD**!

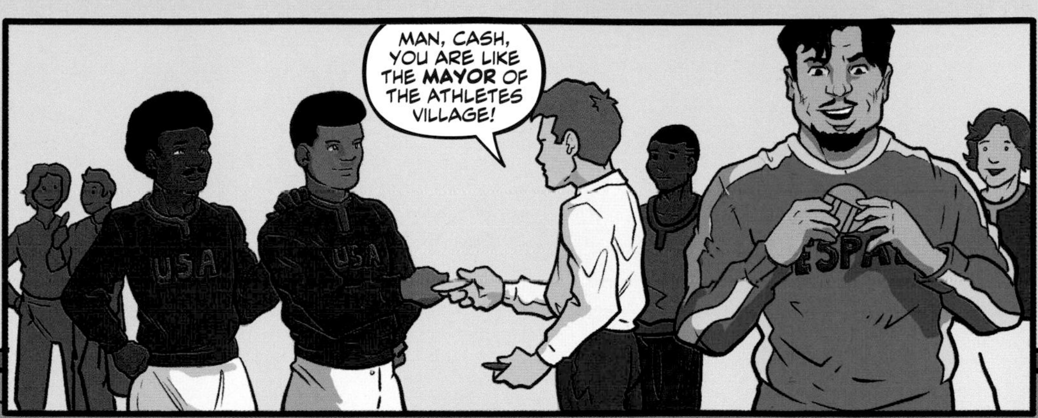
MAN, CASH, YOU ARE LIKE THE **MAYOR** OF THE ATHLETES VILLAGE!
USA
USA
ESPA

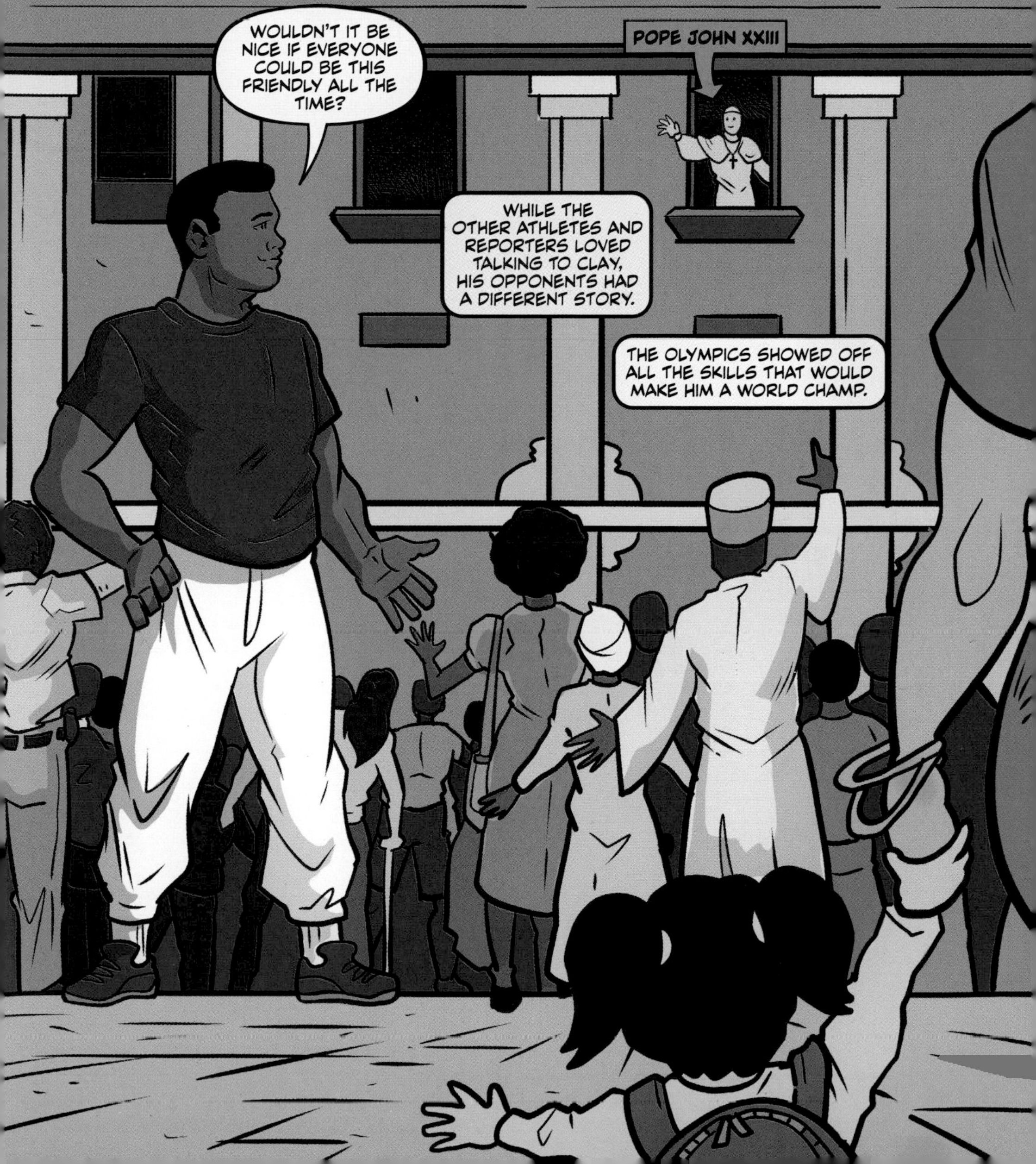
WOULDN'T IT BE NICE IF EVERYONE COULD BE THIS FRIENDLY ALL THE TIME?
POPE JOHN XXIII
WHILE THE OTHER ATHLETES AND REPORTERS LOVED TALKING TO CLAY, HIS OPPONENTS HAD A DIFFERENT STORY.
THE OLYMPICS SHOWED OFF ALL THE SKILLS THAT WOULD MAKE HIM A WORLD CHAMP.

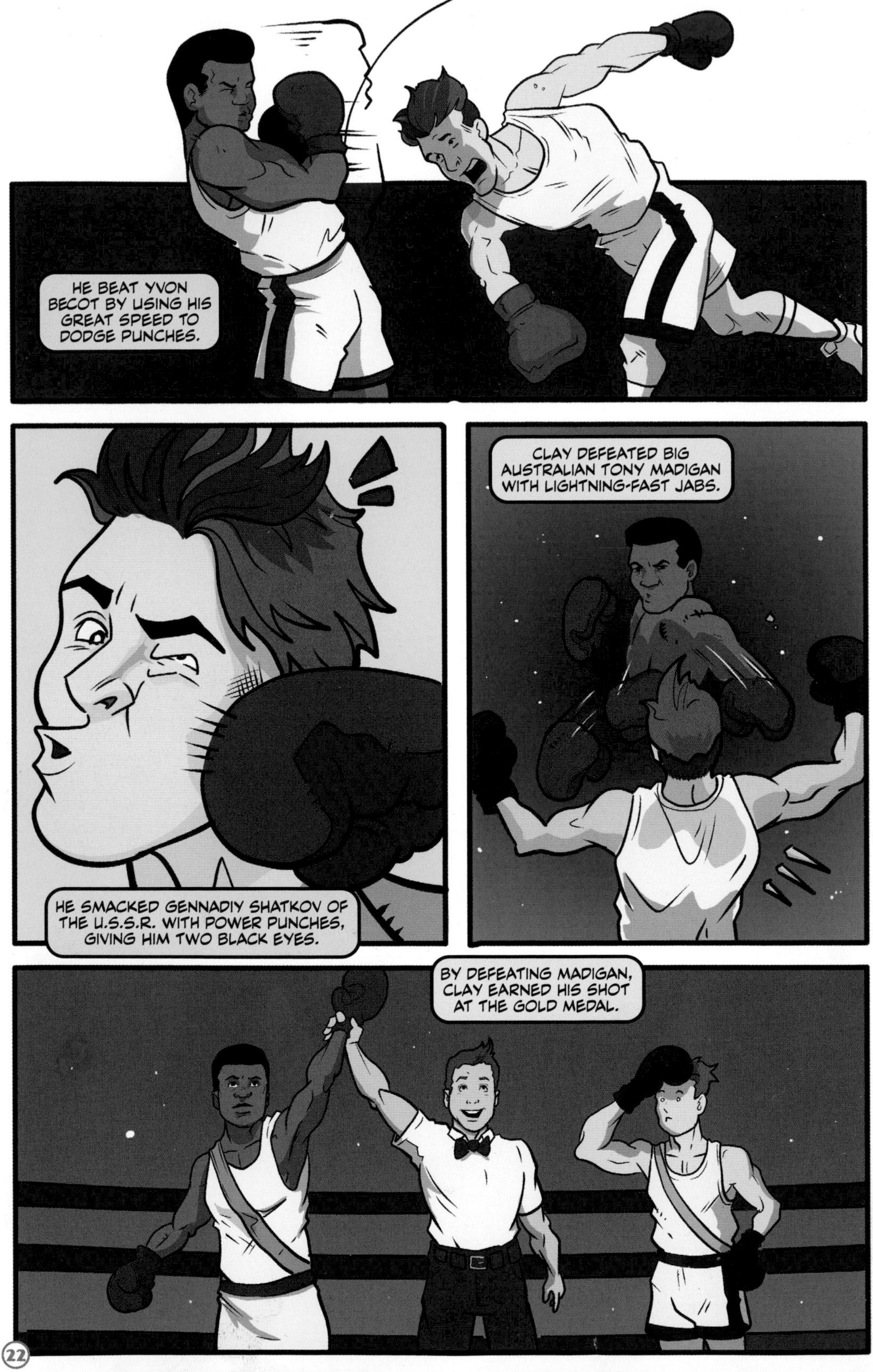
HE BEAT YVON BECOT BY USING HIS GREAT SPEED TO DODGE PUNCHES.
HE SMACKED GENNADIY SHATKOV OF THE U.S.S.R. WITH POWER PUNCHES, GIVING HIM TWO BLACK EYES.
CLAY DEFEATED BIG AUSTRALIAN TONY MADIGAN WITH LIGHTNING-FAST JABS.
BY DEFEATING MADIGAN, CLAY EARNED HIS SHOT AT THE GOLD MEDAL.

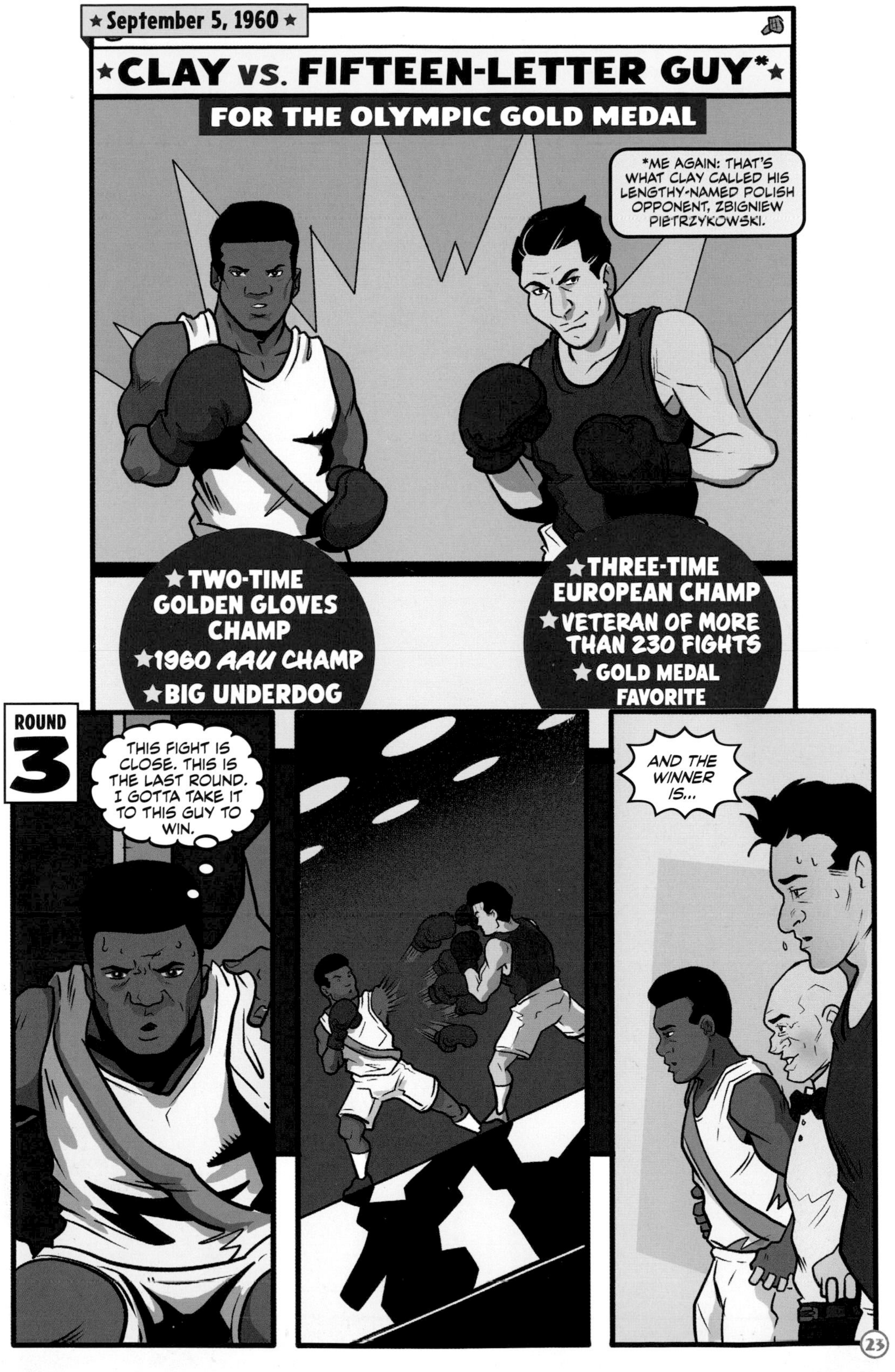

September 5, 1960
CLAY vs. FIFTEEN-LETTER GUY*
FOR THE OLYMPIC GOLD MEDAL
*ME AGAIN: THAT'S WHAT CLAY CALLED HIS LENGTHY-NAMED POLISH OPPONENT, ZBIGNIEW PIETRZYKOWSKI.
TWO-TIME GOLDEN GLOVES CHAMP
1960 AAU CHAMP
BIG UNDERDOG
THREE-TIME EUROPEAN CHAMP
VETERAN OF MORE THAN 230 FIGHTS
GOLD MEDAL FAVORITE
ROUND 3
THIS FIGHT IS CLOSE. THIS IS THE LAST ROUND. I GOTTA TAKE IT TO THIS GUY TO WIN.
AND THE WINNER IS...

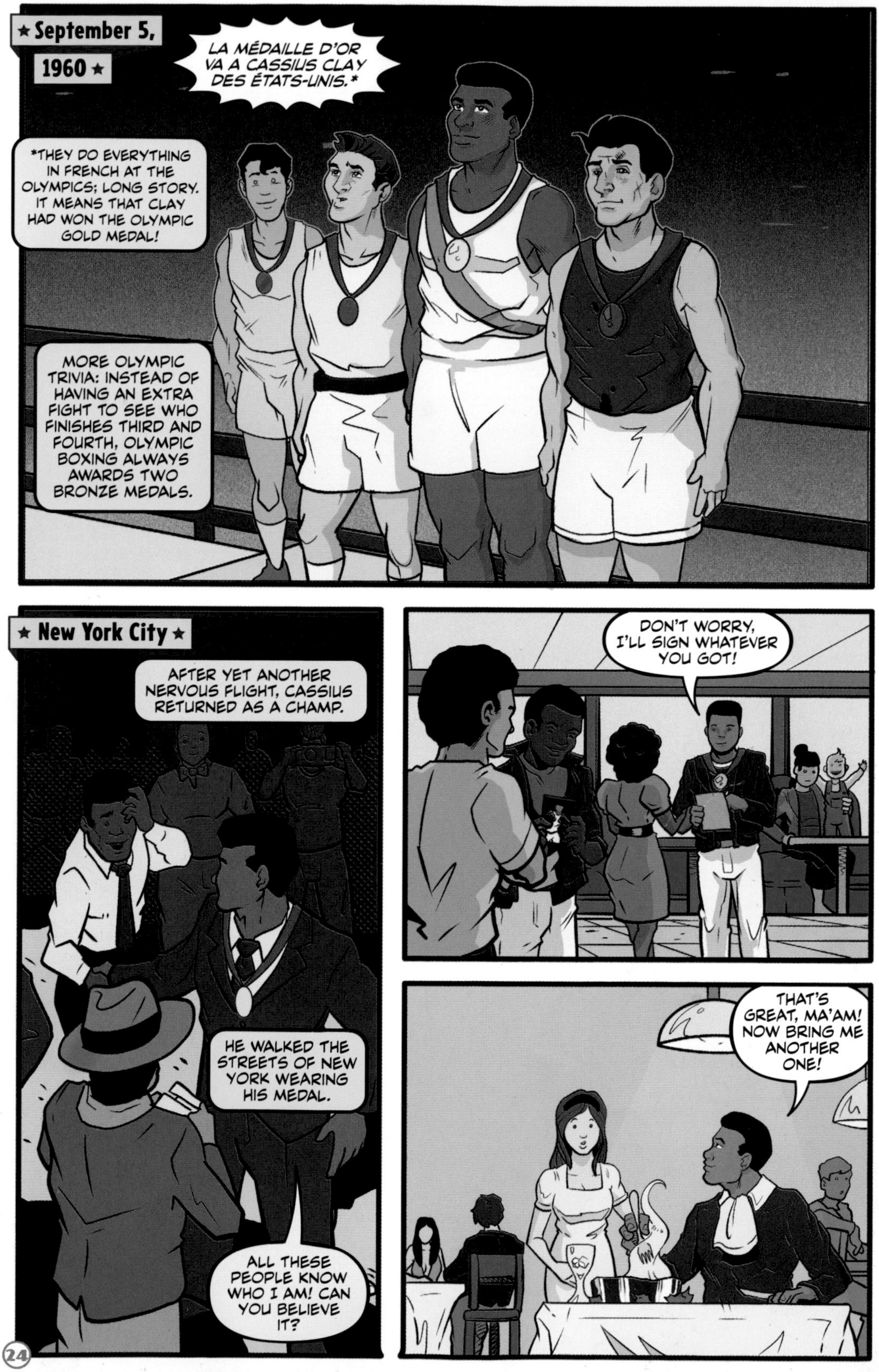
★ September 5, 1960 ★
LA MÉDAILLE D'OR VA A CASSIUS CLAY DES ÉTATS-UNIS.*
*THEY DO EVERYTHING IN FRENCH AT THE OLYMPICS; LONG STORY. IT MEANS THAT CLAY HAD WON THE OLYMPIC GOLD MEDAL!
MORE OLYMPIC TRIVIA: INSTEAD OF HAVING AN EXTRA FIGHT TO SEE WHO FINISHES THIRD AND FOURTH, OLYMPIC BOXING ALWAYS AWARDS TWO BRONZE MEDALS.
★ New York City ★
AFTER YET ANOTHER NERVOUS FLIGHT, CASSIUS RETURNED AS A CHAMP.
HE WALKED THE STREETS OF NEW YORK WEARING HIS MEDAL.
ALL THESE PEOPLE KNOW WHO I AM! CAN YOU BELIEVE IT?
DON'T WORRY, I'LL SIGN WHATEVER YOU GOT!
THAT'S GREAT, MA'AM! NOW BRING ME ANOTHER ONE!

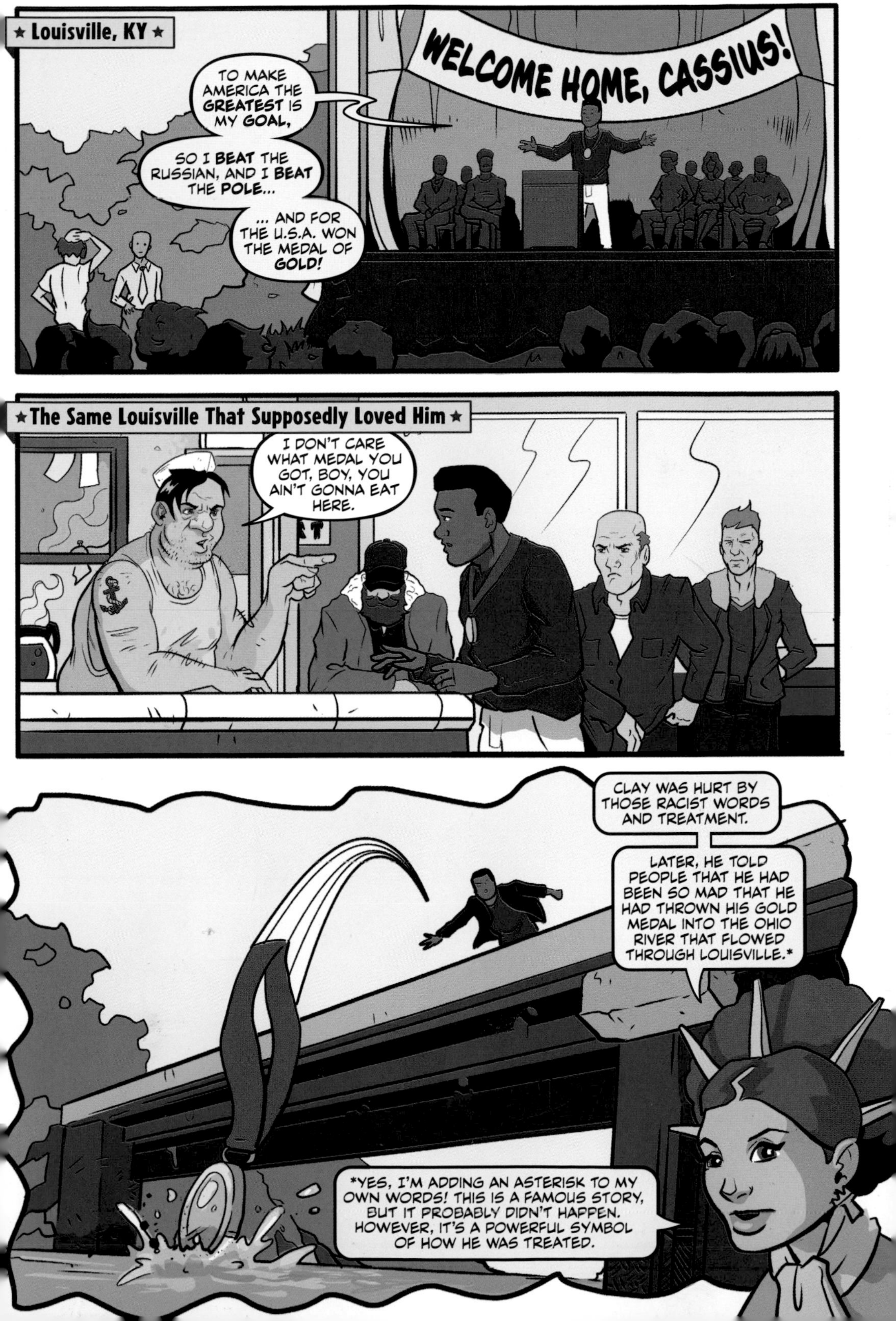

★ Louisville, KY ★
WELCOME HOME, CASSIUS!
TO MAKE AMERICA THE GREATEST IS MY GOAL,
SO I BEAT THE RUSSIAN, AND I BEAT THE POLE...
... AND FOR THE U.S.A. WON THE MEDAL OF GOLD!
★ The Same Louisville That Supposedly Loved Him ★
I DON'T CARE WHAT MEDAL YOU GOT, BOY, YOU AIN'T GONNA EAT HERE.
CLAY WAS HURT BY THOSE RACIST WORDS AND TREATMENT.
LATER, HE TOLD PEOPLE THAT HE HAD BEEN SO MAD THAT HE HAD THROWN HIS GOLD MEDAL INTO THE OHIO RIVER THAT FLOWED THROUGH LOUISVILLE.*
*YES, I'M ADDING AN ASTERISK TO MY OWN WORDS! THIS IS A FAMOUS STORY, BUT IT PROBABLY DIDN'T HAPPEN. HOWEVER, IT'S A POWERFUL SYMBOL OF HOW HE WAS TREATED.

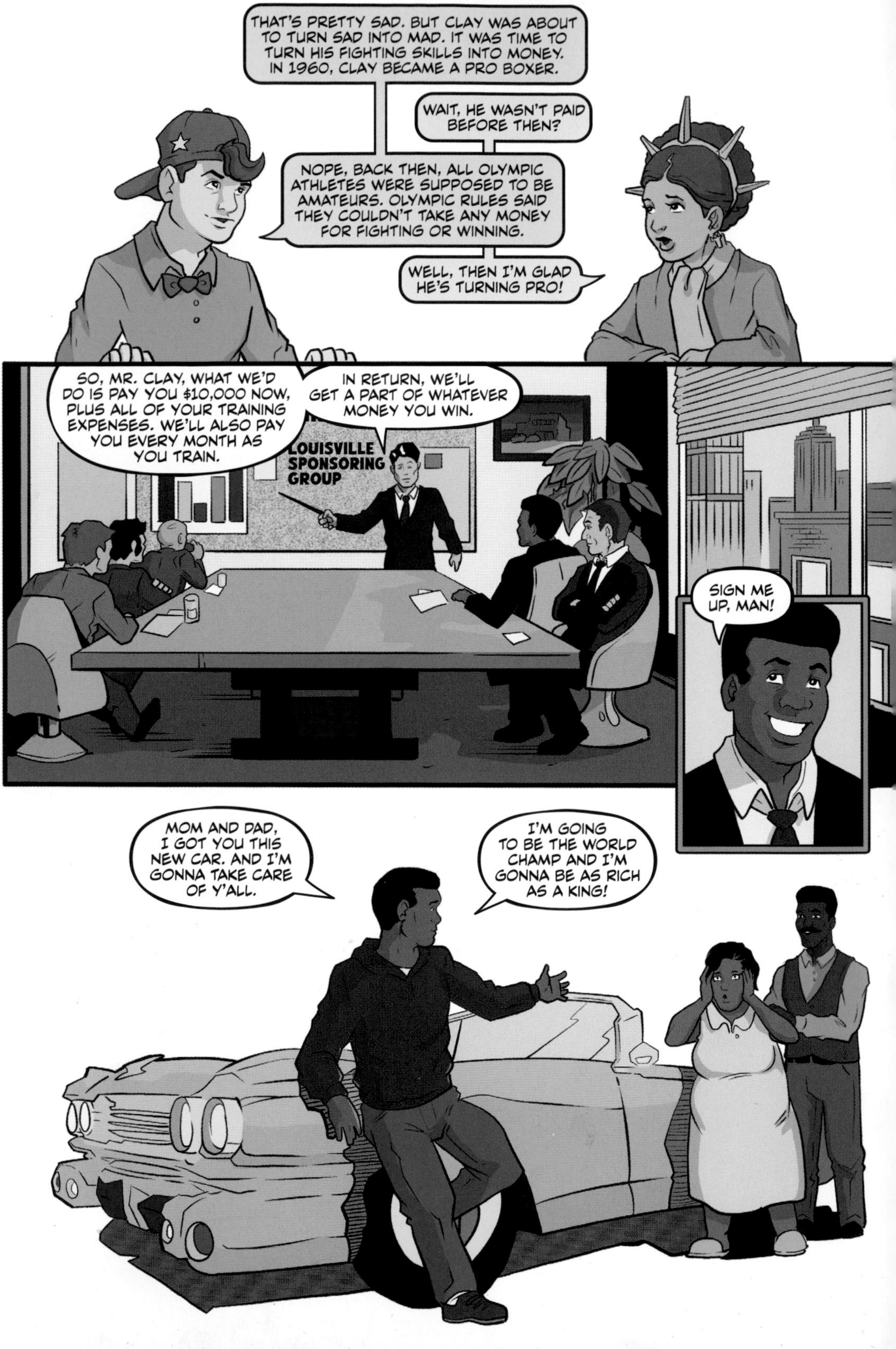
THAT'S PRETTY SAD. BUT CLAY WAS ABOUT TO TURN SAD INTO MAD. IT WAS TIME TO TURN HIS FIGHTING SKILLS INTO MONEY. IN 1960, CLAY BECAME A PRO BOXER.
WAIT, HE WASN'T PAID BEFORE THEN?
NOPE, BACK THEN, ALL OLYMPIC ATHLETES WERE SUPPOSED TO BE AMATEURS. OLYMPIC RULES SAID THEY COULDN'T TAKE ANY MONEY FOR FIGHTING OR WINNING.
WELL, THEN I'M GLAD HE'S TURNING PRO!
SO, MR. CLAY, WHAT WE'D DO IS PAY YOU $10,000 NOW, PLUS ALL OF YOUR TRAINING EXPENSES. WE'LL ALSO PAY YOU EVERY MONTH AS YOU TRAIN.
IN RETURN, WE'LL GET A PART OF WHATEVER MONEY YOU WIN.
LOUISVILLE SPONSORING GROUP
SIGN ME UP, MAN!
MOM AND DAD, I GOT YOU THIS NEW CAR. AND I'M GONNA TAKE CARE OF Y'ALL.
I'M GOING TO BE THE WORLD CHAMP AND I'M GONNA BE AS RICH AS A KING!

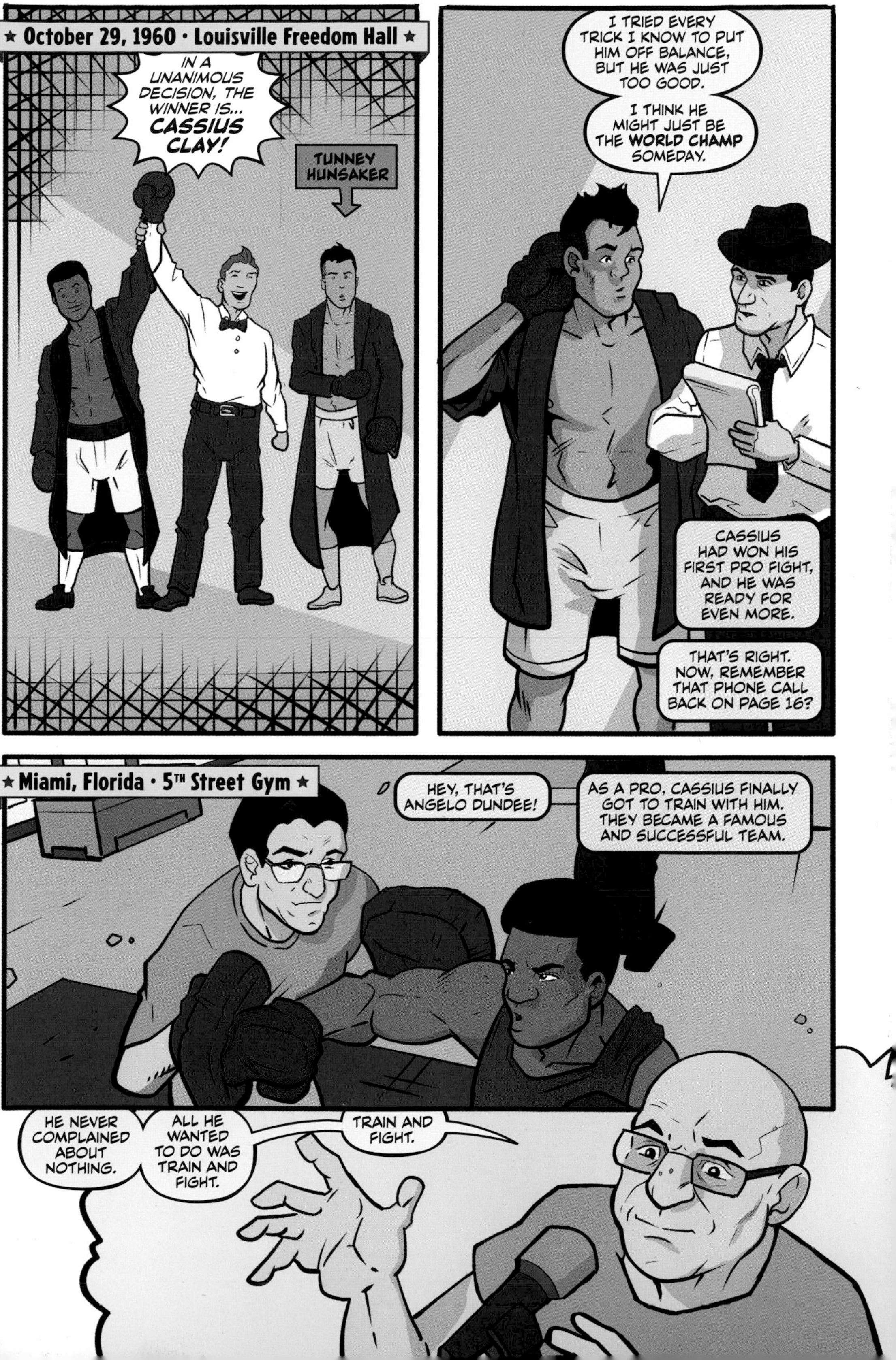
October 29, 1960 • Louisville Freedom Hall
IN A UNANIMOUS DECISION, THE WINNER IS... CASSIUS CLAY!
TUNNEY HUNSAKER
I TRIED EVERY TRICK I KNOW TO PUT HIM OFF BALANCE, BUT HE WAS JUST TOO GOOD.
I THINK HE MIGHT JUST BE THE WORLD CHAMP SOMEDAY.
CASSIUS HAD WON HIS FIRST PRO FIGHT, AND HE WAS READY FOR EVEN MORE.
THAT'S RIGHT. NOW, REMEMBER THAT PHONE CALL BACK ON PAGE 16?
Miami, Florida • 5TH Street Gym
HEY, THAT'S ANGELO DUNDEE!
AS A PRO, CASSIUS FINALLY GOT TO TRAIN WITH HIM. THEY BECAME A FAMOUS AND SUCCESSFUL TEAM.
HE NEVER COMPLAINED ABOUT NOTHING.
ALL HE WANTED TO DO WAS TRAIN AND FIGHT.
TRAIN AND FIGHT.

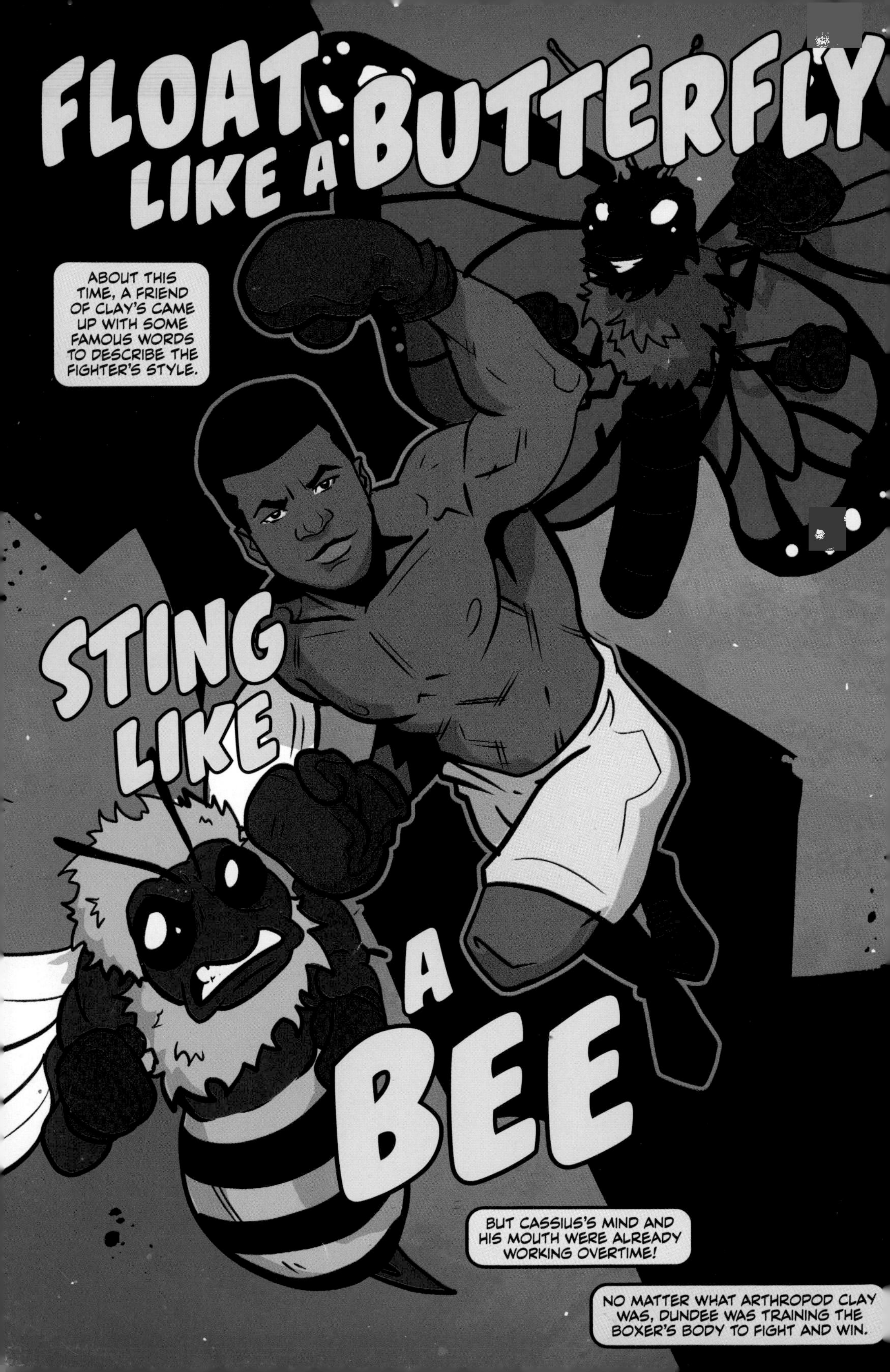
FLOAT LIKE A BUTTERFLY
ABOUT THIS TIME, A FRIEND OF CLAY'S CAME UP WITH SOME FAMOUS WORDS TO DESCRIBE THE FIGHTER'S STYLE.
STING LIKE A BEE
BUT CASSIUS'S MIND AND HIS MOUTH WERE ALREADY WORKING OVERTIME!
NO MATTER WHAT ARTHROPOD CLAY WAS, DUNDEE WAS TRAINING THE BOXER'S BODY TO FIGHT AND WIN.

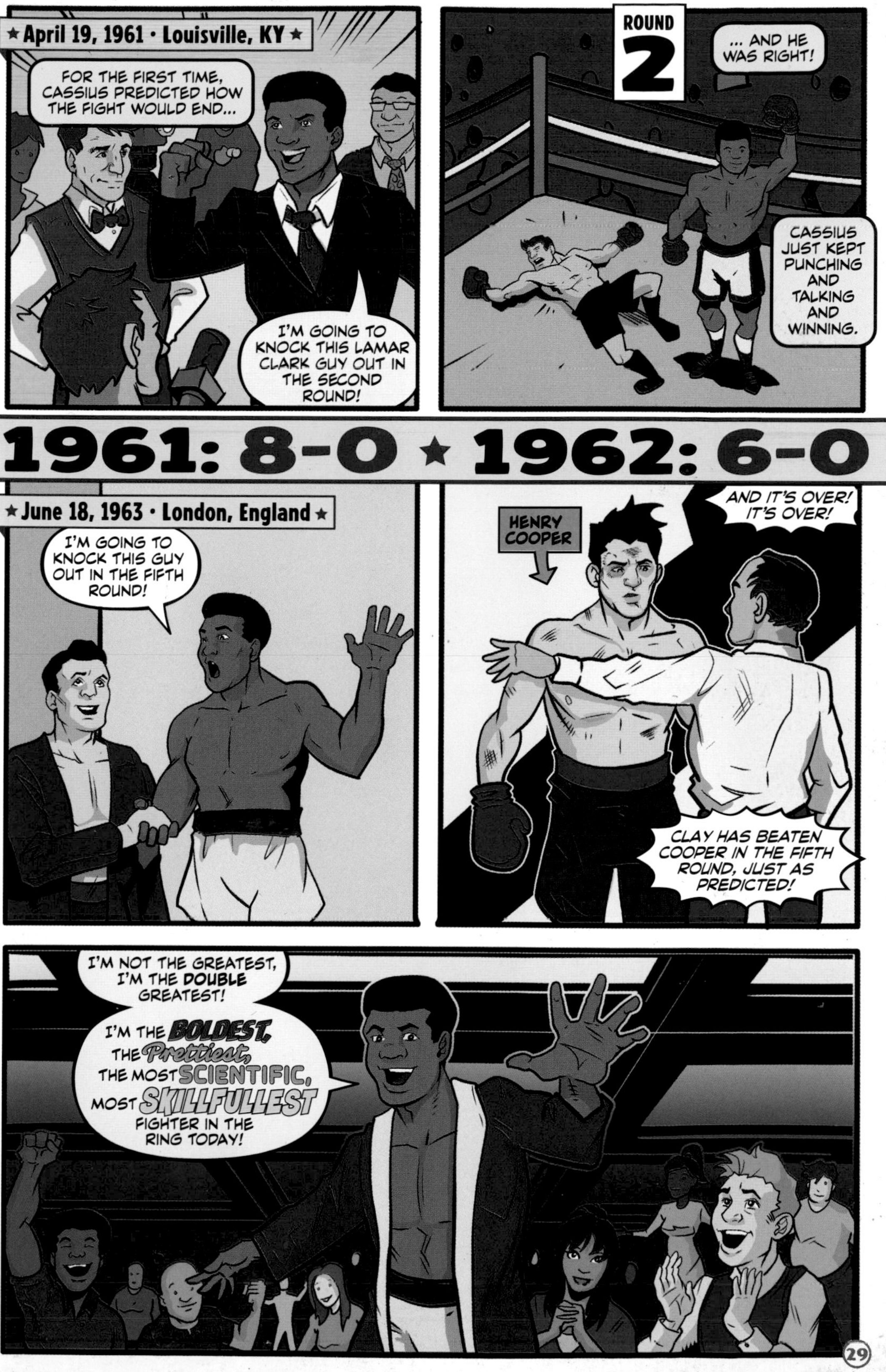
★ April 19, 1961 • Louisville, KY ★
FOR THE FIRST TIME, CASSIUS PREDICTED HOW THE FIGHT WOULD END...
I'M GOING TO KNOCK THIS LAMAR CLARK GUY OUT IN THE SECOND ROUND!
ROUND 2
... AND HE WAS RIGHT!
CASSIUS JUST KEPT PUNCHING AND TALKING AND WINNING.
1961: 8-0 ★ 1962: 6-0
★ June 18, 1963 • London, England ★
I'M GOING TO KNOCK THIS GUY OUT IN THE FIFTH ROUND!
HENRY COOPER
AND IT'S OVER! IT'S OVER!
CLAY HAS BEATEN COOPER IN THE FIFTH ROUND, JUST AS PREDICTED!
I'M NOT THE GREATEST, I'M THE DOUBLE GREATEST!
I'M THE BOLDEST, THE Prettiest, THE MOST SCIENTIFIC, MOST SKILLFULLEST FIGHTER IN THE RING TODAY!

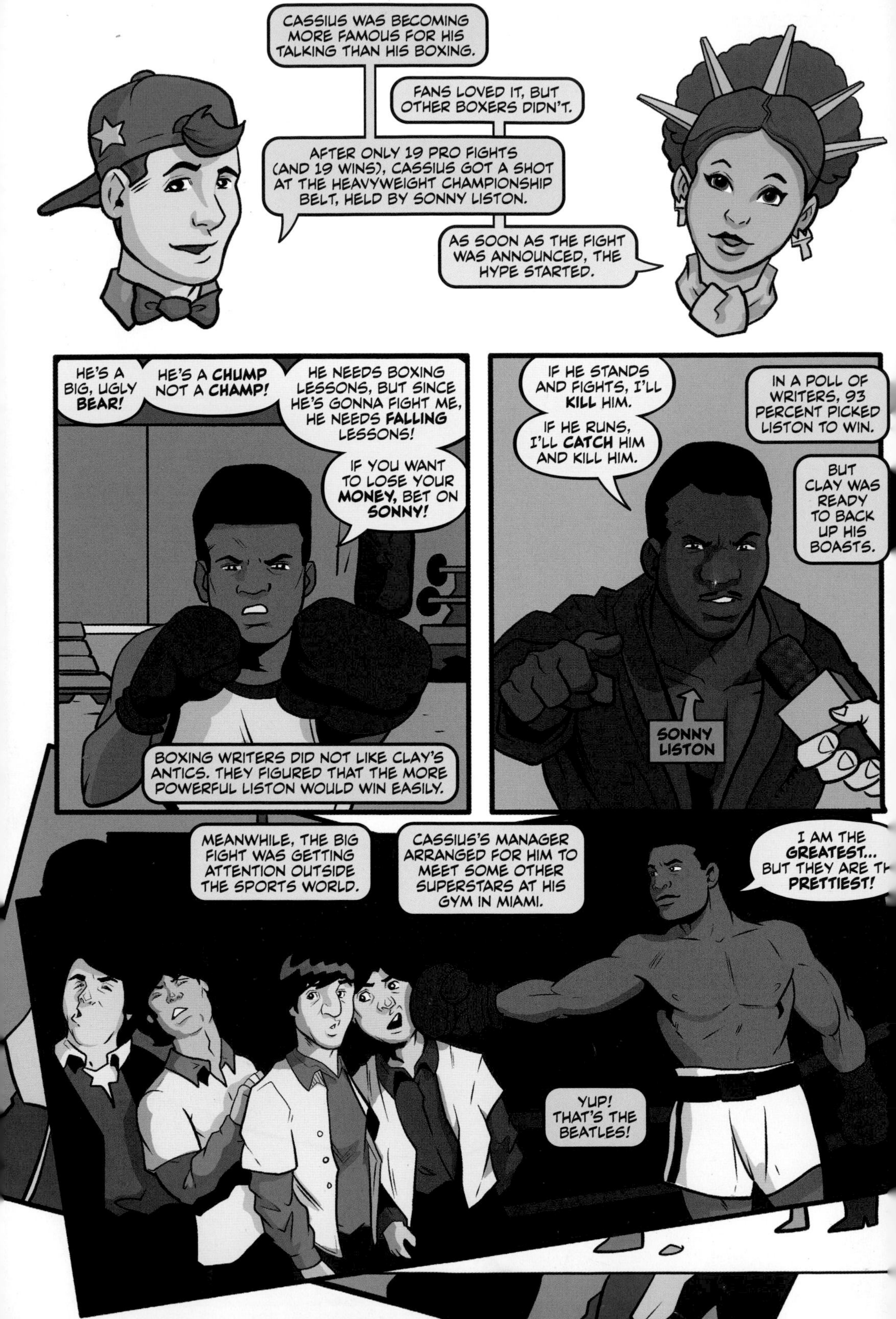
CASSIUS WAS BECOMING MORE FAMOUS FOR HIS TALKING THAN HIS BOXING.
FANS LOVED IT, BUT OTHER BOXERS DIDN'T.
AFTER ONLY 19 PRO FIGHTS (AND 19 WINS), CASSIUS GOT A SHOT AT THE HEAVYWEIGHT CHAMPIONSHIP BELT, HELD BY SONNY LISTON.
AS SOON AS THE FIGHT WAS ANNOUNCED, THE HYPE STARTED.
HE'S A BIG, UGLY **BEAR!**
HE'S A **CHUMP** NOT A **CHAMP!**
HE NEEDS BOXING LESSONS, BUT SINCE HE'S GONNA FIGHT ME, HE NEEDS **FALLING** LESSONS!
IF YOU WANT TO LOSE YOUR **MONEY,** BET ON **SONNY!**
BOXING WRITERS DID NOT LIKE CLAY'S ANTICS. THEY FIGURED THAT THE MORE POWERFUL LISTON WOULD WIN EASILY.
IF HE STANDS AND FIGHTS, I'LL **KILL** HIM.
IF HE RUNS, I'LL **CATCH** HIM AND KILL HIM.
IN A POLL OF WRITERS, 93 PERCENT PICKED LISTON TO WIN.
BUT CLAY WAS READY TO BACK UP HIS BOASTS.
SONNY LISTON
MEANWHILE, THE BIG FIGHT WAS GETTING ATTENTION OUTSIDE THE SPORTS WORLD.
CASSIUS'S MANAGER ARRANGED FOR HIM TO MEET SOME OTHER SUPERSTARS AT HIS GYM IN MIAMI.
I AM THE **GREATEST...** BUT THEY ARE TH **PRETTIEST!**
YUP! THAT'S THE BEATLES!

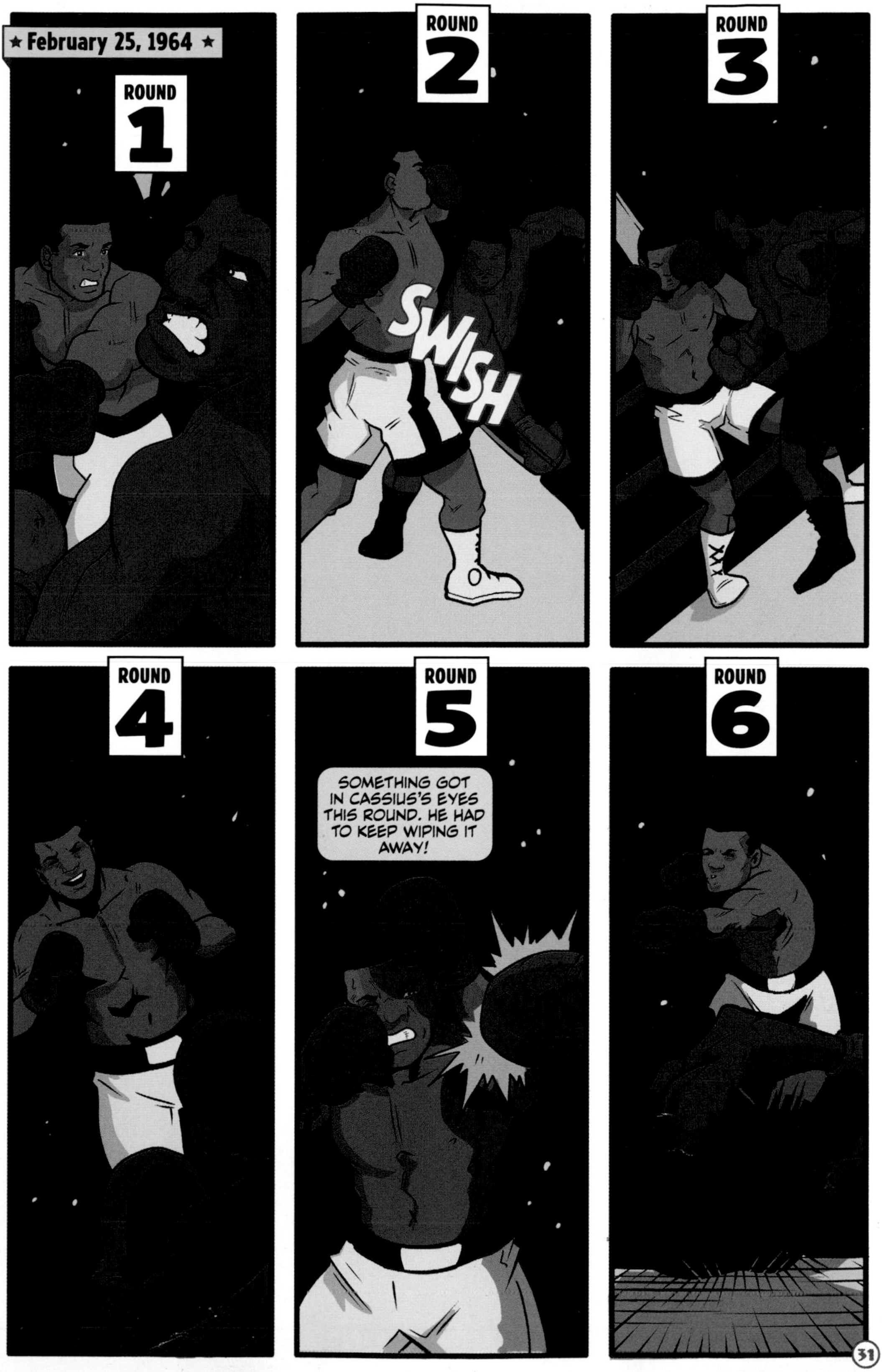
February 25, 1964
ROUND 1
ROUND 2
SWISH
ROUND 3
ROUND 4
ROUND 5
SOMETHING GOT IN CASSIUS'S EYES THIS ROUND. HE HAD TO KEEP WIPING IT AWAY!
ROUND 6

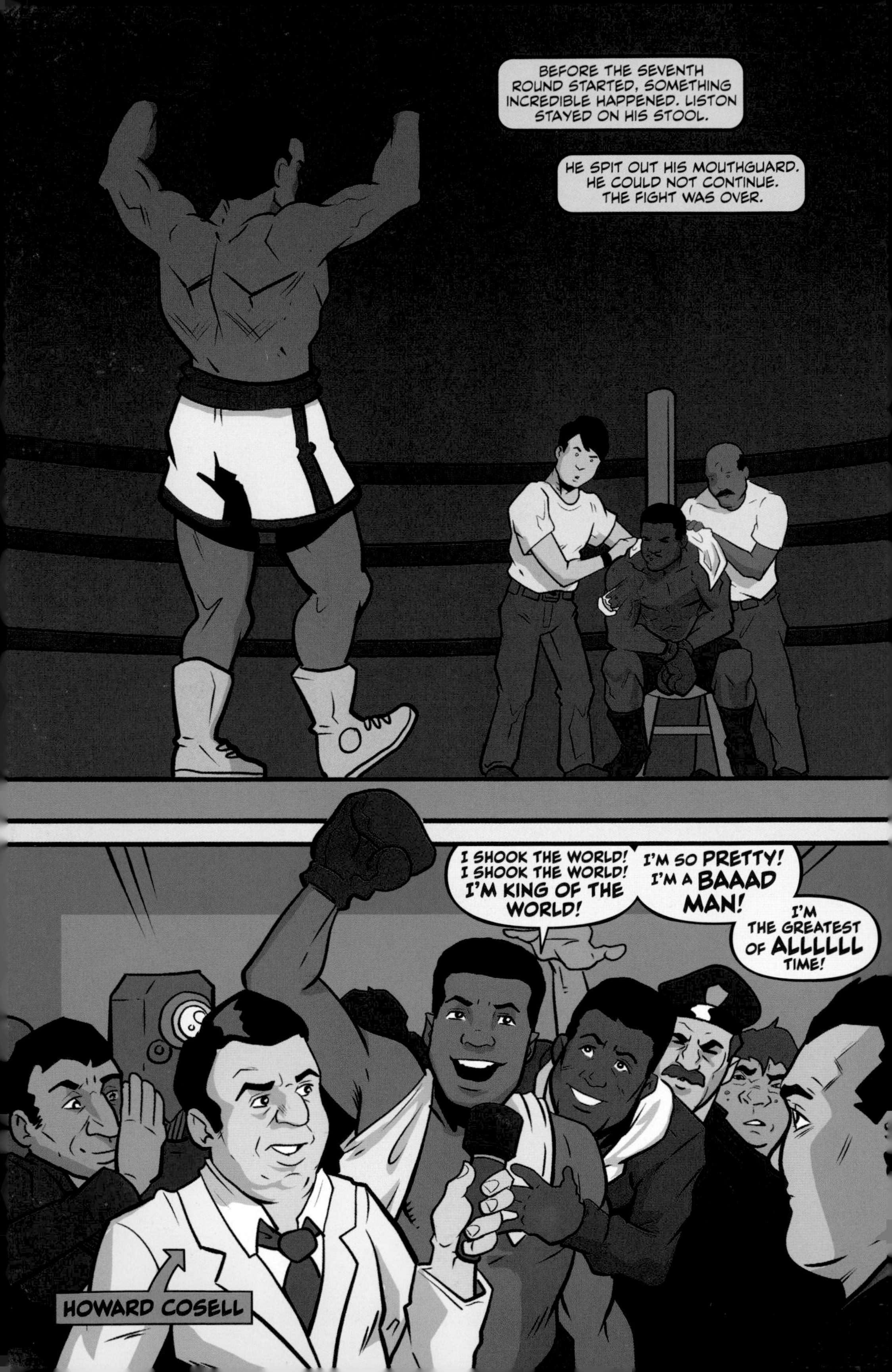
BEFORE THE SEVENTH ROUND STARTED, SOMETHING INCREDIBLE HAPPENED. LISTON STAYED ON HIS STOOL.
HE SPIT OUT HIS MOUTHGUARD. HE COULD NOT CONTINUE. THE FIGHT WAS OVER.
I SHOOK THE WORLD! I SHOOK THE WORLD! I'M KING OF THE WORLD!
I'M SO PRETTY! I'M A BAAAD MAN!
I'M THE GREATEST OF ALLLLLL TIME!
HOWARD COSELL

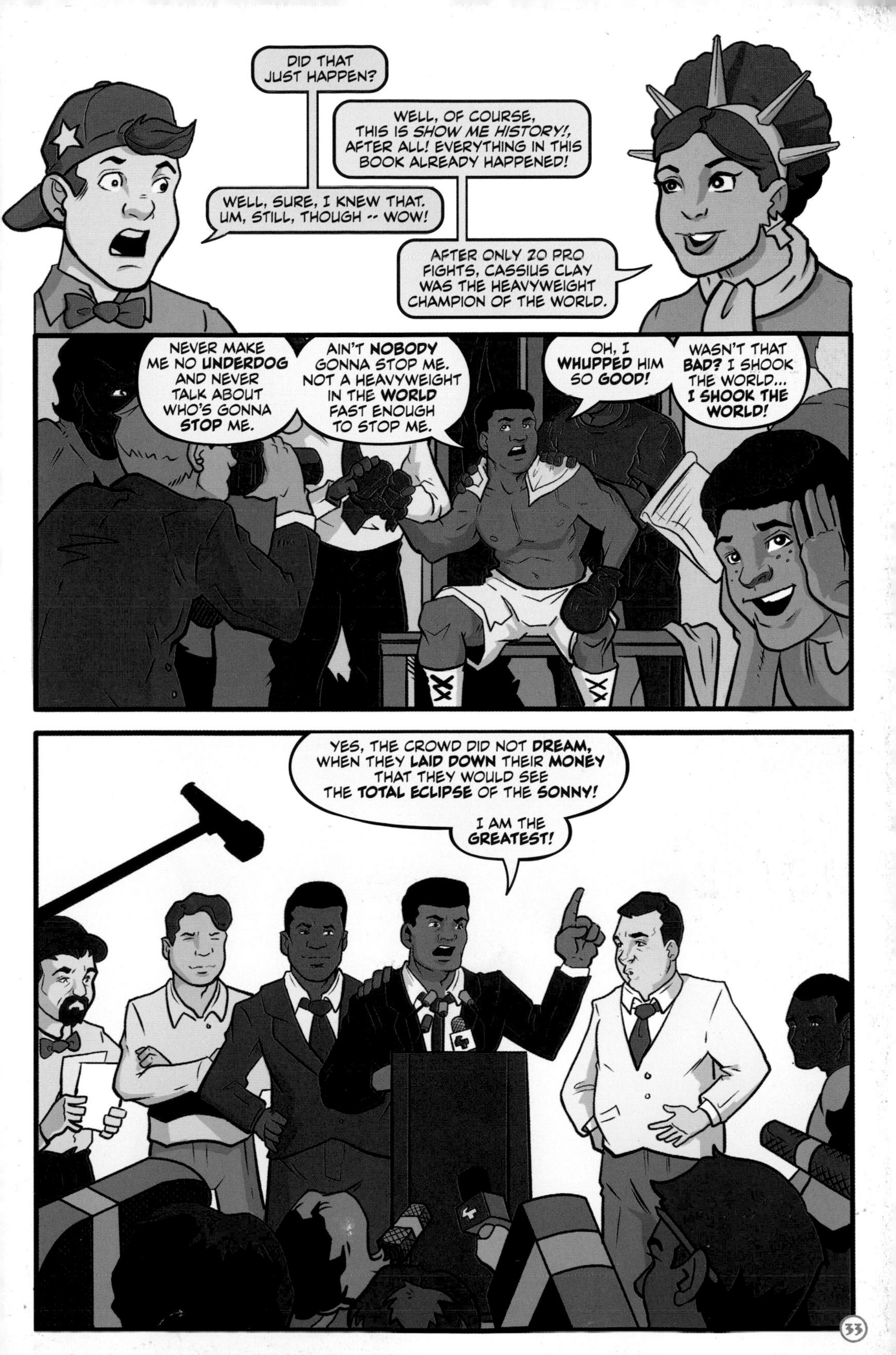
DID THAT JUST HAPPEN?
WELL, OF COURSE, THIS IS *SHOW ME HISTORY!*, AFTER ALL! EVERYTHING IN THIS BOOK ALREADY HAPPENED!
WELL, SURE, I KNEW THAT. UM, STILL, THOUGH -- WOW!
AFTER ONLY 20 PRO FIGHTS, CASSIUS CLAY WAS THE HEAVYWEIGHT CHAMPION OF THE WORLD.
NEVER MAKE ME NO **UNDERDOG** AND NEVER TALK ABOUT WHO'S GONNA **STOP** ME.
AIN'T **NOBODY** GONNA STOP ME. NOT A HEAVYWEIGHT IN THE **WORLD** FAST ENOUGH TO STOP ME.
OH, I **WHUPPED** HIM SO **GOOD!**
WASN'T THAT **BAD?** I SHOOK THE WORLD... **I SHOOK THE WORLD!**
YES, THE CROWD DID NOT **DREAM,** WHEN THEY **LAID DOWN** THEIR **MONEY** THAT THEY WOULD SEE THE **TOTAL ECLIPSE** OF THE **SONNY!**
I AM THE **GREATEST!**

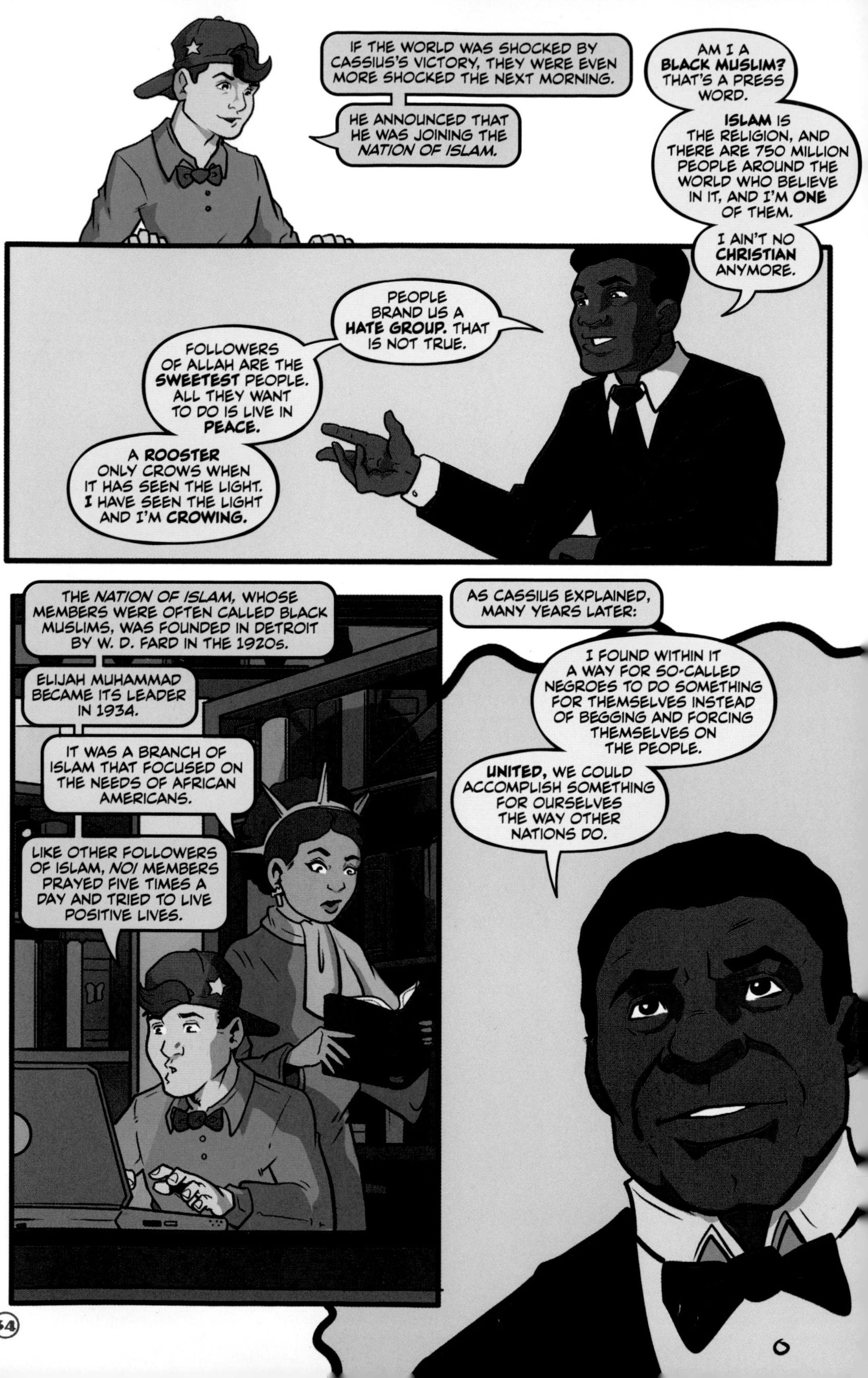
IF THE WORLD WAS SHOCKED BY CASSIUS'S VICTORY, THEY WERE EVEN MORE SHOCKED THE NEXT MORNING.
HE ANNOUNCED THAT HE WAS JOINING THE *NATION OF ISLAM.*
AM I A **BLACK MUSLIM?** THAT'S A PRESS WORD.
ISLAM IS THE RELIGION, AND THERE ARE 750 MILLION PEOPLE AROUND THE WORLD WHO BELIEVE IN IT, AND I'M **ONE** OF THEM.
I AIN'T NO **CHRISTIAN** ANYMORE.
PEOPLE BRAND US A **HATE GROUP.** THAT IS NOT TRUE.
FOLLOWERS OF ALLAH ARE THE **SWEETEST** PEOPLE. ALL THEY WANT TO DO IS LIVE IN **PEACE.**
A **ROOSTER** ONLY CROWS WHEN IT HAS SEEN THE LIGHT. **I** HAVE SEEN THE LIGHT AND I'M **CROWING.**
THE *NATION OF ISLAM,* WHOSE MEMBERS WERE OFTEN CALLED BLACK MUSLIMS, WAS FOUNDED IN DETROIT BY W. D. FARD IN THE 1920s.
ELIJAH MUHAMMAD BECAME ITS LEADER IN 1934.
IT WAS A BRANCH OF ISLAM THAT FOCUSED ON THE NEEDS OF AFRICAN AMERICANS.
LIKE OTHER FOLLOWERS OF ISLAM, *NOI* MEMBERS PRAYED FIVE TIMES A DAY AND TRIED TO LIVE POSITIVE LIVES.
AS CASSIUS EXPLAINED, MANY YEARS LATER:
I FOUND WITHIN IT A WAY FOR SO-CALLED NEGROES TO DO SOMETHING FOR THEMSELVES INSTEAD OF BEGGING AND FORCING THEMSELVES ON THE PEOPLE.
UNITED, WE COULD ACCOMPLISH SOMETHING FOR OURSELVES THE WAY OTHER NATIONS DO.

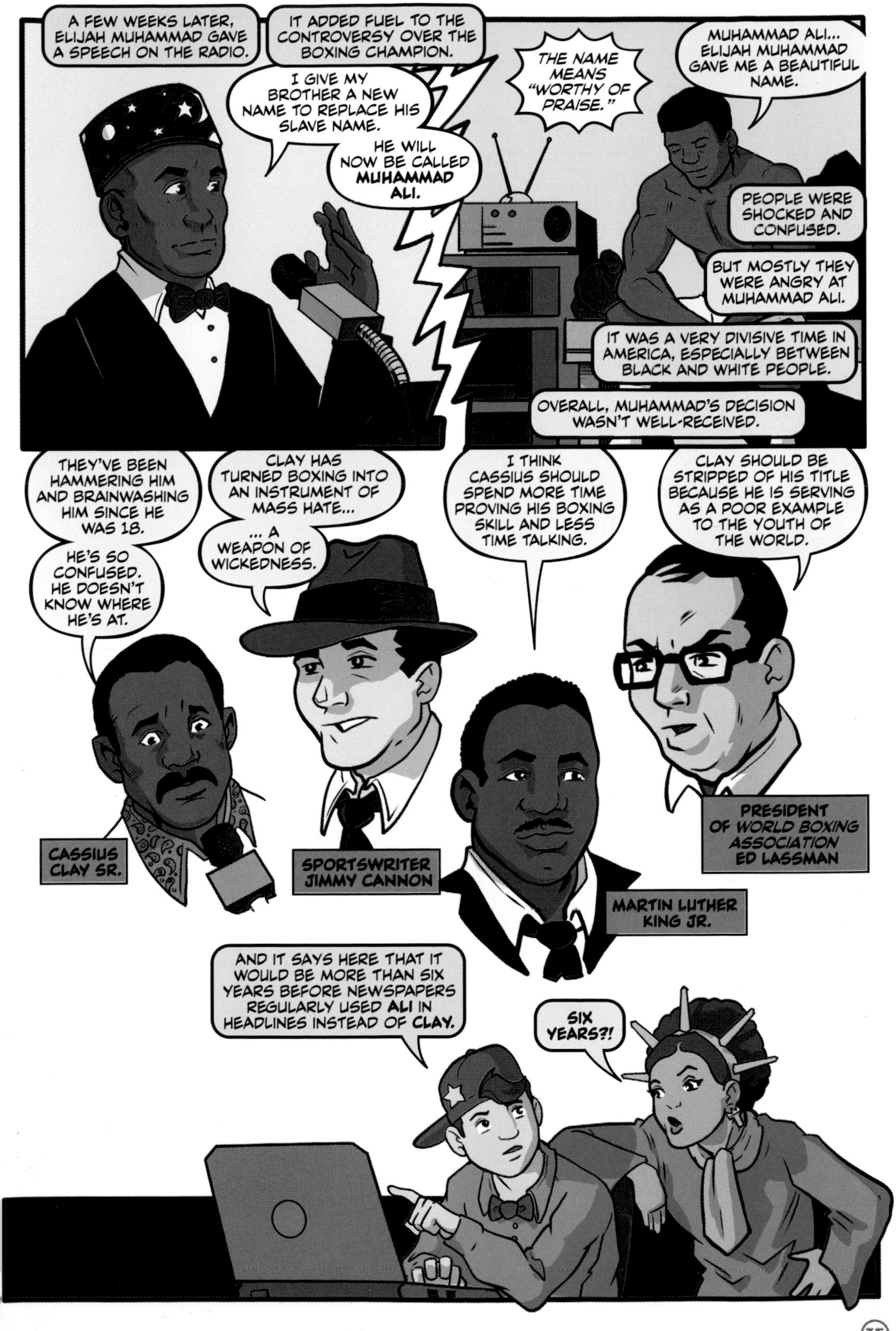
A FEW WEEKS LATER, ELIJAH MUHAMMAD GAVE A SPEECH ON THE RADIO.
IT ADDED FUEL TO THE CONTROVERSY OVER THE BOXING CHAMPION.
I GIVE MY BROTHER A NEW NAME TO REPLACE HIS SLAVE NAME.
HE WILL NOW BE CALLED **MUHAMMAD ALI.**
THE NAME MEANS "WORTHY OF PRAISE."
MUHAMMAD ALI... ELIJAH MUHAMMAD GAVE ME A BEAUTIFUL NAME.
PEOPLE WERE SHOCKED AND CONFUSED.
BUT MOSTLY THEY WERE ANGRY AT MUHAMMAD ALI.
IT WAS A VERY DIVISIVE TIME IN AMERICA, ESPECIALLY BETWEEN BLACK AND WHITE PEOPLE.
OVERALL, MUHAMMAD'S DECISION WASN'T WELL-RECEIVED.
THEY'VE BEEN HAMMERING HIM AND BRAINWASHING HIM SINCE HE WAS 18.
HE'S SO CONFUSED. HE DOESN'T KNOW WHERE HE'S AT.
CASSIUS CLAY SR.
CLAY HAS TURNED BOXING INTO AN INSTRUMENT OF MASS HATE...
... A WEAPON OF WICKEDNESS.
SPORTSWRITER JIMMY CANNON
I THINK CASSIUS SHOULD SPEND MORE TIME PROVING HIS BOXING SKILL AND LESS TIME TALKING.
MARTIN LUTHER KING JR.
CLAY SHOULD BE STRIPPED OF HIS TITLE BECAUSE HE IS SERVING AS A POOR EXAMPLE TO THE YOUTH OF THE WORLD.
PRESIDENT OF *WORLD BOXING ASSOCIATION* ED LASSMAN
AND IT SAYS HERE THAT IT WOULD BE MORE THAN SIX YEARS BEFORE NEWSPAPERS REGULARLY USED **ALI** IN HEADLINES INSTEAD OF **CLAY.**
SIX YEARS?!

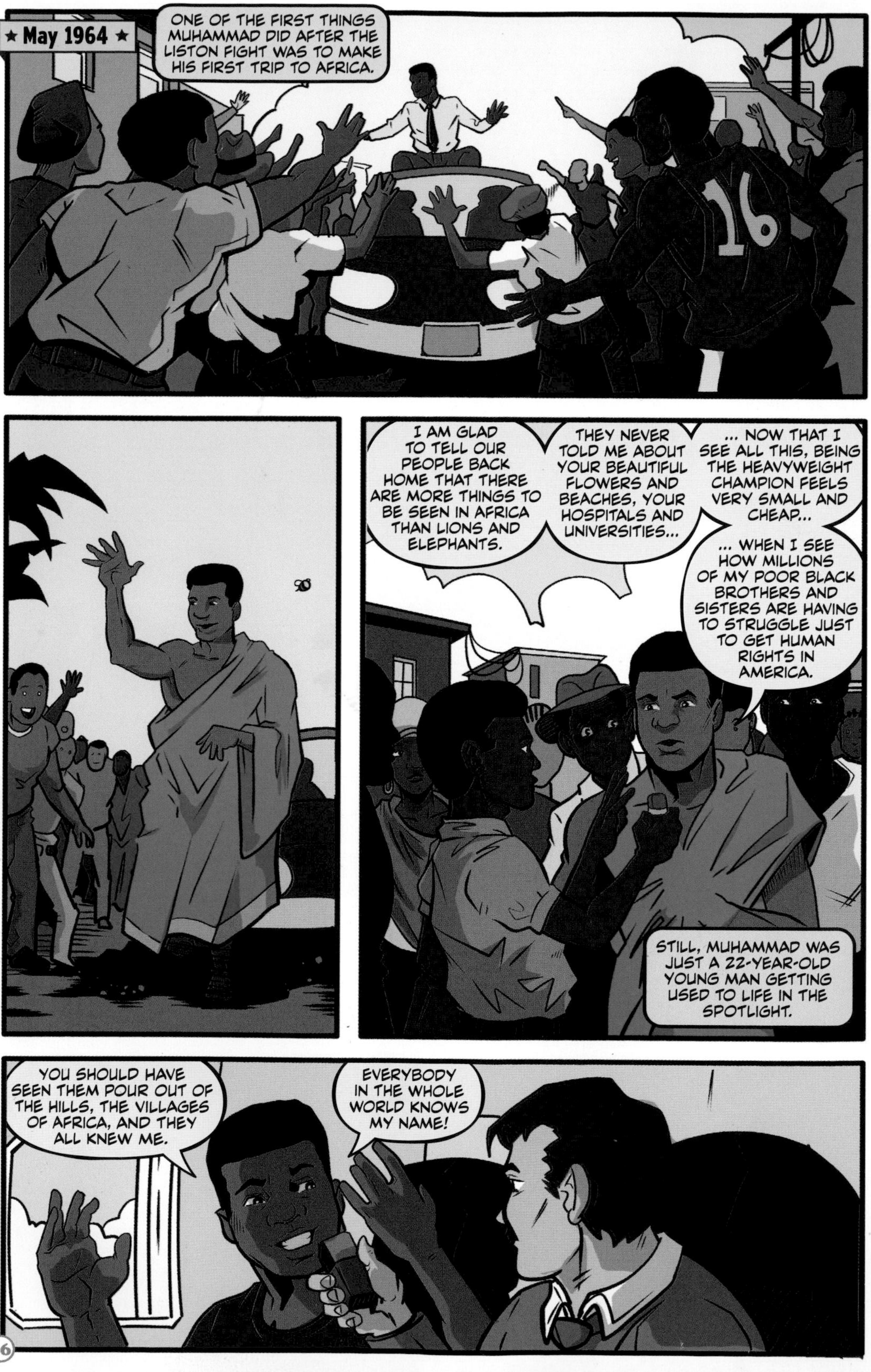
May 1964
ONE OF THE FIRST THINGS MUHAMMAD DID AFTER THE LISTON FIGHT WAS TO MAKE HIS FIRST TRIP TO AFRICA.
16
I AM GLAD TO TELL OUR PEOPLE BACK HOME THAT THERE ARE MORE THINGS TO BE SEEN IN AFRICA THAN LIONS AND ELEPHANTS.
THEY NEVER TOLD ME ABOUT YOUR BEAUTIFUL FLOWERS AND BEACHES, YOUR HOSPITALS AND UNIVERSITIES...
... NOW THAT I SEE ALL THIS, BEING THE HEAVYWEIGHT CHAMPION FEELS VERY SMALL AND CHEAP...
... WHEN I SEE HOW MILLIONS OF MY POOR BLACK BROTHERS AND SISTERS ARE HAVING TO STRUGGLE JUST TO GET HUMAN RIGHTS IN AMERICA.
STILL, MUHAMMAD WAS JUST A 22-YEAR-OLD YOUNG MAN GETTING USED TO LIFE IN THE SPOTLIGHT.
YOU SHOULD HAVE SEEN THEM POUR OUT OF THE HILLS, THE VILLAGES OF AFRICA, AND THEY ALL KNEW ME.
EVERYBODY IN THE WHOLE WORLD KNOWS MY NAME!

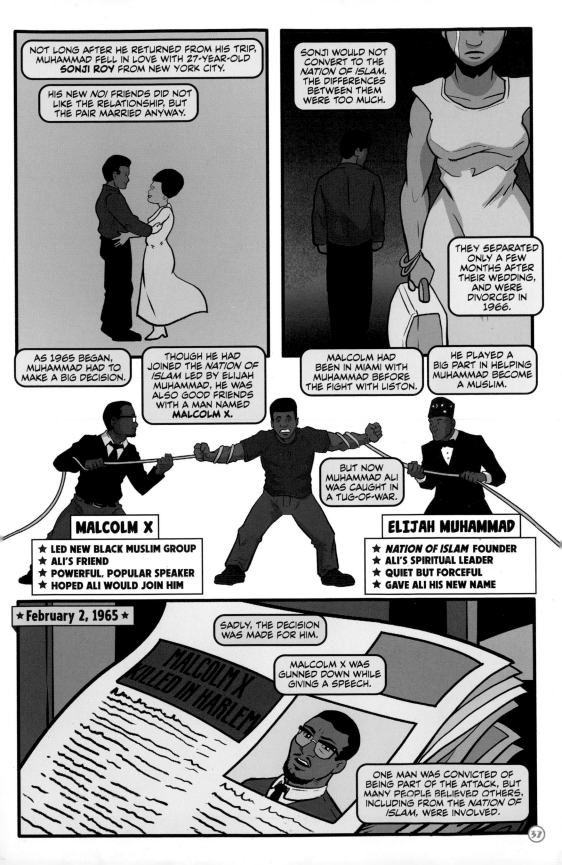

NOT LONG AFTER HE RETURNED FROM HIS TRIP, MUHAMMAD FELL IN LOVE WITH 27-YEAR-OLD **SONJI ROY** FROM NEW YORK CITY.

HIS NEW *NOI* FRIENDS DID NOT LIKE THE RELATIONSHIP, BUT THE PAIR MARRIED ANYWAY.

SONJI WOULD NOT CONVERT TO THE *NATION OF ISLAM*. THE DIFFERENCES BETWEEN THEM WERE TOO MUCH.

THEY SEPARATED ONLY A FEW MONTHS AFTER THEIR WEDDING, AND WERE DIVORCED IN 1966.

AS 1965 BEGAN, MUHAMMAD HAD TO MAKE A BIG DECISION.

THOUGH HE HAD JOINED THE *NATION OF ISLAM* LED BY ELIJAH MUHAMMAD, HE WAS ALSO GOOD FRIENDS WITH A MAN NAMED **MALCOLM X.**

MALCOLM HAD BEEN IN MIAMI WITH MUHAMMAD BEFORE THE FIGHT WITH LISTON.

HE PLAYED A BIG PART IN HELPING MUHAMMAD BECOME A MUSLIM.

BUT NOW MUHAMMAD ALI WAS CAUGHT IN A TUG-OF-WAR.

MALCOLM X
★ LED NEW BLACK MUSLIM GROUP
★ ALI'S FRIEND
★ POWERFUL, POPULAR SPEAKER
★ HOPED ALI WOULD JOIN HIM

ELIJAH MUHAMMAD
★ *NATION OF ISLAM* FOUNDER
★ ALI'S SPIRITUAL LEADER
★ QUIET BUT FORCEFUL
★ GAVE ALI HIS NEW NAME

★ February 2, 1965 ★

SADLY, THE DECISION WAS MADE FOR HIM.

MALCOLM X WAS GUNNED DOWN WHILE GIVING A SPEECH.

MALCOLM X KILLED IN HARLEM

ONE MAN WAS CONVICTED OF BEING PART OF THE ATTACK, BUT MANY PEOPLE BELIEVED OTHERS, INCLUDING FROM THE *NATION OF ISLAM*, WERE INVOLVED.

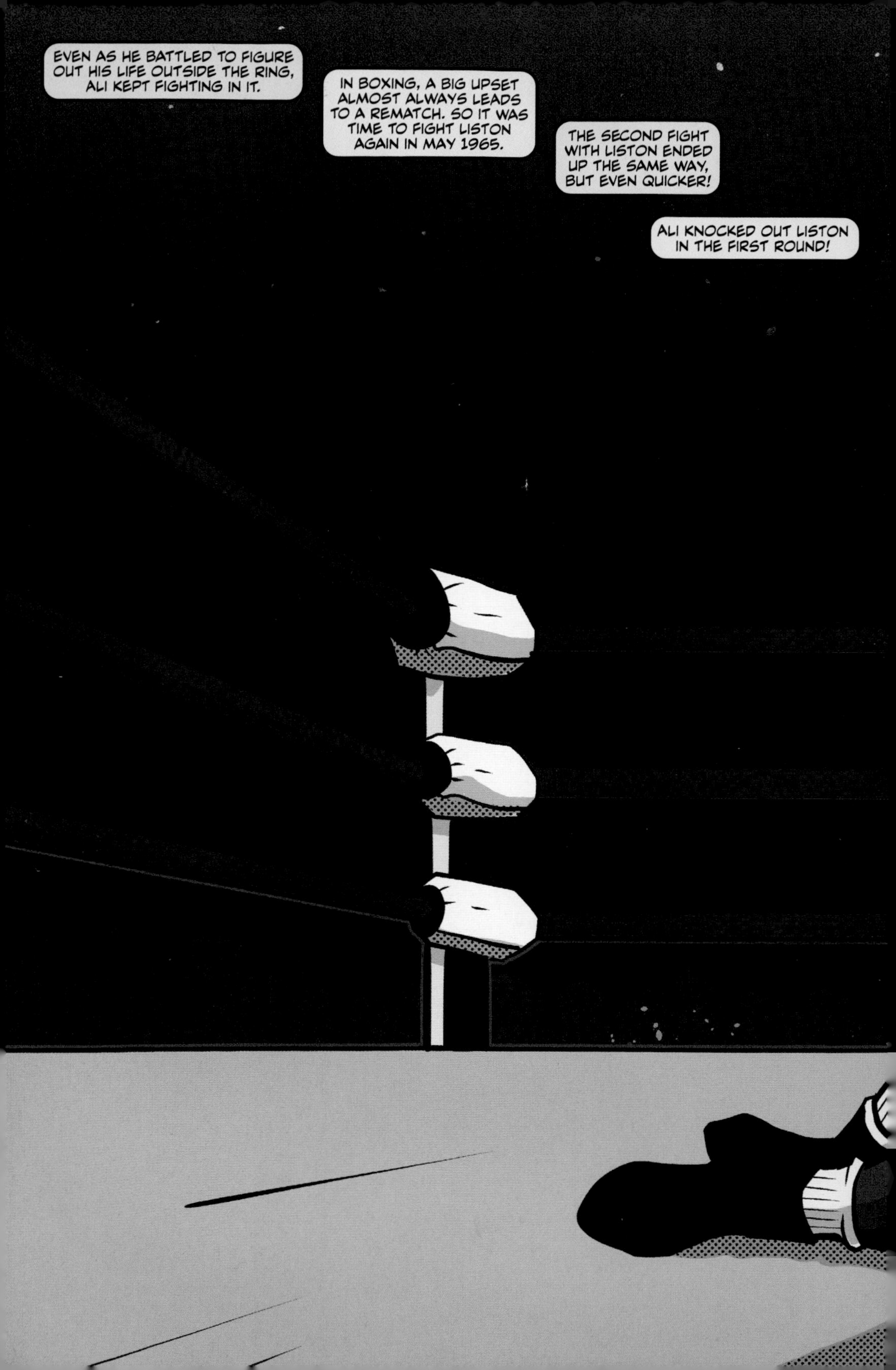
EVEN AS HE BATTLED TO FIGURE OUT HIS LIFE OUTSIDE THE RING, ALI KEPT FIGHTING IN IT.
IN BOXING, A BIG UPSET ALMOST ALWAYS LEADS TO A REMATCH. SO IT WAS TIME TO FIGHT LISTON AGAIN IN MAY 1965.
THE SECOND FIGHT WITH LISTON ENDED UP THE SAME WAY, BUT EVEN QUICKER!
ALI KNOCKED OUT LISTON IN THE FIRST ROUND!

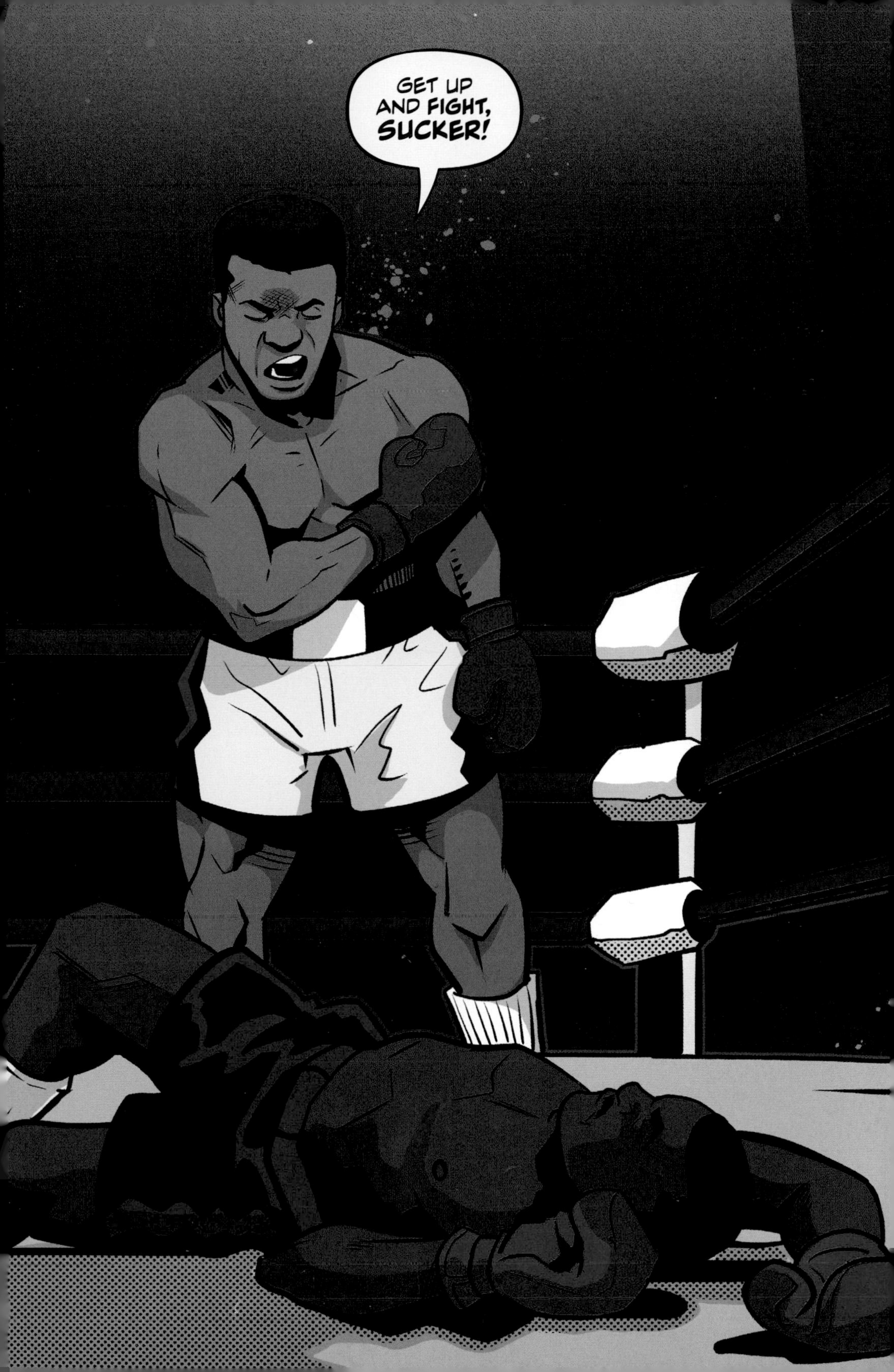
GET UP AND FIGHT, SUCKER!

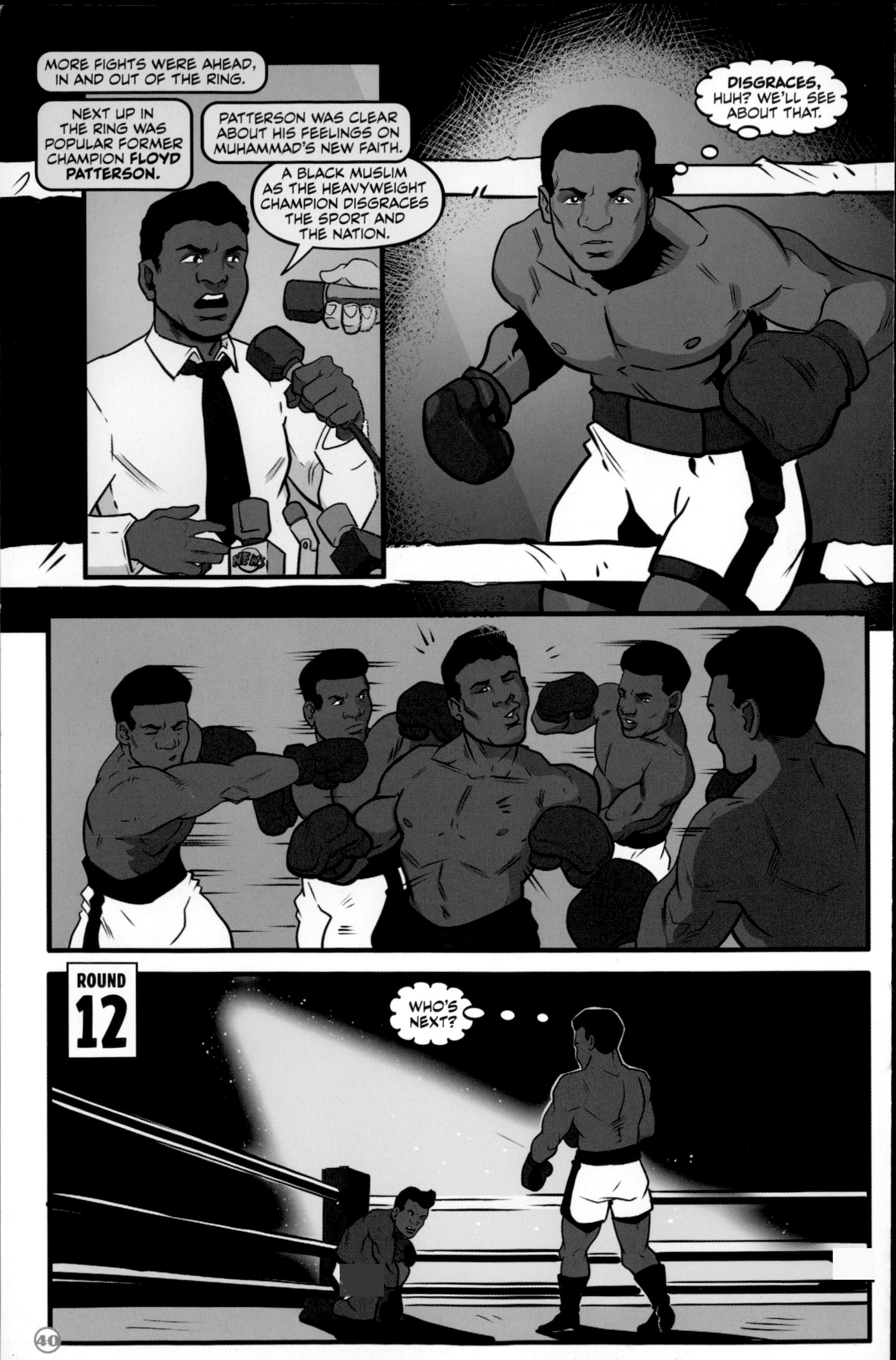
MORE FIGHTS WERE AHEAD, IN AND OUT OF THE RING.
NEXT UP IN THE RING WAS POPULAR FORMER CHAMPION FLOYD PATTERSON.
PATTERSON WAS CLEAR ABOUT HIS FEELINGS ON MUHAMMAD'S NEW FAITH.
A BLACK MUSLIM AS THE HEAVYWEIGHT CHAMPION DISGRACES THE SPORT AND THE NATION.
DISGRACES, HUH? WE'LL SEE ABOUT THAT.
NEWS
ROUND 12
WHO'S NEXT?

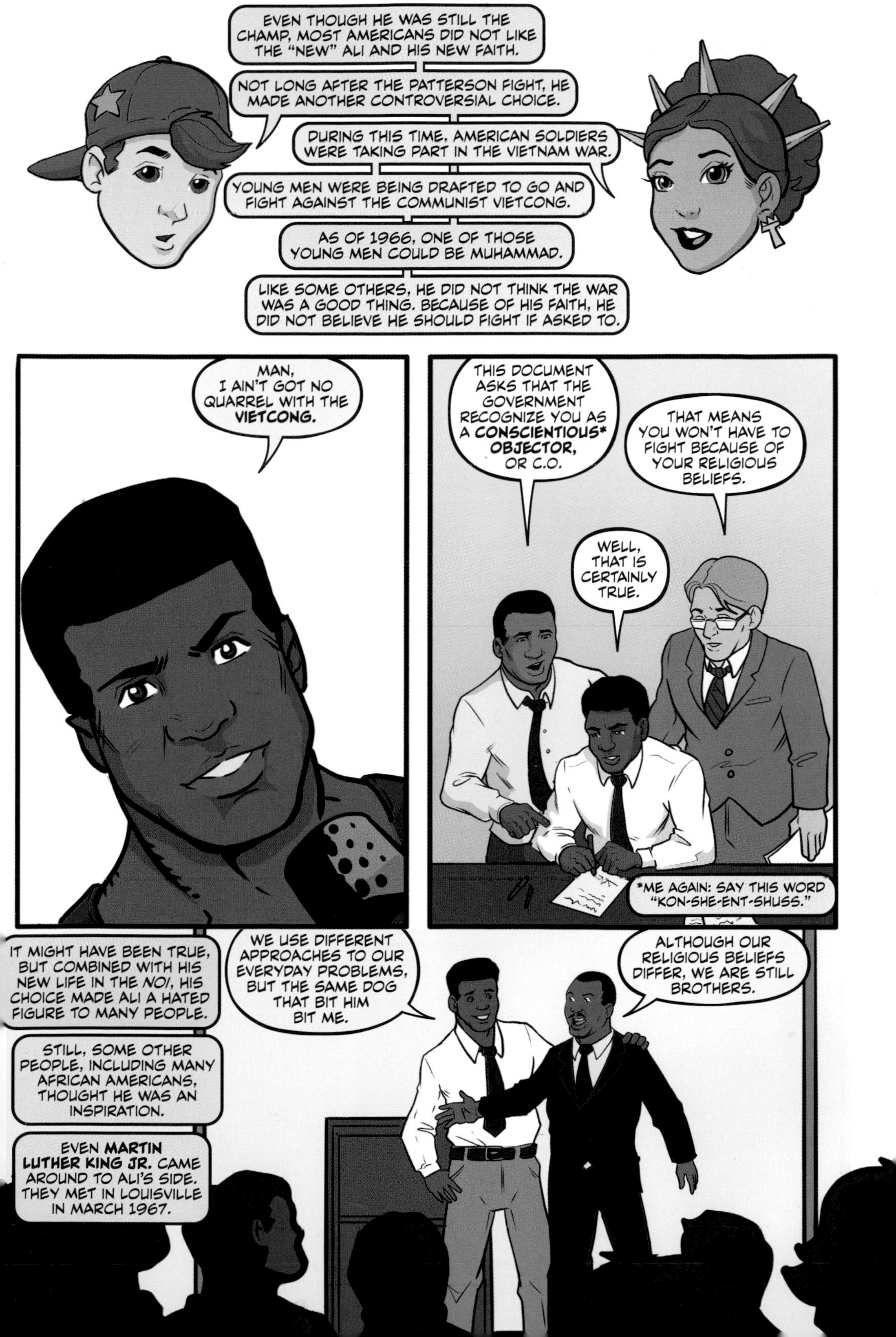
EVEN THOUGH HE WAS STILL THE CHAMP, MOST AMERICANS DID NOT LIKE THE "NEW" ALI AND HIS NEW FAITH.
NOT LONG AFTER THE PATTERSON FIGHT, HE MADE ANOTHER CONTROVERSIAL CHOICE.
DURING THIS TIME, AMERICAN SOLDIERS WERE TAKING PART IN THE VIETNAM WAR.
YOUNG MEN WERE BEING DRAFTED TO GO AND FIGHT AGAINST THE COMMUNIST VIETCONG.
AS OF 1966, ONE OF THOSE YOUNG MEN COULD BE MUHAMMAD.
LIKE SOME OTHERS, HE DID NOT THINK THE WAR WAS A GOOD THING. BECAUSE OF HIS FAITH, HE DID NOT BELIEVE HE SHOULD FIGHT IF ASKED TO.
MAN, I AIN'T GOT NO QUARREL WITH THE **VIETCONG.**
THIS DOCUMENT ASKS THAT THE GOVERNMENT RECOGNIZE YOU AS A **CONSCIENTIOUS* OBJECTOR,** OR C.O.
THAT MEANS YOU WON'T HAVE TO FIGHT BECAUSE OF YOUR RELIGIOUS BELIEFS.
WELL, THAT IS CERTAINLY TRUE.
*ME AGAIN: SAY THIS WORD "KON-SHE-ENT-SHUSS."
IT MIGHT HAVE BEEN TRUE, BUT COMBINED WITH HIS NEW LIFE IN THE *NOI*, HIS CHOICE MADE ALI A HATED FIGURE TO MANY PEOPLE.
STILL, SOME OTHER PEOPLE, INCLUDING MANY AFRICAN AMERICANS, THOUGHT HE WAS AN INSPIRATION.
EVEN **MARTIN LUTHER KING JR.** CAME AROUND TO ALI'S SIDE. THEY MET IN LOUISVILLE IN MARCH 1967.
WE USE DIFFERENT APPROACHES TO OUR EVERYDAY PROBLEMS, BUT THE SAME DOG THAT BIT HIM BIT ME.
ALTHOUGH OUR RELIGIOUS BELIEFS DIFFER, WE ARE STILL BROTHERS.

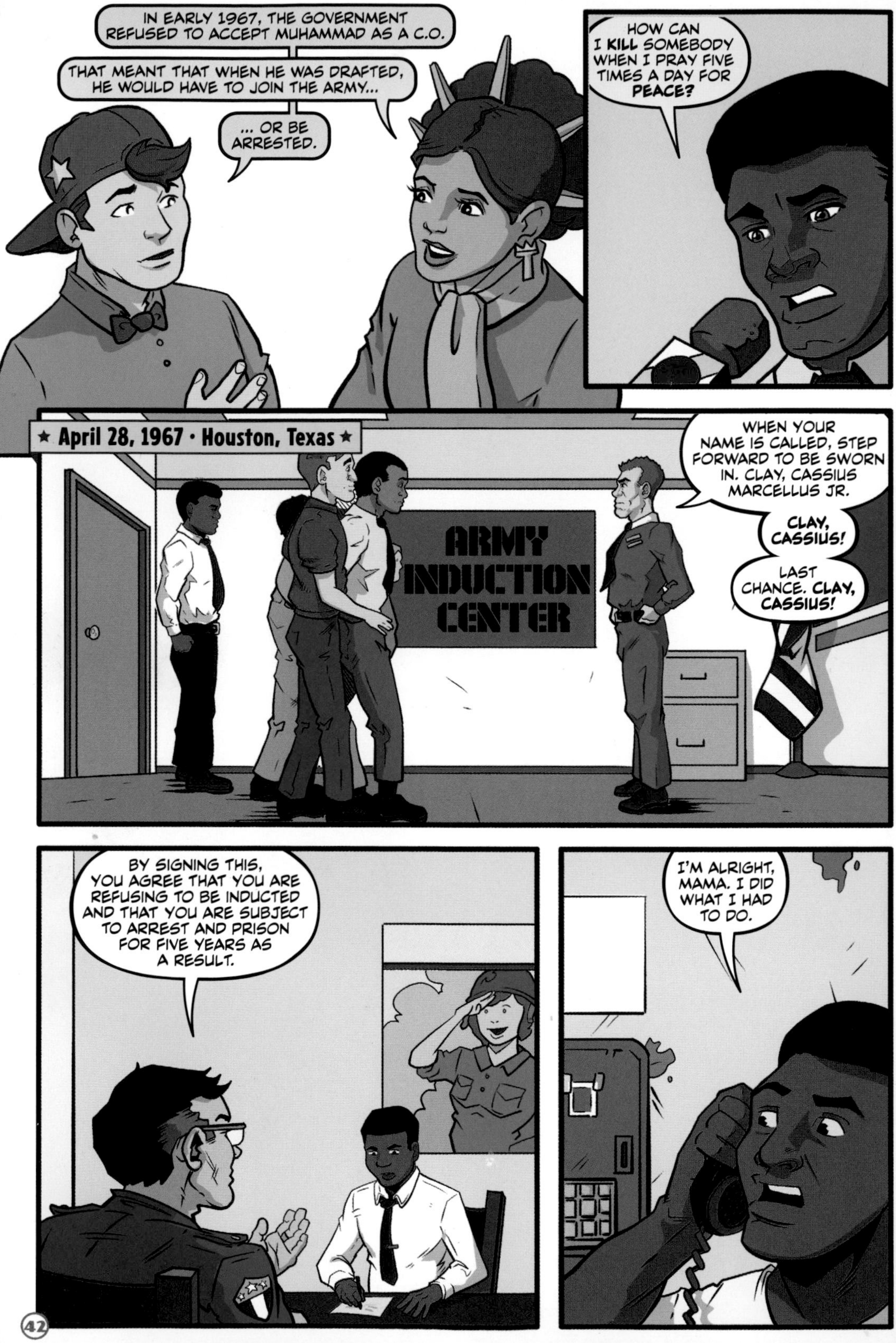
IN EARLY 1967, THE GOVERNMENT REFUSED TO ACCEPT MUHAMMAD AS A C.O.
THAT MEANT THAT WHEN HE WAS DRAFTED, HE WOULD HAVE TO JOIN THE ARMY...
... OR BE ARRESTED.
HOW CAN I KILL SOMEBODY WHEN I PRAY FIVE TIMES A DAY FOR PEACE?
★ April 28, 1967 • Houston, Texas ★
ARMY INDUCTION CENTER
WHEN YOUR NAME IS CALLED, STEP FORWARD TO BE SWORN IN. CLAY, CASSIUS MARCELLUS JR.
CLAY, CASSIUS!
LAST CHANCE. CLAY, CASSIUS!
BY SIGNING THIS, YOU AGREE THAT YOU ARE REFUSING TO BE INDUCTED AND THAT YOU ARE SUBJECT TO ARREST AND PRISON FOR FIVE YEARS AS A RESULT.
I'M ALRIGHT, MAMA. I DID WHAT I HAD TO DO.

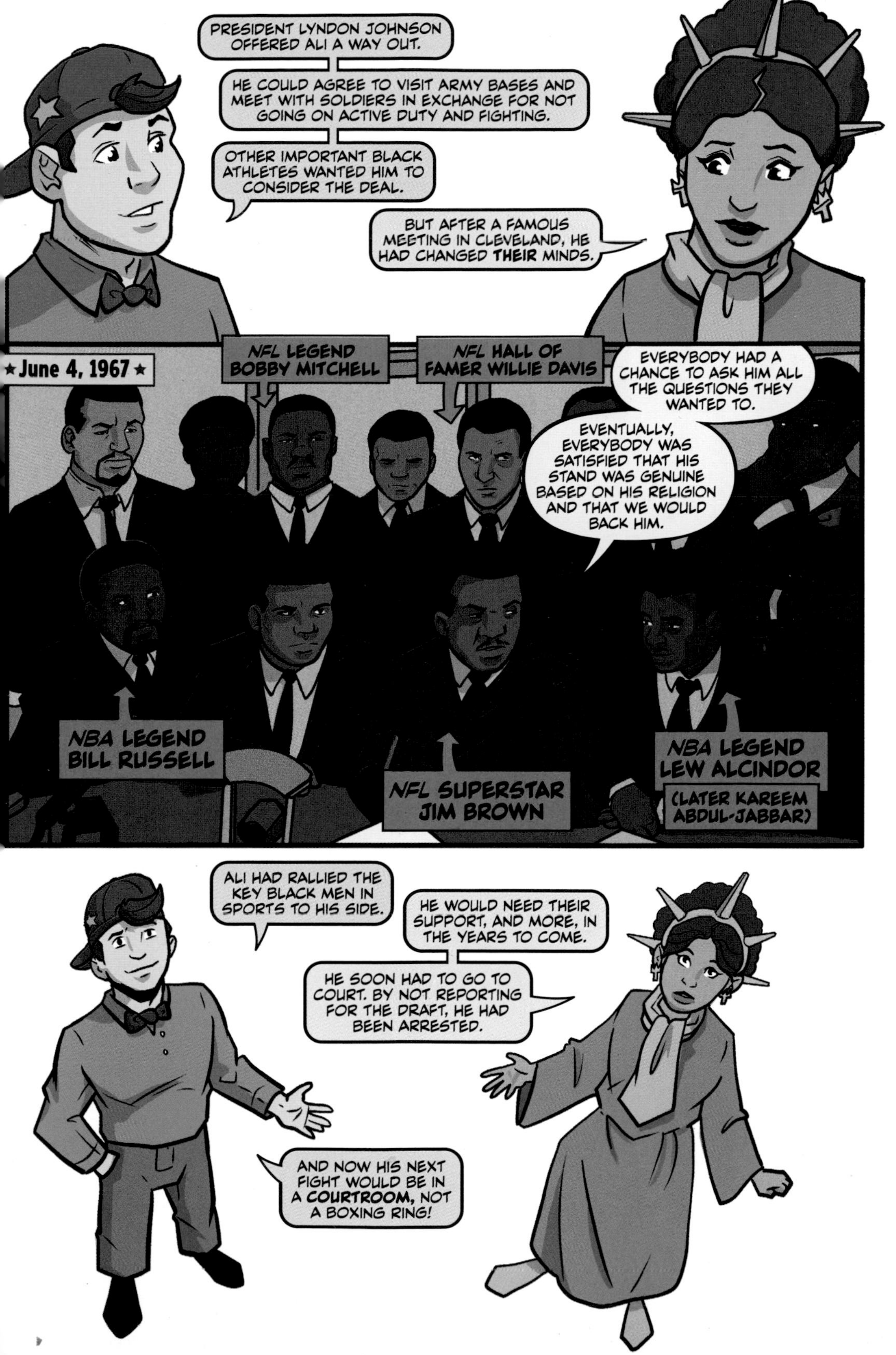
PRESIDENT LYNDON JOHNSON OFFERED ALI A WAY OUT.
HE COULD AGREE TO VISIT ARMY BASES AND MEET WITH SOLDIERS IN EXCHANGE FOR NOT GOING ON ACTIVE DUTY AND FIGHTING.
OTHER IMPORTANT BLACK ATHLETES WANTED HIM TO CONSIDER THE DEAL.
BUT AFTER A FAMOUS MEETING IN CLEVELAND, HE HAD CHANGED **THEIR** MINDS.
★June 4, 1967★
NFL LEGEND BOBBY MITCHELL
NFL HALL OF FAMER WILLIE DAVIS
EVERYBODY HAD A CHANCE TO ASK HIM ALL THE QUESTIONS THEY WANTED TO.
EVENTUALLY, EVERYBODY WAS SATISFIED THAT HIS STAND WAS GENUINE BASED ON HIS RELIGION AND THAT WE WOULD BACK HIM.
NBA LEGEND BILL RUSSELL
NFL SUPERSTAR JIM BROWN
NBA LEGEND LEW ALCINDOR
(LATER KAREEM ABDUL-JABBAR)
ALI HAD RALLIED THE KEY BLACK MEN IN SPORTS TO HIS SIDE.
HE WOULD NEED THEIR SUPPORT, AND MORE, IN THE YEARS TO COME.
HE SOON HAD TO GO TO COURT. BY NOT REPORTING FOR THE DRAFT, HE HAD BEEN ARRESTED.
AND NOW HIS NEXT FIGHT WOULD BE IN A **COURTROOM**, NOT A BOXING RING!

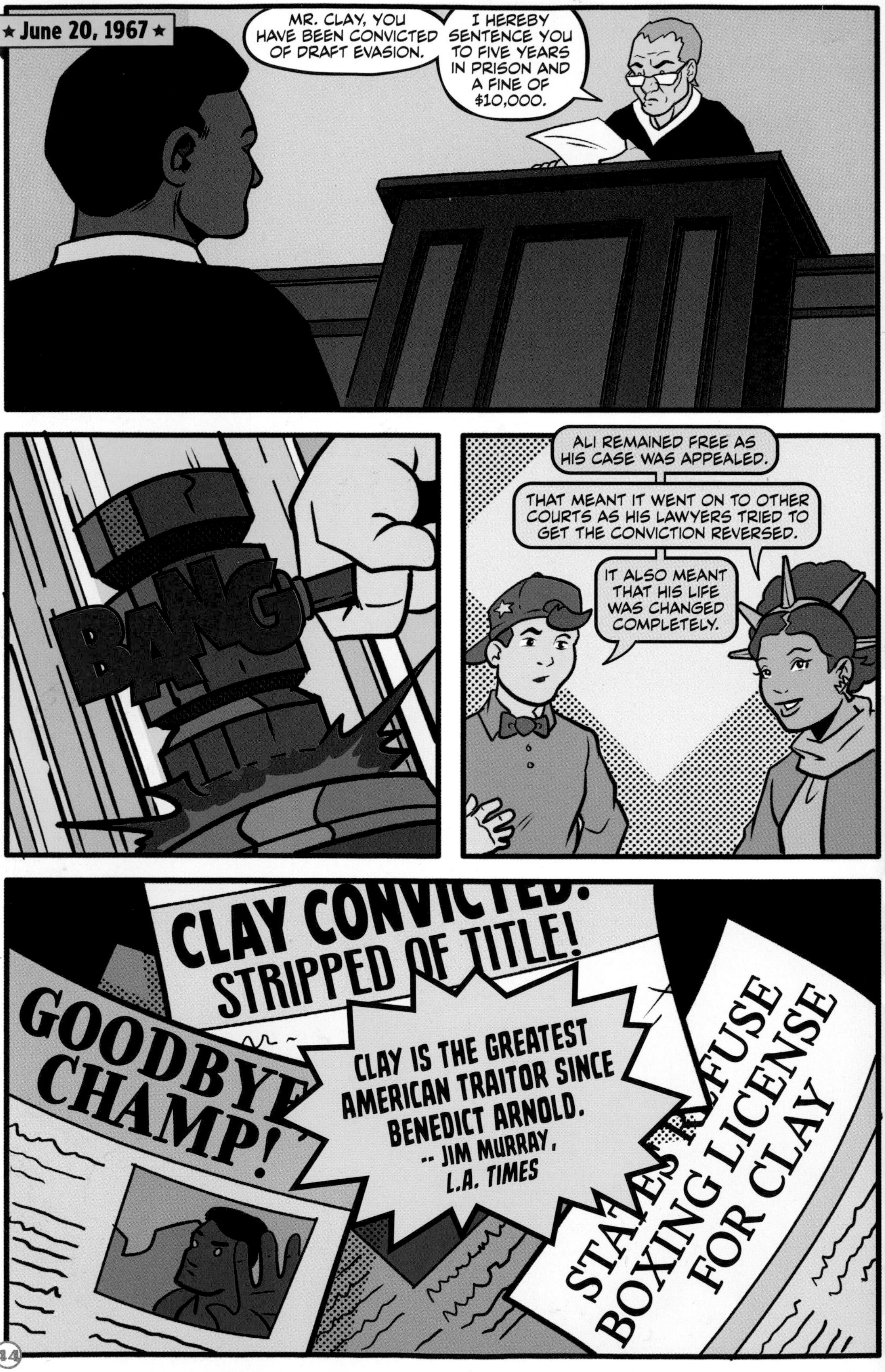
★ June 20, 1967 ★
MR. CLAY, YOU HAVE BEEN CONVICTED OF DRAFT EVASION.
I HEREBY SENTENCE YOU TO FIVE YEARS IN PRISON AND A FINE OF $10,000.
BANG
ALI REMAINED FREE AS HIS CASE WAS APPEALED.
THAT MEANT IT WENT ON TO OTHER COURTS AS HIS LAWYERS TRIED TO GET THE CONVICTION REVERSED.
IT ALSO MEANT THAT HIS LIFE WAS CHANGED COMPLETELY.
CLAY CONVICTED!
STRIPPED OF TITLE!
GOODBYE CHAMP!
CLAY IS THE GREATEST AMERICAN TRAITOR SINCE BENEDICT ARNOLD.
-- JIM MURRAY, L.A. TIMES
STATES REFUSE BOXING LICENSE FOR CLAY

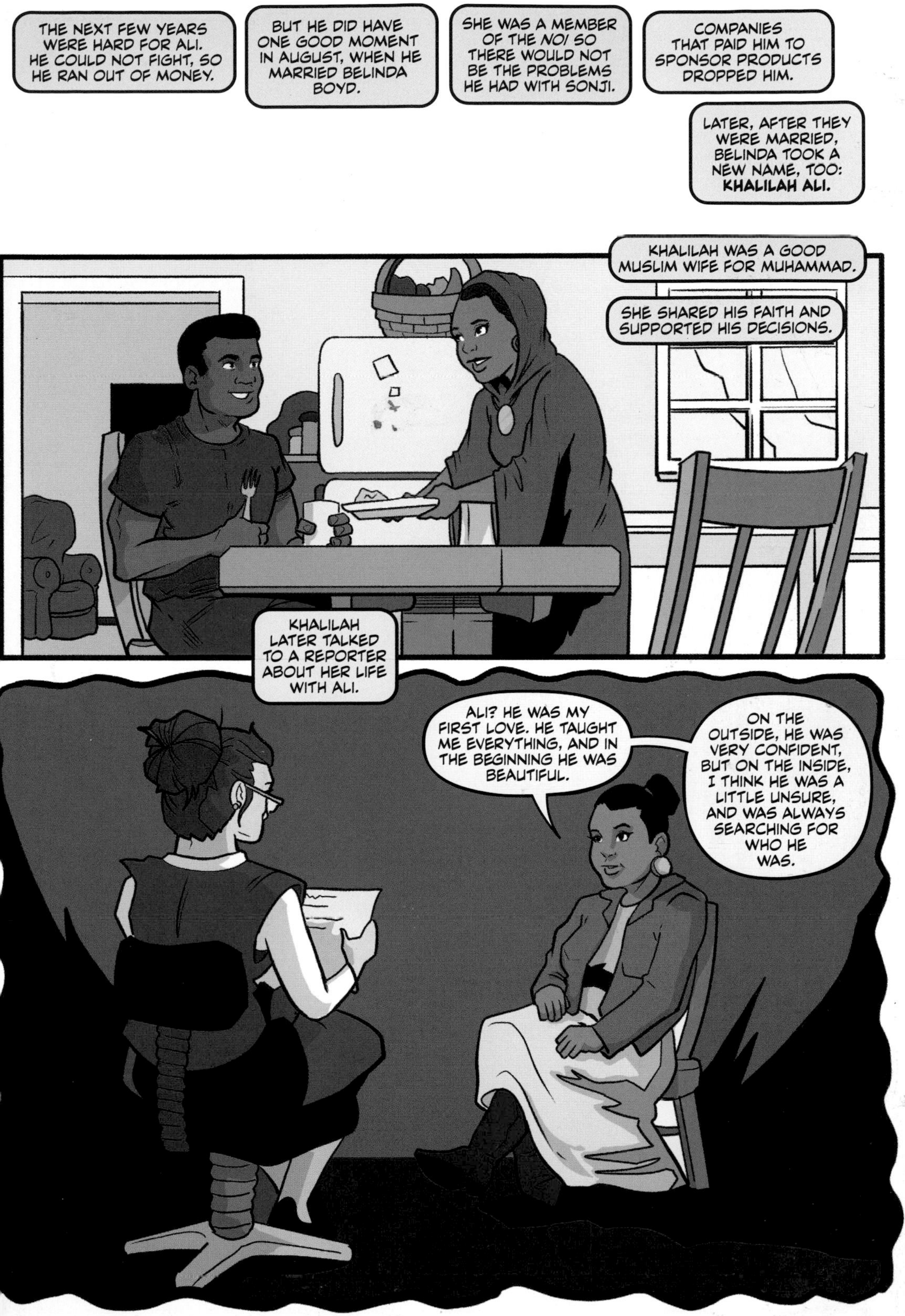
THE NEXT FEW YEARS WERE HARD FOR ALI. HE COULD NOT FIGHT, SO HE RAN OUT OF MONEY.
BUT HE DID HAVE ONE GOOD MOMENT IN AUGUST, WHEN HE MARRIED BELINDA BOYD.
SHE WAS A MEMBER OF THE *NOI* SO THERE WOULD NOT BE THE PROBLEMS HE HAD WITH SONJI.
COMPANIES THAT PAID HIM TO SPONSOR PRODUCTS DROPPED HIM.
LATER, AFTER THEY WERE MARRIED, BELINDA TOOK A NEW NAME, TOO: **KHALILAH ALI.**
KHALILAH WAS A GOOD MUSLIM WIFE FOR MUHAMMAD.
SHE SHARED HIS FAITH AND SUPPORTED HIS DECISIONS.
KHALILAH LATER TALKED TO A REPORTER ABOUT HER LIFE WITH ALI.
ALI? HE WAS MY FIRST LOVE. HE TAUGHT ME EVERYTHING, AND IN THE BEGINNING HE WAS BEAUTIFUL.
ON THE OUTSIDE, HE WAS VERY CONFIDENT, BUT ON THE INSIDE, I THINK HE WAS A LITTLE UNSURE, AND WAS ALWAYS SEARCHING FOR WHO HE WAS.

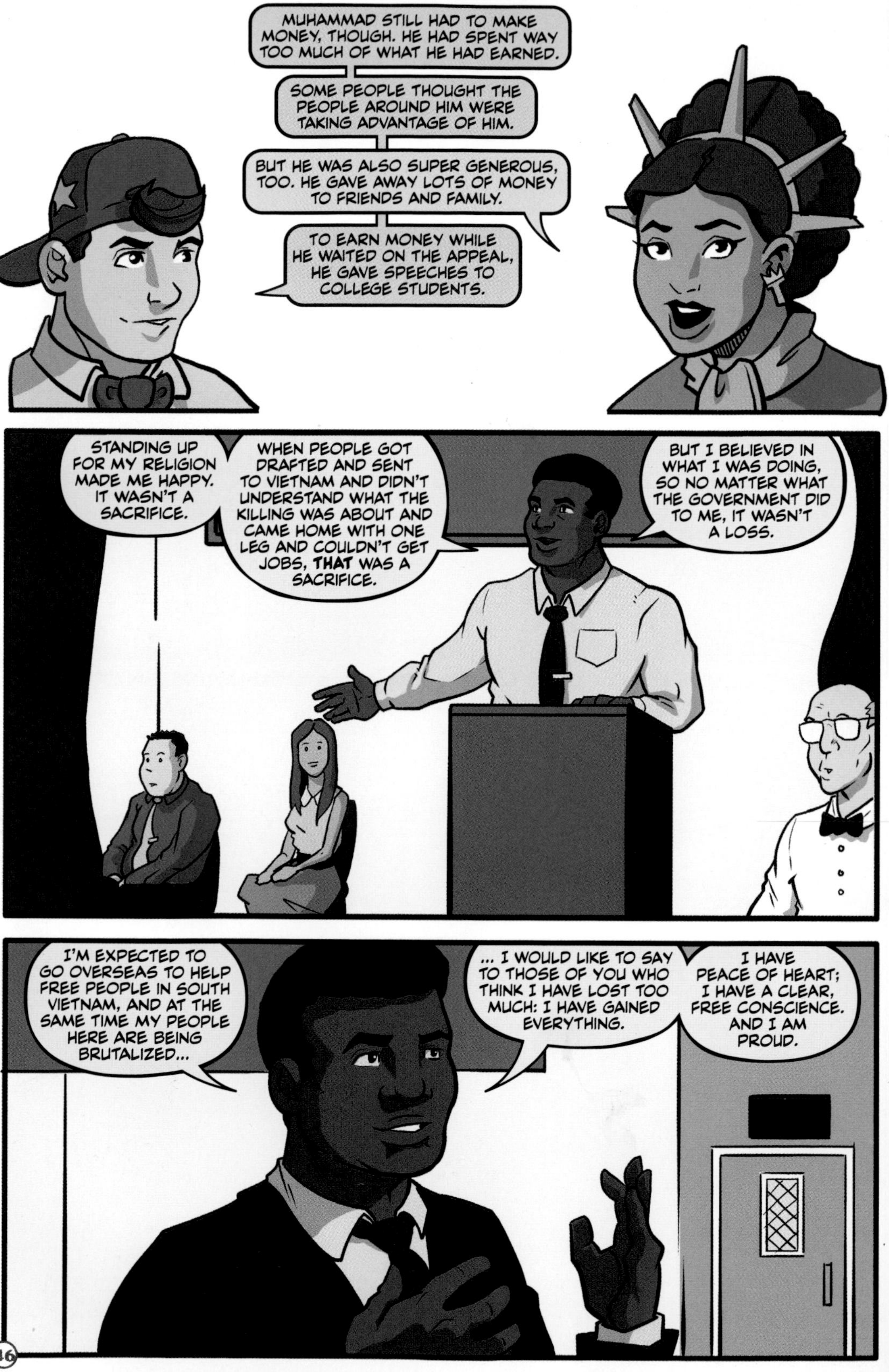
MUHAMMAD STILL HAD TO MAKE MONEY, THOUGH. HE HAD SPENT WAY TOO MUCH OF WHAT HE HAD EARNED.
SOME PEOPLE THOUGHT THE PEOPLE AROUND HIM WERE TAKING ADVANTAGE OF HIM.
BUT HE WAS ALSO SUPER GENEROUS, TOO. HE GAVE AWAY LOTS OF MONEY TO FRIENDS AND FAMILY.
TO EARN MONEY WHILE HE WAITED ON THE APPEAL, HE GAVE SPEECHES TO COLLEGE STUDENTS.
STANDING UP FOR MY RELIGION MADE ME HAPPY. IT WASN'T A SACRIFICE.
WHEN PEOPLE GOT DRAFTED AND SENT TO VIETNAM AND DIDN'T UNDERSTAND WHAT THE KILLING WAS ABOUT AND CAME HOME WITH ONE LEG AND COULDN'T GET JOBS, **THAT** WAS A SACRIFICE.
BUT I BELIEVED IN WHAT I WAS DOING, SO NO MATTER WHAT THE GOVERNMENT DID TO ME, IT WASN'T A LOSS.
I'M EXPECTED TO GO OVERSEAS TO HELP FREE PEOPLE IN SOUTH VIETNAM, AND AT THE SAME TIME MY PEOPLE HERE ARE BEING BRUTALIZED...
... I WOULD LIKE TO SAY TO THOSE OF YOU WHO THINK I HAVE LOST TOO MUCH: I HAVE GAINED EVERYTHING.
I HAVE PEACE OF HEART; I HAVE A CLEAR, FREE CONSCIENCE. AND I AM PROUD.

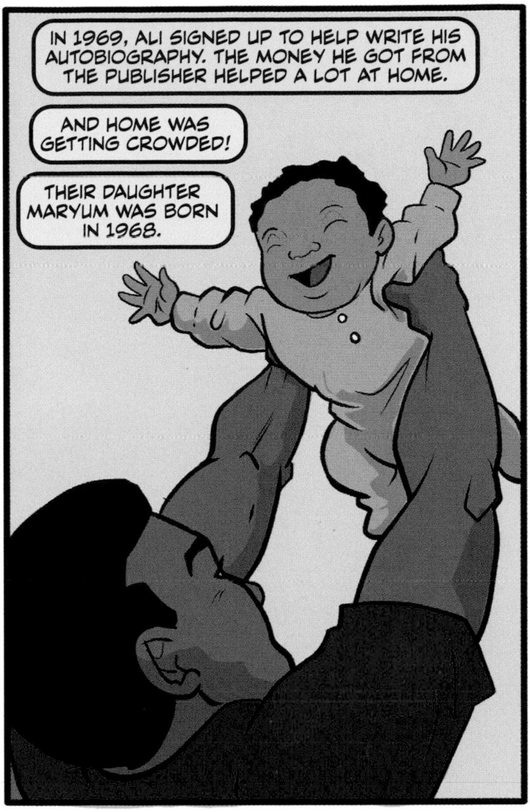
IN 1969, ALI SIGNED UP TO HELP WRITE HIS AUTOBIOGRAPHY. THE MONEY HE GOT FROM THE PUBLISHER HELPED A LOT AT HOME.
AND HOME WAS GETTING CROWDED!
THEIR DAUGHTER MARYUM WAS BORN IN 1968.

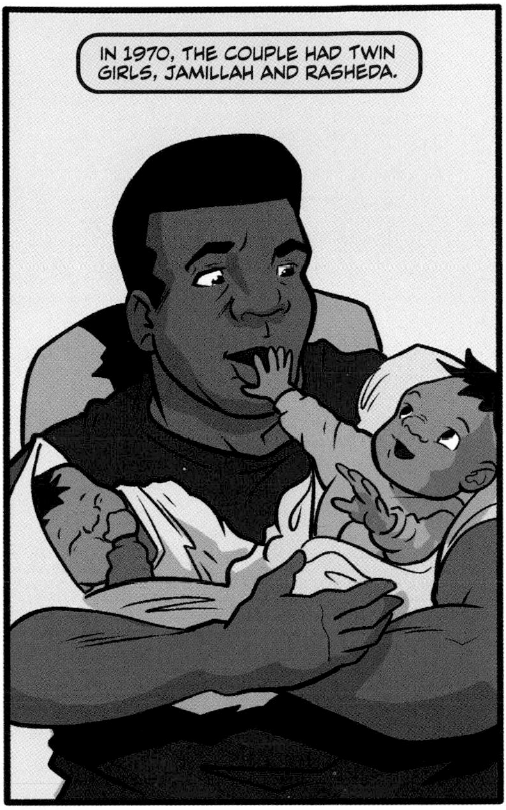
IN 1970, THE COUPLE HAD TWIN GIRLS, JAMILLAH AND RASHEDA.

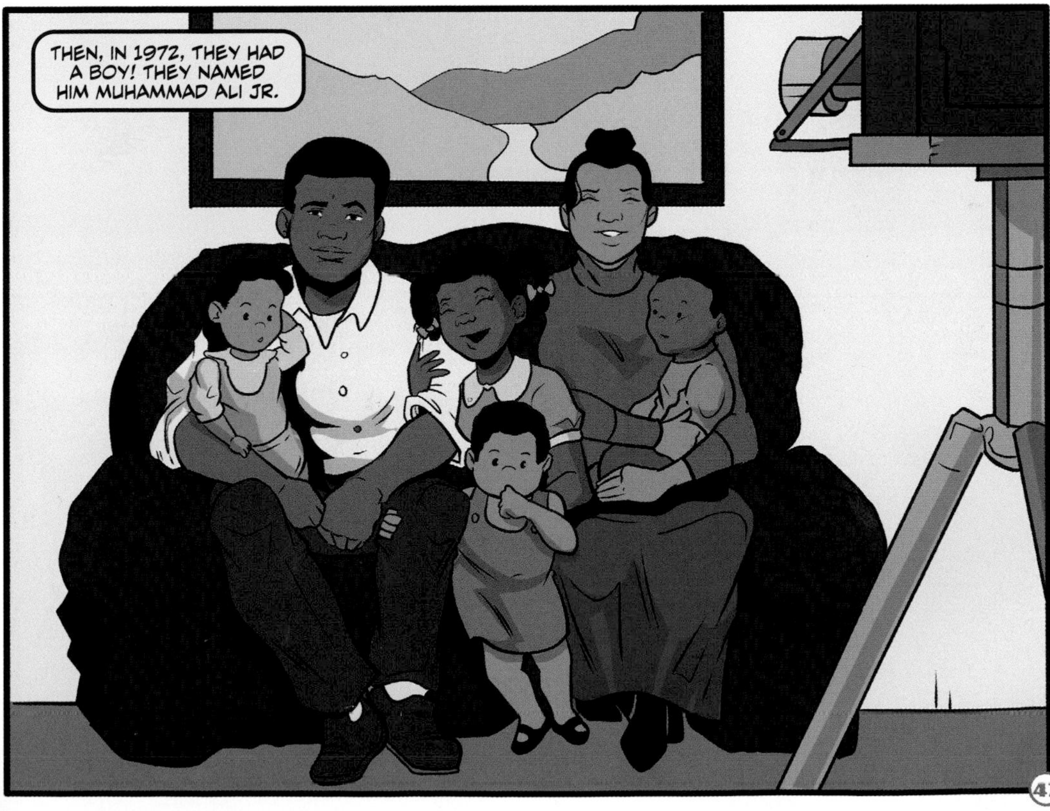
THEN, IN 1972, THEY HAD A BOY! THEY NAMED HIM MUHAMMAD ALI JR.

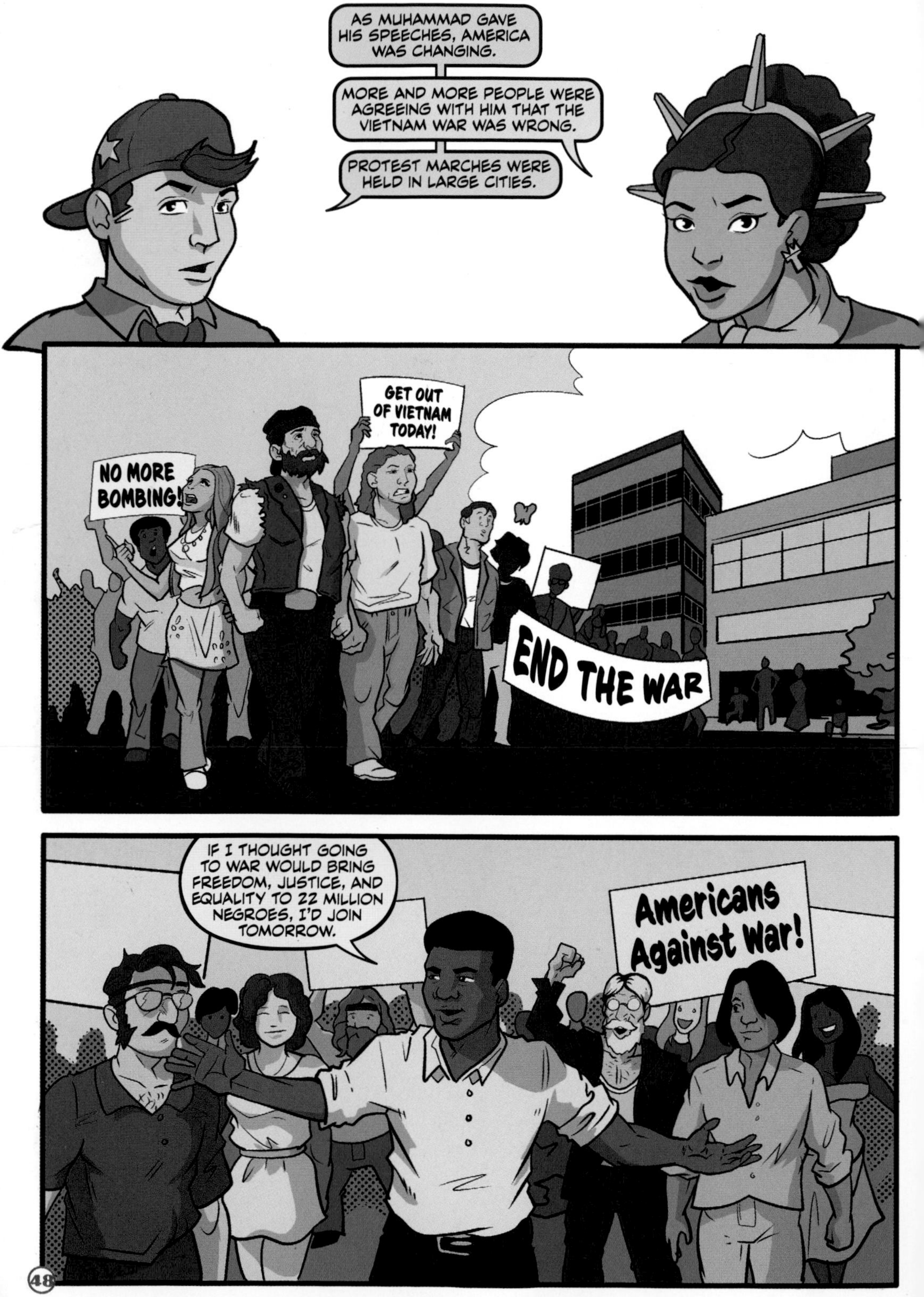
AS MUHAMMAD GAVE HIS SPEECHES, AMERICA WAS CHANGING.
MORE AND MORE PEOPLE WERE AGREEING WITH HIM THAT THE VIETNAM WAR WAS WRONG.
PROTEST MARCHES WERE HELD IN LARGE CITIES.
NO MORE BOMBING!
GET OUT OF VIETNAM TODAY!
END THE WAR
IF I THOUGHT GOING TO WAR WOULD BRING FREEDOM, JUSTICE, AND EQUALITY TO 22 MILLION NEGROES, I'D JOIN TOMORROW.
Americans Against War!

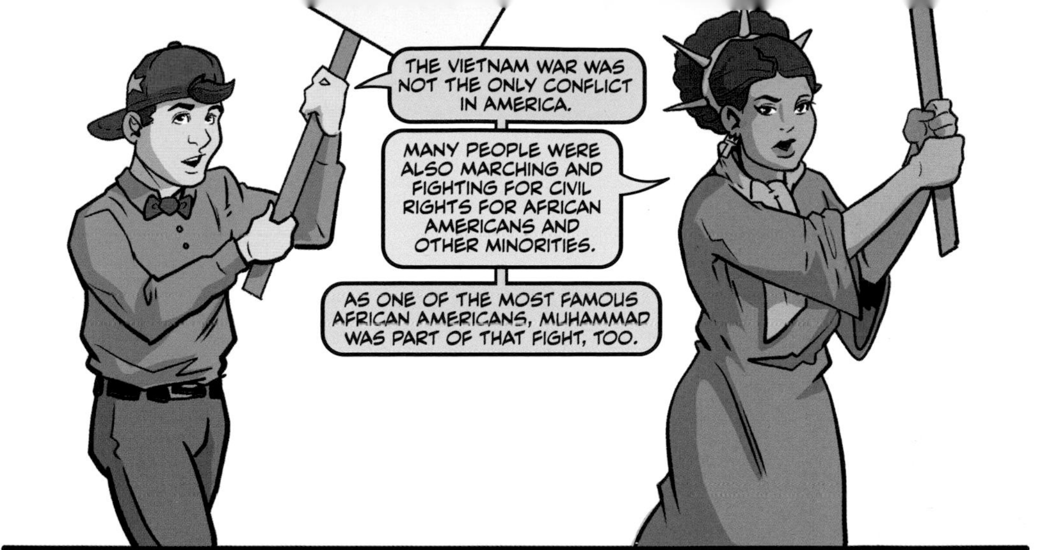
THE VIETNAM WAR WAS NOT THE ONLY CONFLICT IN AMERICA.
MANY PEOPLE WERE ALSO MARCHING AND FIGHTING FOR CIVIL RIGHTS FOR AFRICAN AMERICANS AND OTHER MINORITIES.
AS ONE OF THE MOST FAMOUS AFRICAN AMERICANS, MUHAMMAD WAS PART OF THAT FIGHT, TOO.

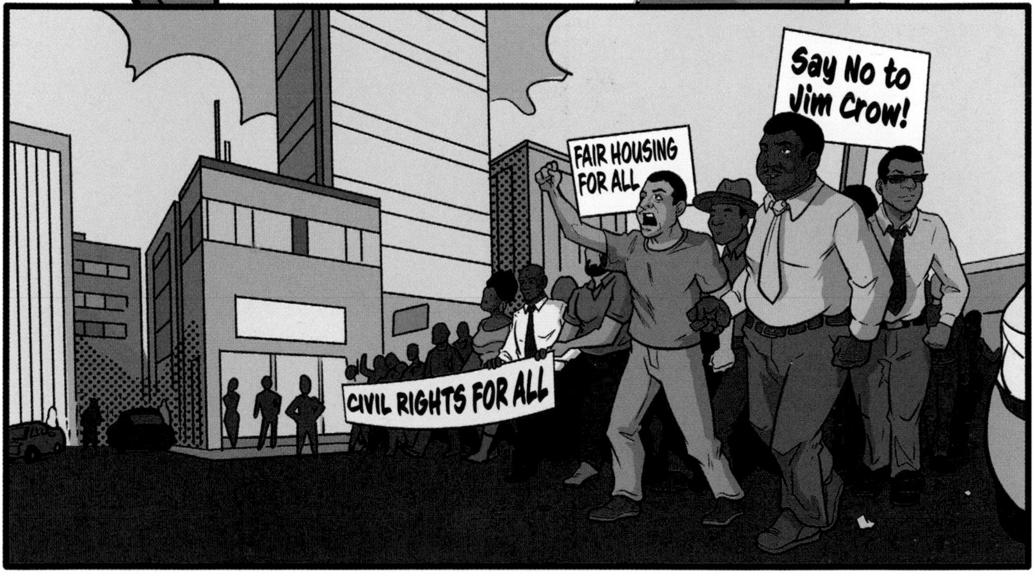
Say No to Jim Crow!
FAIR HOUSING FOR ALL
CIVIL RIGHTS FOR ALL

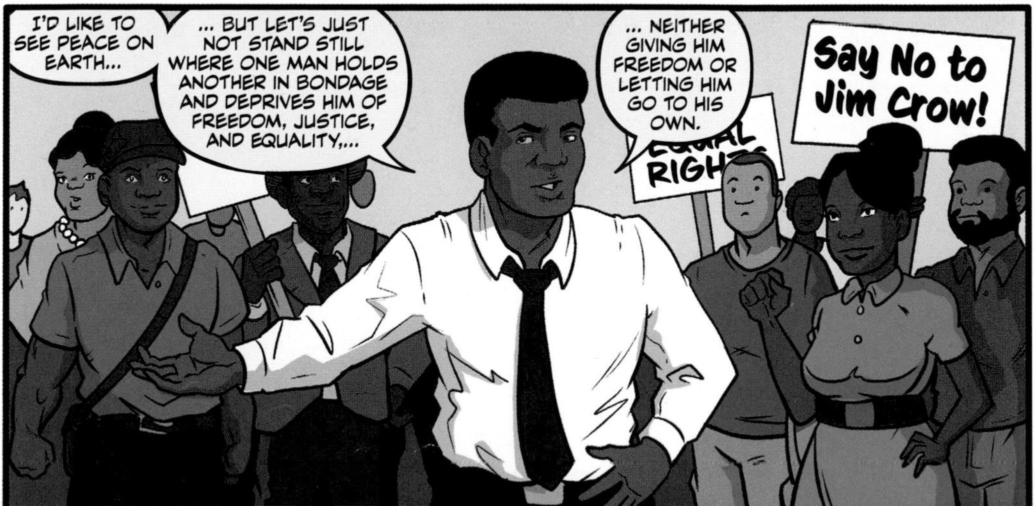
I'D LIKE TO SEE PEACE ON EARTH...
... BUT LET'S JUST NOT STAND STILL WHERE ONE MAN HOLDS ANOTHER IN BONDAGE AND DEPRIVES HIM OF FREEDOM, JUSTICE, AND EQUALITY,...
... NEITHER GIVING HIM FREEDOM OR LETTING HIM GO TO HIS OWN.
Say No to Jim Crow!

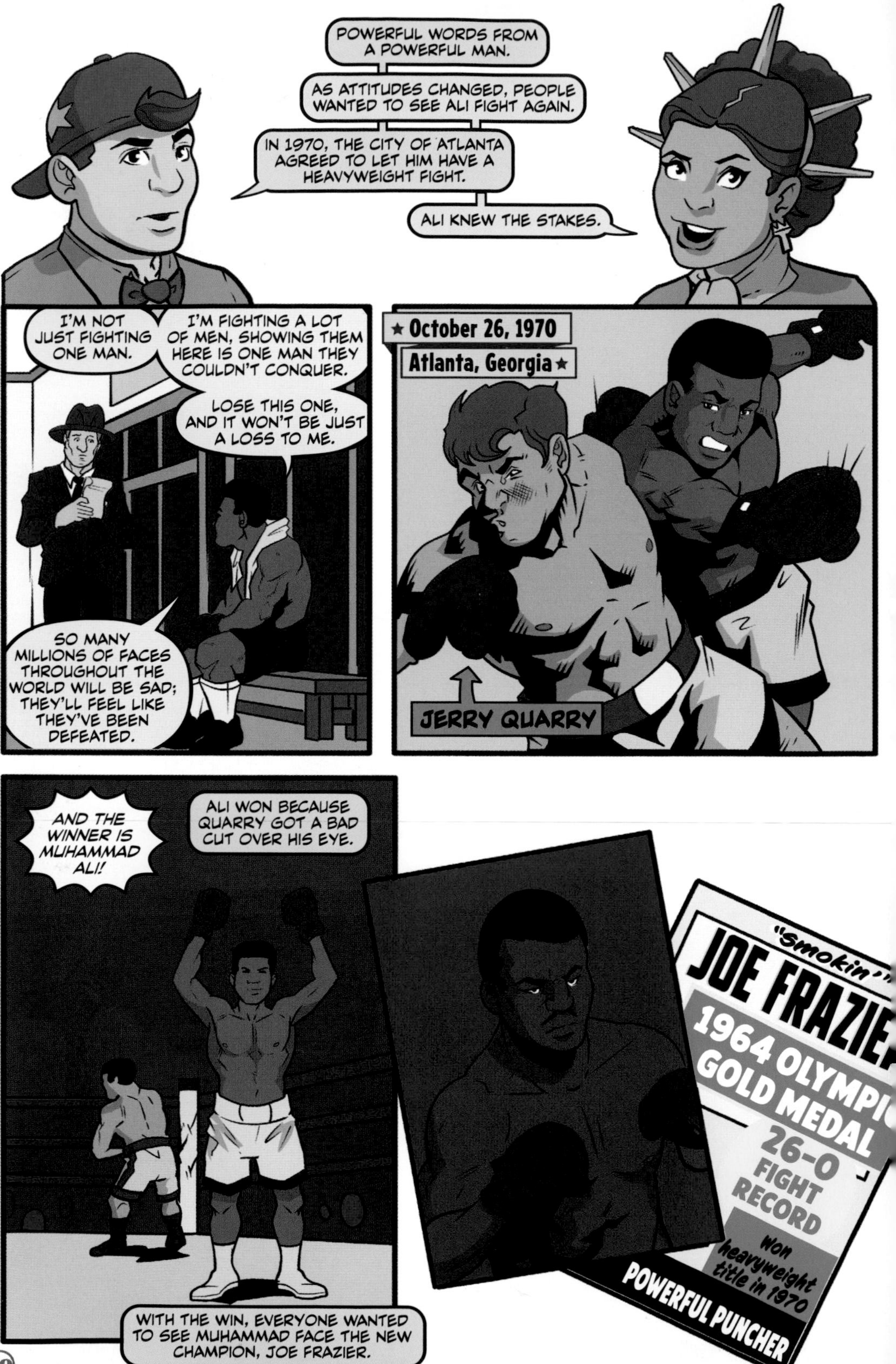
POWERFUL WORDS FROM A POWERFUL MAN.
AS ATTITUDES CHANGED, PEOPLE WANTED TO SEE ALI FIGHT AGAIN.
IN 1970, THE CITY OF ATLANTA AGREED TO LET HIM HAVE A HEAVYWEIGHT FIGHT.
ALI KNEW THE STAKES.
I'M NOT JUST FIGHTING ONE MAN.
I'M FIGHTING A LOT OF MEN, SHOWING THEM HERE IS ONE MAN THEY COULDN'T CONQUER.
LOSE THIS ONE, AND IT WON'T BE JUST A LOSS TO ME.
SO MANY MILLIONS OF FACES THROUGHOUT THE WORLD WILL BE SAD; THEY'LL FEEL LIKE THEY'VE BEEN DEFEATED.
October 26, 1970
Atlanta, Georgia
JERRY QUARRY
AND THE WINNER IS MUHAMMAD ALI!
ALI WON BECAUSE QUARRY GOT A BAD CUT OVER HIS EYE.
"Smokin'"
JOE FRAZIE
1964 OLYMPI
GOLD MEDAL
26-0 FIGHT RECORD
won heavyweight title in 1970
POWERFUL PUNCHER
WITH THE WIN, EVERYONE WANTED TO SEE MUHAMMAD FACE THE NEW CHAMPION, JOE FRAZIER.

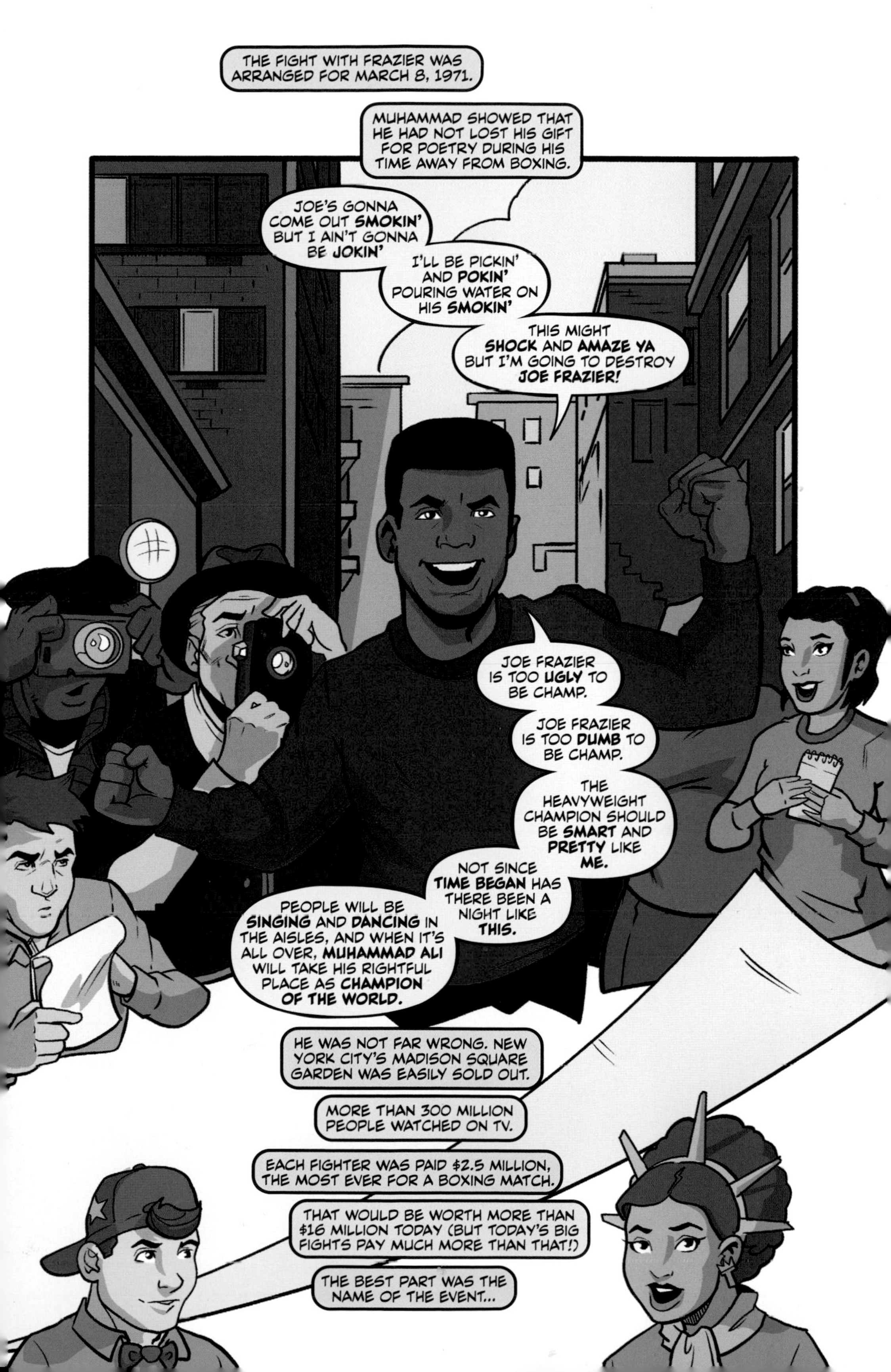
THE FIGHT WITH FRAZIER WAS ARRANGED FOR MARCH 8, 1971.
MUHAMMAD SHOWED THAT HE HAD NOT LOST HIS GIFT FOR POETRY DURING HIS TIME AWAY FROM BOXING.
JOE'S GONNA COME OUT **SMOKIN'** BUT I AIN'T GONNA BE **JOKIN'**
I'LL BE PICKIN' AND **POKIN'** POURING WATER ON HIS **SMOKIN'**
THIS MIGHT **SHOCK** AND **AMAZE YA** BUT I'M GOING TO DESTROY **JOE FRAZIER!**
JOE FRAZIER IS TOO **UGLY** TO BE CHAMP.
JOE FRAZIER IS TOO **DUMB** TO BE CHAMP.
THE HEAVYWEIGHT CHAMPION SHOULD BE **SMART** AND **PRETTY** LIKE **ME.**
NOT SINCE **TIME BEGAN** HAS THERE BEEN A NIGHT LIKE **THIS.**
PEOPLE WILL BE **SINGING** AND **DANCING** IN THE AISLES, AND WHEN IT'S ALL OVER, **MUHAMMAD ALI** WILL TAKE HIS RIGHTFUL PLACE AS **CHAMPION OF THE WORLD.**
HE WAS NOT FAR WRONG. NEW YORK CITY'S MADISON SQUARE GARDEN WAS EASILY SOLD OUT.
MORE THAN 300 MILLION PEOPLE WATCHED ON TV.
EACH FIGHTER WAS PAID $2.5 MILLION, THE MOST EVER FOR A BOXING MATCH.
THAT WOULD BE WORTH MORE THAN $16 MILLION TODAY (BUT TODAY'S BIG FIGHTS PAY MUCH MORE THAN THAT!)
THE BEST PART WAS THE NAME OF THE EVENT...

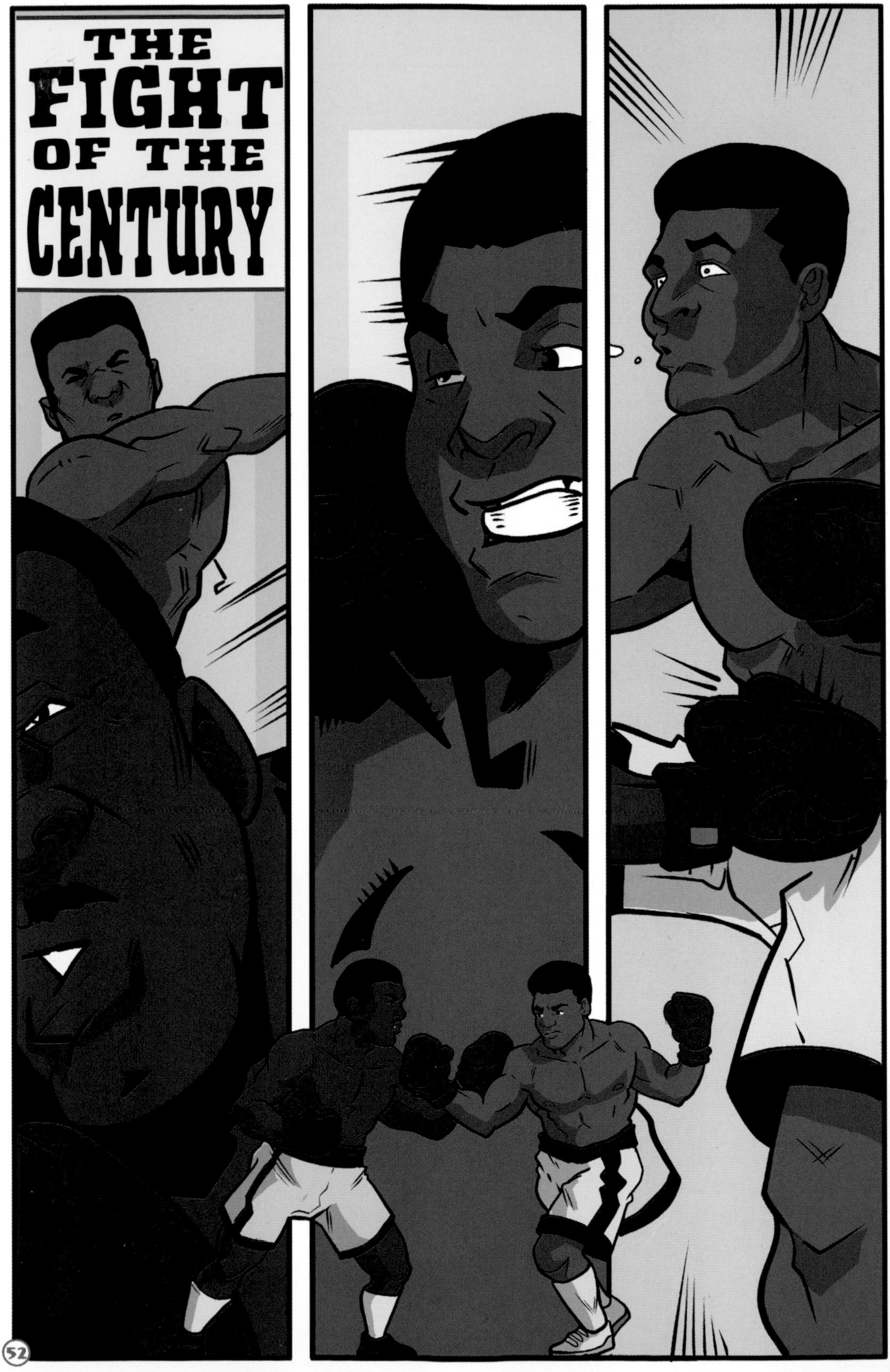
THE FIGHT OF THE CENTURY

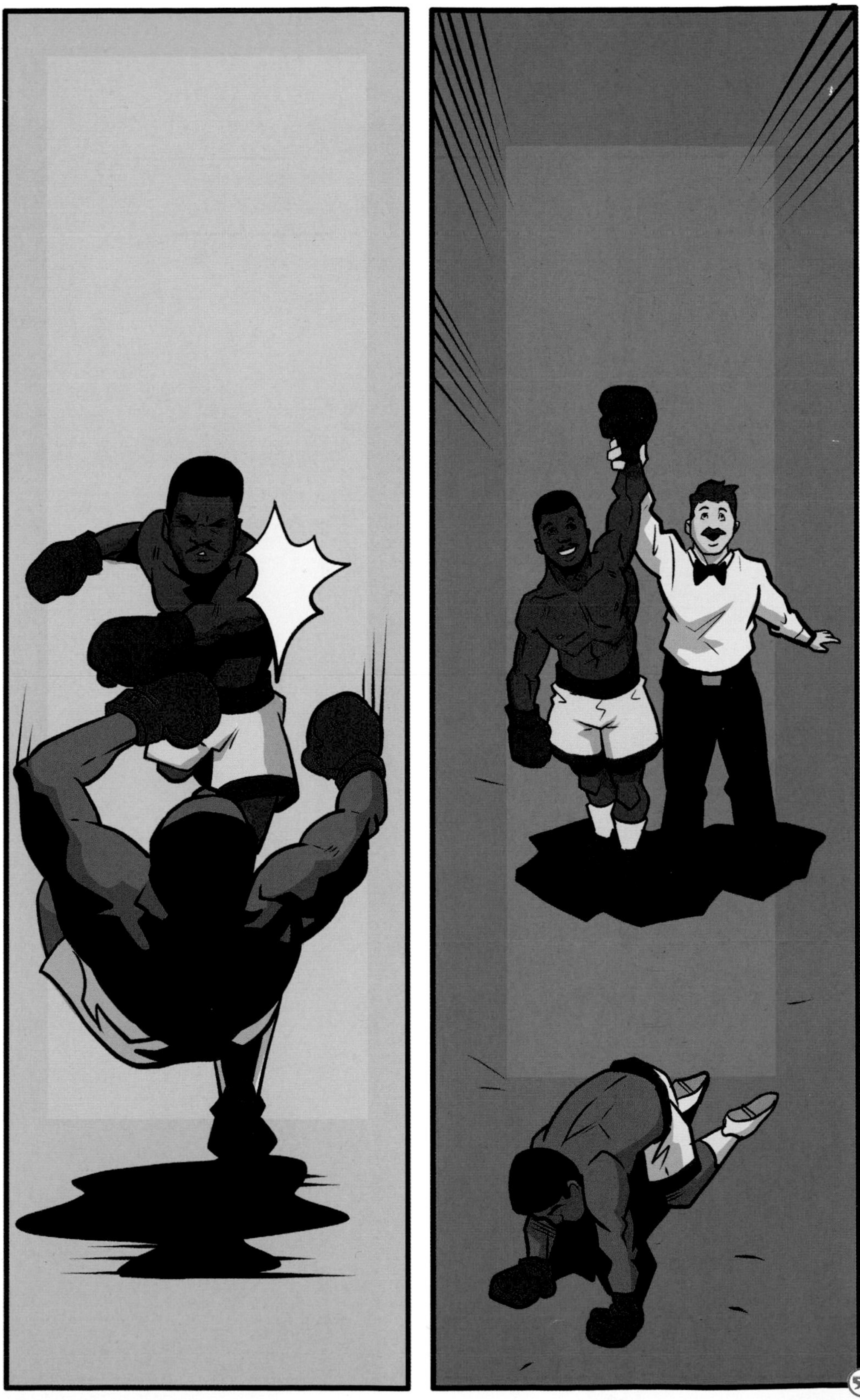

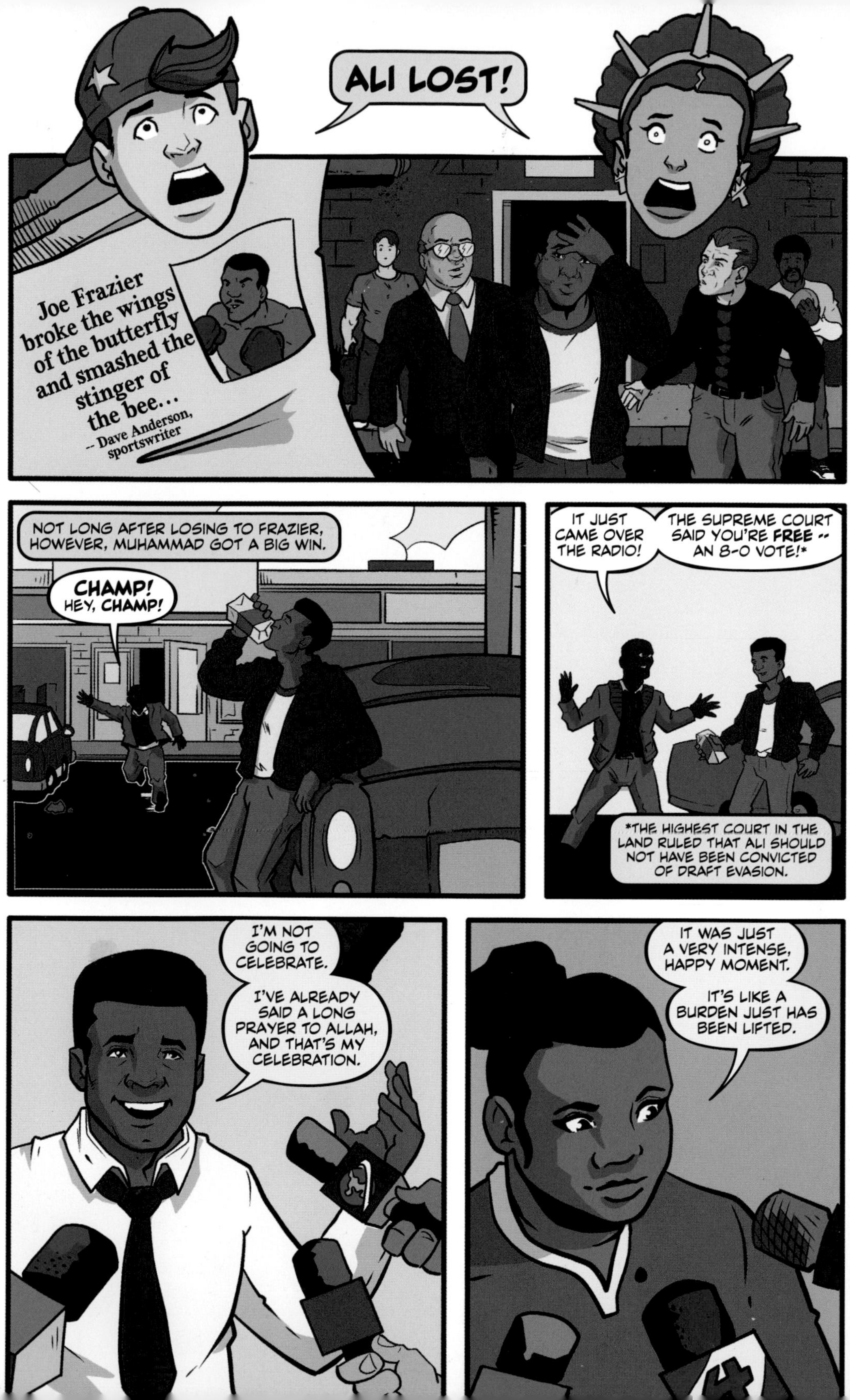
ALI LOST!
Joe Frazier broke the wings of the butterfly and smashed the stinger of the bee...
-- Dave Anderson, sportswriter
NOT LONG AFTER LOSING TO FRAZIER, HOWEVER, MUHAMMAD GOT A BIG WIN.
CHAMP! HEY, CHAMP!
IT JUST CAME OVER THE RADIO!
THE SUPREME COURT SAID YOU'RE FREE -- AN 8-0 VOTE!*
*THE HIGHEST COURT IN THE LAND RULED THAT ALI SHOULD NOT HAVE BEEN CONVICTED OF DRAFT EVASION.
I'M NOT GOING TO CELEBRATE.
I'VE ALREADY SAID A LONG PRAYER TO ALLAH, AND THAT'S MY CELEBRATION.
IT WAS JUST A VERY INTENSE, HAPPY MOMENT.
IT'S LIKE A BURDEN JUST HAS BEEN LIFTED.

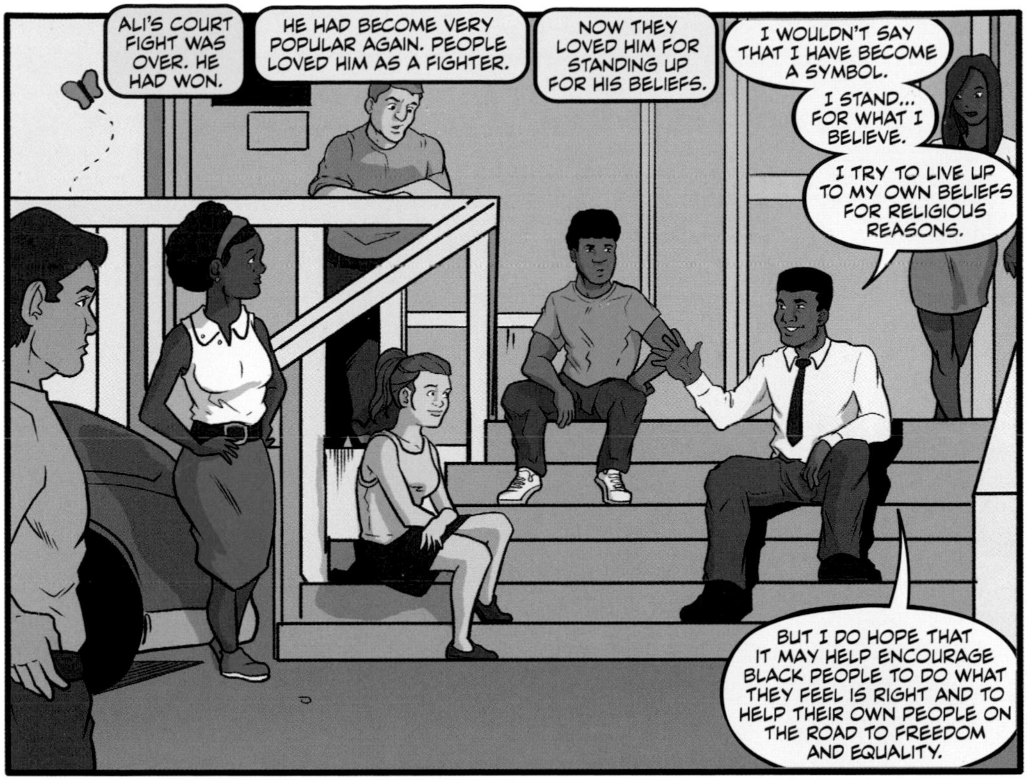
ALI'S COURT FIGHT WAS OVER. HE HAD WON.
HE HAD BECOME VERY POPULAR AGAIN. PEOPLE LOVED HIM AS A FIGHTER.
NOW THEY LOVED HIM FOR STANDING UP FOR HIS BELIEFS.
I WOULDN'T SAY THAT I HAVE BECOME A SYMBOL.
I STAND... FOR WHAT I BELIEVE.
I TRY TO LIVE UP TO MY OWN BELIEFS FOR RELIGIOUS REASONS.
BUT I DO HOPE THAT IT MAY HELP ENCOURAGE BLACK PEOPLE TO DO WHAT THEY FEEL IS RIGHT AND TO HELP THEIR OWN PEOPLE ON THE ROAD TO FREEDOM AND EQUALITY.

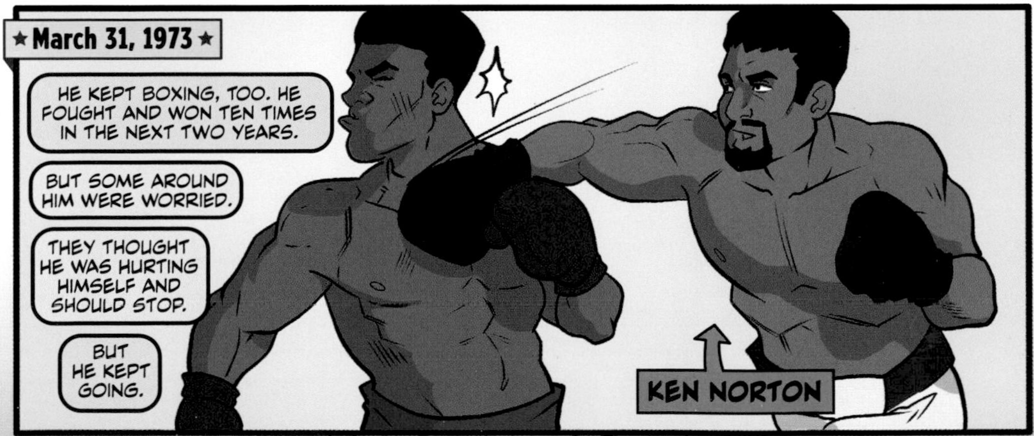
★ March 31, 1973 ★
HE KEPT BOXING, TOO. HE FOUGHT AND WON TEN TIMES IN THE NEXT TWO YEARS.
BUT SOME AROUND HIM WERE WORRIED.
THEY THOUGHT HE WAS HURTING HIMSELF AND SHOULD STOP.
BUT HE KEPT GOING.
KEN NORTON

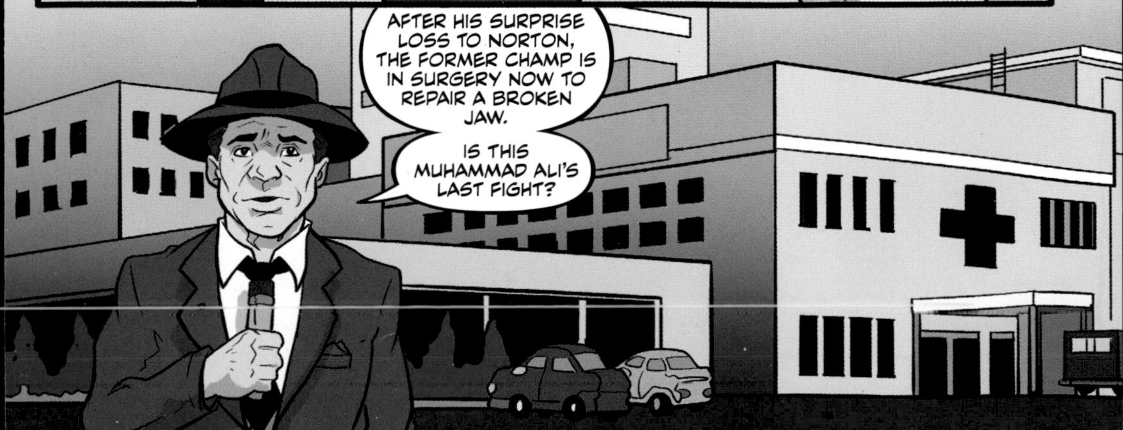
AFTER HIS SURPRISE LOSS TO NORTON, THE FORMER CHAMP IS IN SURGERY NOW TO REPAIR A BROKEN JAW.
IS THIS MUHAMMAD ALI'S LAST FIGHT?

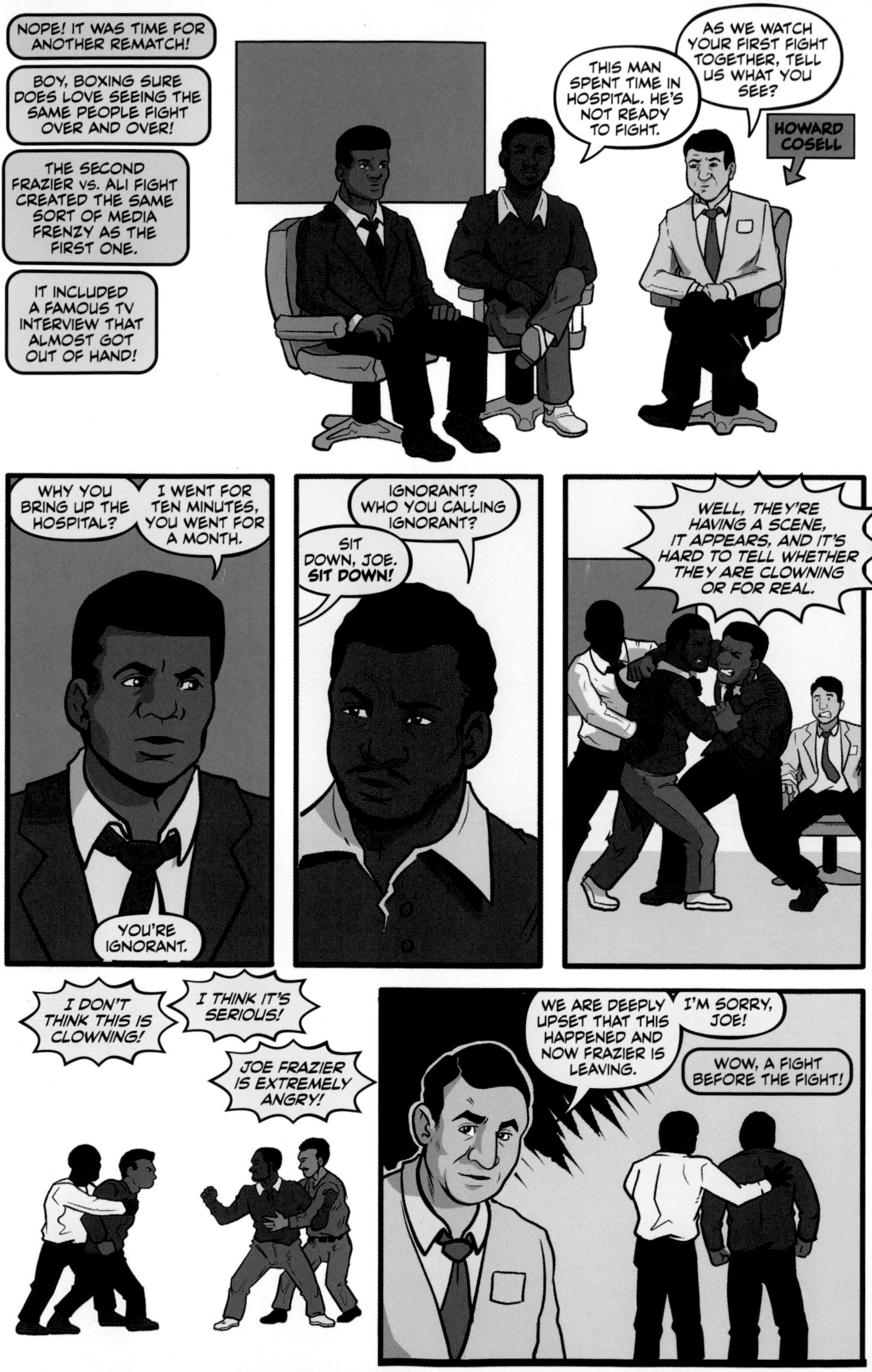
NOPE! IT WAS TIME FOR ANOTHER REMATCH!
BOY, BOXING SURE DOES LOVE SEEING THE SAME PEOPLE FIGHT OVER AND OVER!
THE SECOND FRAZIER VS. ALI FIGHT CREATED THE SAME SORT OF MEDIA FRENZY AS THE FIRST ONE.
IT INCLUDED A FAMOUS TV INTERVIEW THAT ALMOST GOT OUT OF HAND!
AS WE WATCH YOUR FIRST FIGHT TOGETHER, TELL US WHAT YOU SEE?
THIS MAN SPENT TIME IN HOSPITAL. HE'S NOT READY TO FIGHT.
HOWARD COSELL
WHY YOU BRING UP THE HOSPITAL?
I WENT FOR TEN MINUTES, YOU WENT FOR A MONTH.
YOU'RE IGNORANT.
IGNORANT? WHO YOU CALLING IGNORANT?
SIT DOWN, JOE. **SIT DOWN!**
WELL, THEY'RE HAVING A SCENE, IT APPEARS, AND IT'S HARD TO TELL WHETHER THEY ARE CLOWNING OR FOR REAL.
I DON'T THINK THIS IS CLOWNING!
I THINK IT'S SERIOUS!
JOE FRAZIER IS EXTREMELY ANGRY!
WE ARE DEEPLY UPSET THAT THIS HAPPENED AND NOW FRAZIER IS LEAVING.
I'M SORRY, JOE!
WOW, A FIGHT BEFORE THE FIGHT!

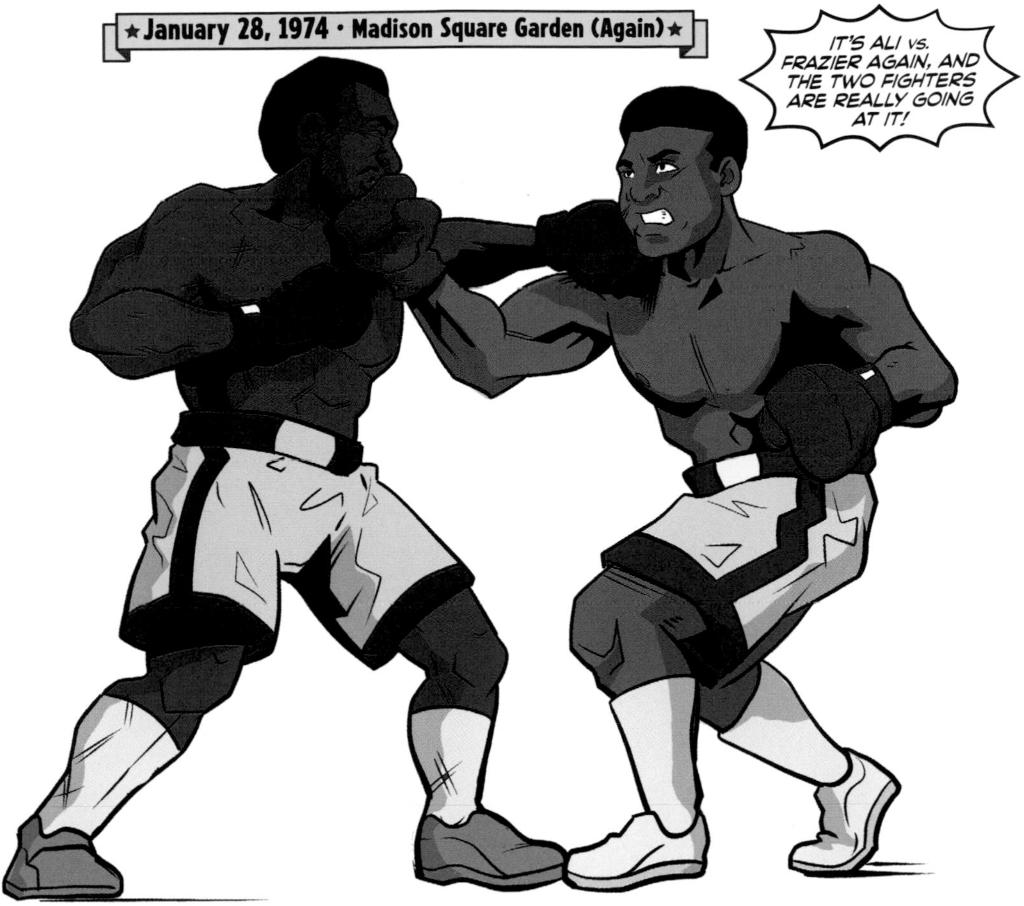
January 28, 1974 • Madison Square Garden (Again)
IT'S ALI vs. FRAZIER AGAIN, AND THE TWO FIGHTERS ARE REALLY GOING AT IT!

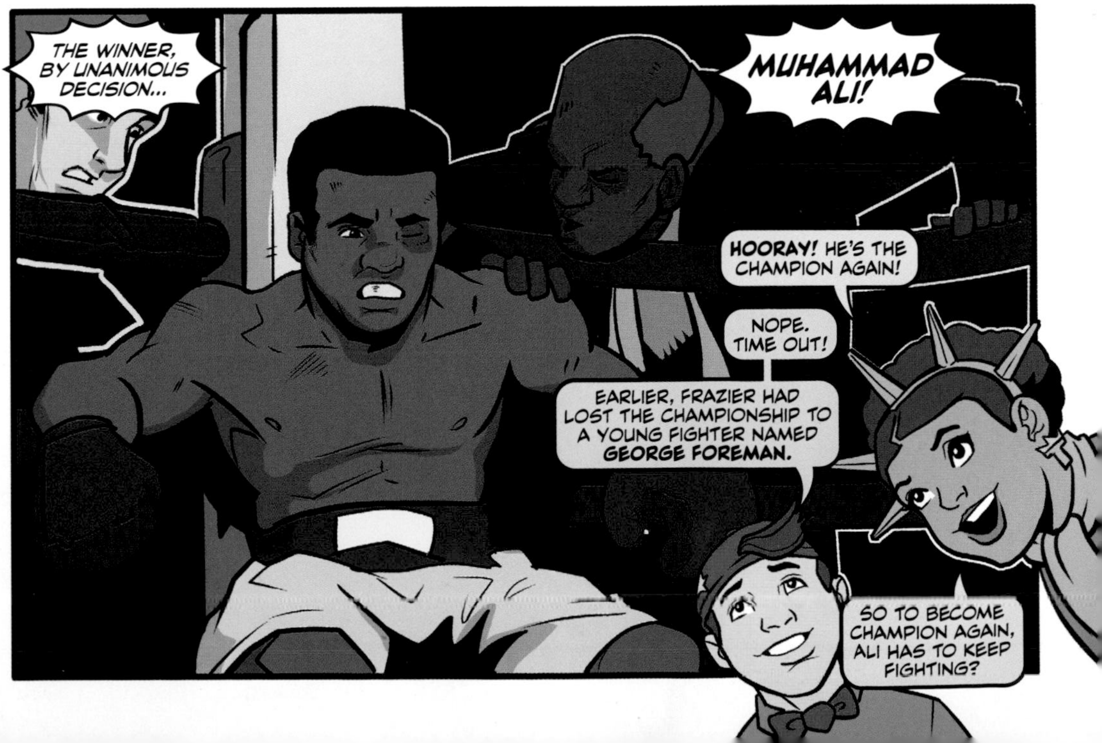
THE WINNER, BY UNANIMOUS DECISION...
MUHAMMAD ALI!
HOORAY! HE'S THE CHAMPION AGAIN!
NOPE. TIME OUT!
EARLIER, FRAZIER HAD LOST THE CHAMPIONSHIP TO A YOUNG FIGHTER NAMED GEORGE FOREMAN.
SO TO BECOME CHAMPION AGAIN, ALI HAS TO KEEP FIGHTING?

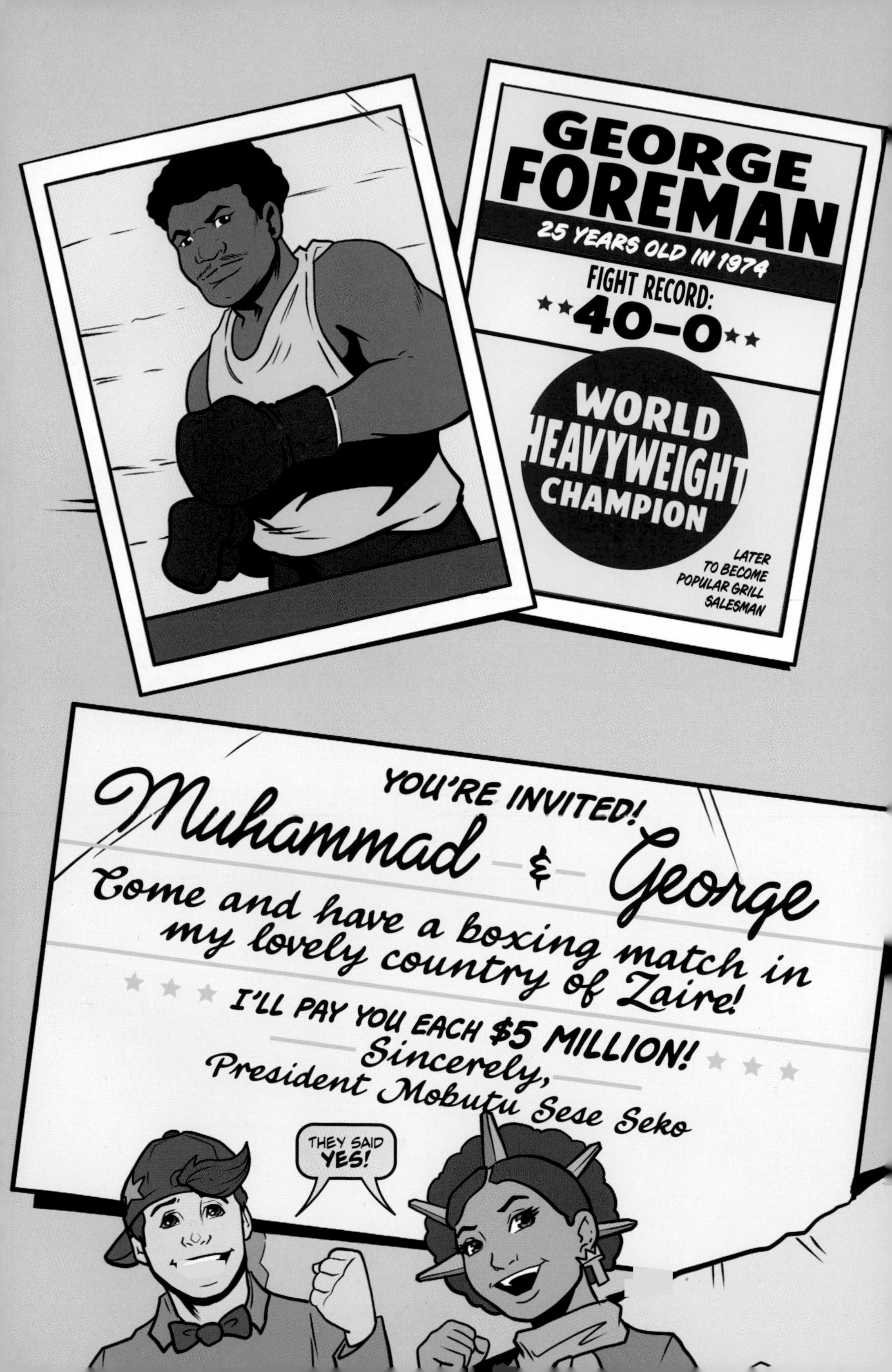
GEORGE FOREMAN
25 YEARS OLD IN 1974
FIGHT RECORD: 40-0
WORLD HEAVYWEIGHT CHAMPION
LATER TO BECOME POPULAR GRILL SALESMAN
YOU'RE INVITED!
Muhammad & George
Come and have a boxing match in my lovely country of Zaire!
I'LL PAY YOU EACH $5 MILLION!
Sincerely,
President Mobutu Sese Seko
THEY SAID YES!

MUHAMMAD SPENT A LOT OF TIME GETTING READY FOR GEORGE FOREMAN.

HE DID MOST OF IT AT HIS PERSONAL TRAINING CAMP.

LOVE YOU, DADDY!

GO GET 'EM, CHAMP!

HI, CHAMP!

AS MUHAMMAD TRAINED, BOXING EXPERTS FELT LIKE HE WOULD HAVE TROUBLE WITH FOREMAN.

FOREMAN WAS YOUNGER, STRONGER, AND MORE POWERFUL.

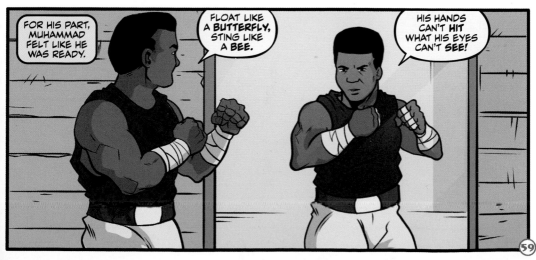

FOR HIS PART, MUHAMMAD FELT LIKE HE WAS READY.

FLOAT LIKE A **BUTTERFLY**, STING LIKE A BEE.

HIS HANDS CAN'T **HIT** WHAT HIS EYES CAN'T **SEE!**

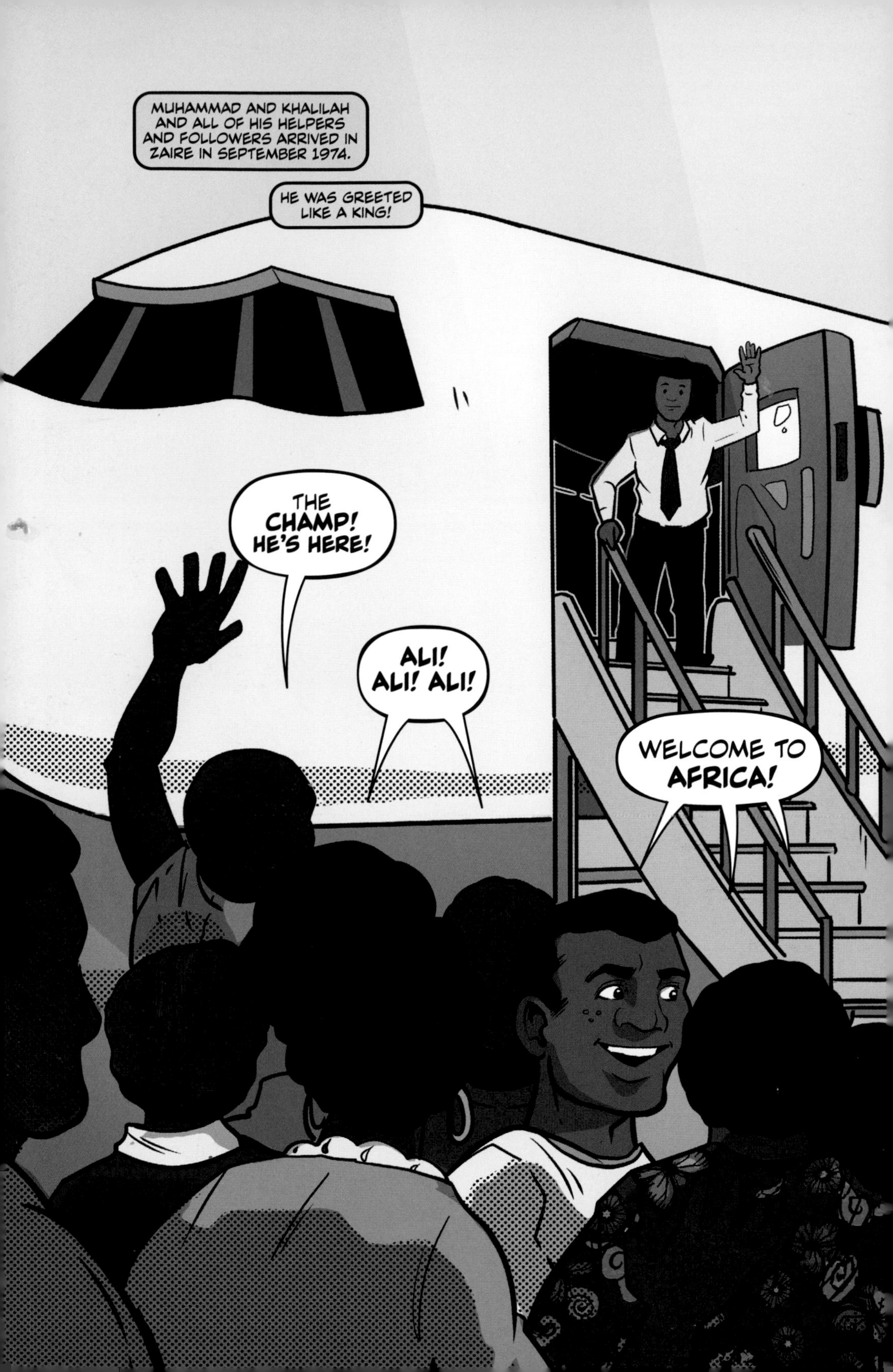
MUHAMMAD AND KHALILAH AND ALL OF HIS HELPERS AND FOLLOWERS ARRIVED IN ZAIRE IN SEPTEMBER 1974.
HE WAS GREETED LIKE A KING!
THE CHAMP! HE'S HERE!
ALI! ALI! ALI!
WELCOME TO AFRICA!

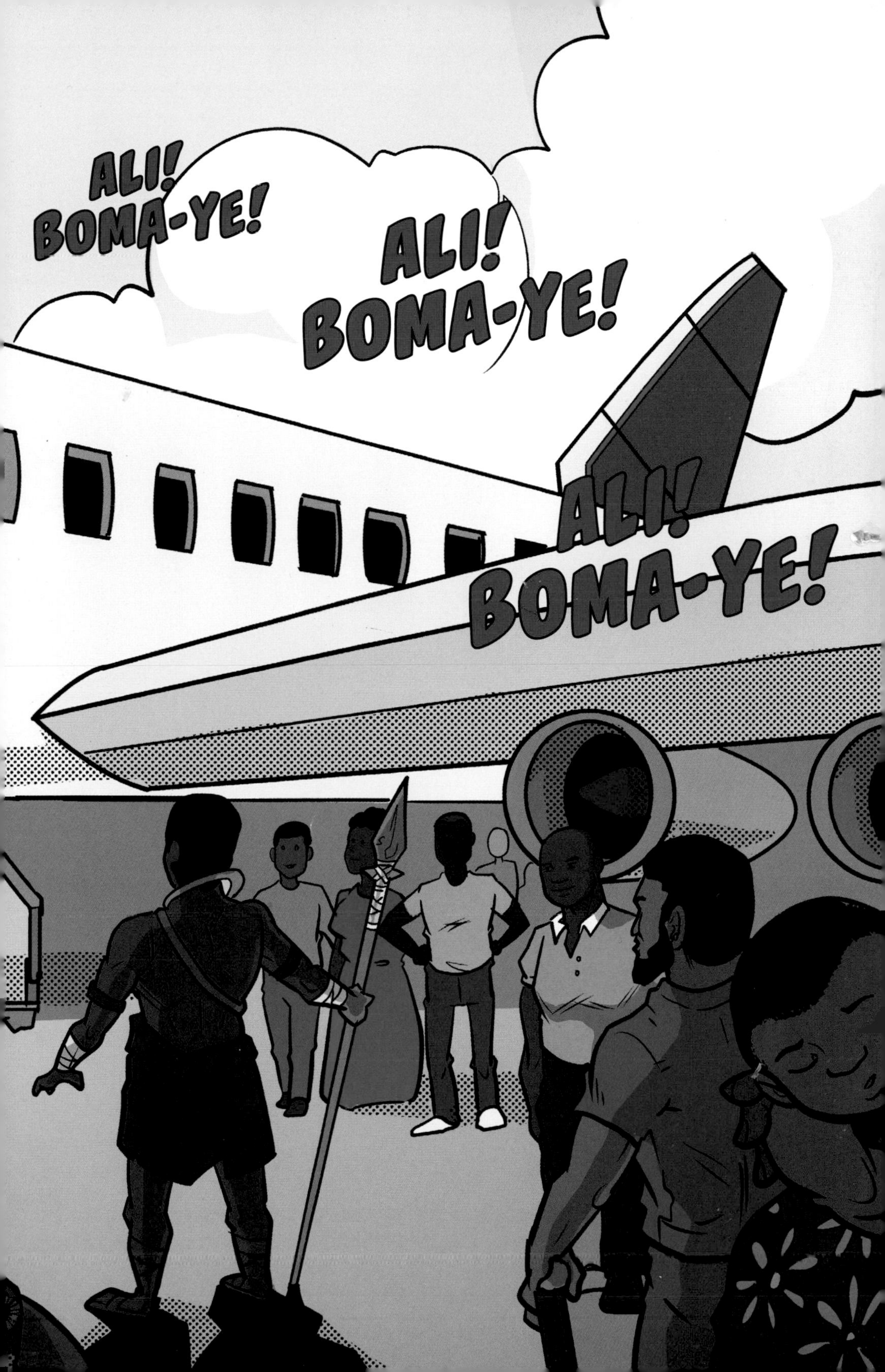
ALI! BOMA-YE!
ALI! BOMA-YE!
ALI! BOMA-YE!

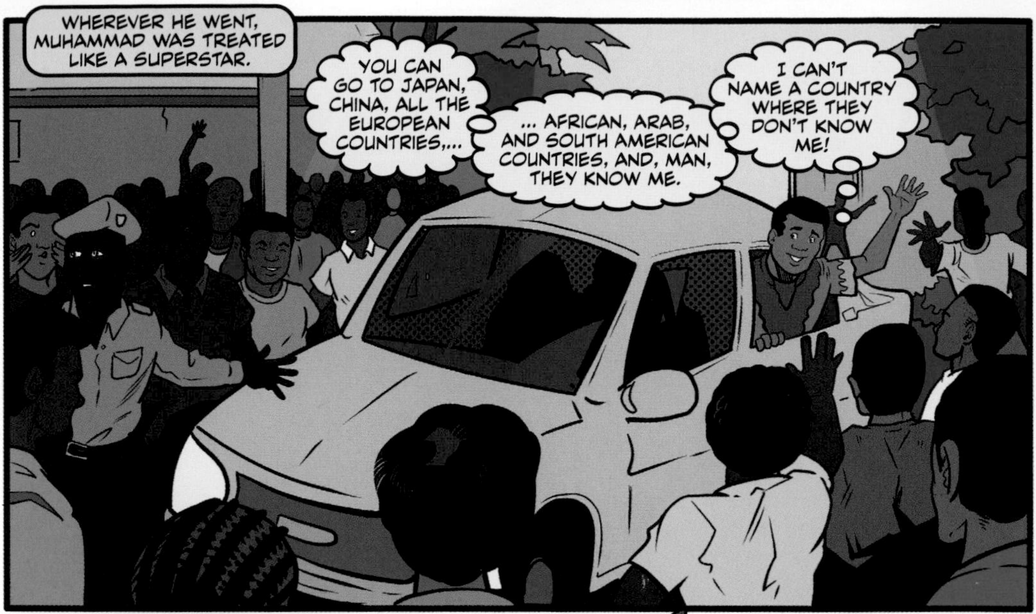
WHEREVER HE WENT, MUHAMMAD WAS TREATED LIKE A SUPERSTAR.
YOU CAN GO TO JAPAN, CHINA, ALL THE EUROPEAN COUNTRIES,...
... AFRICAN, ARAB, AND SOUTH AMERICAN COUNTRIES, AND, MAN, THEY KNOW ME.
I CAN'T NAME A COUNTRY WHERE THEY DON'T KNOW ME!

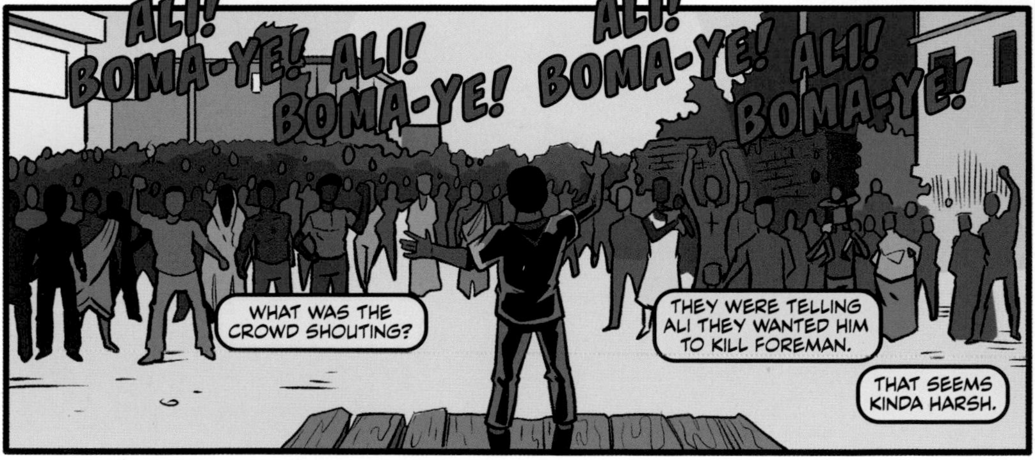
ALI! BOMA-YE! ALI! BOMA-YE! ALI! BOMA-YE! ALI! BOMA-YE!
WHAT WAS THE CROWD SHOUTING?
THEY WERE TELLING ALI THEY WANTED HIM TO KILL FOREMAN.
THAT SEEMS KINDA HARSH.

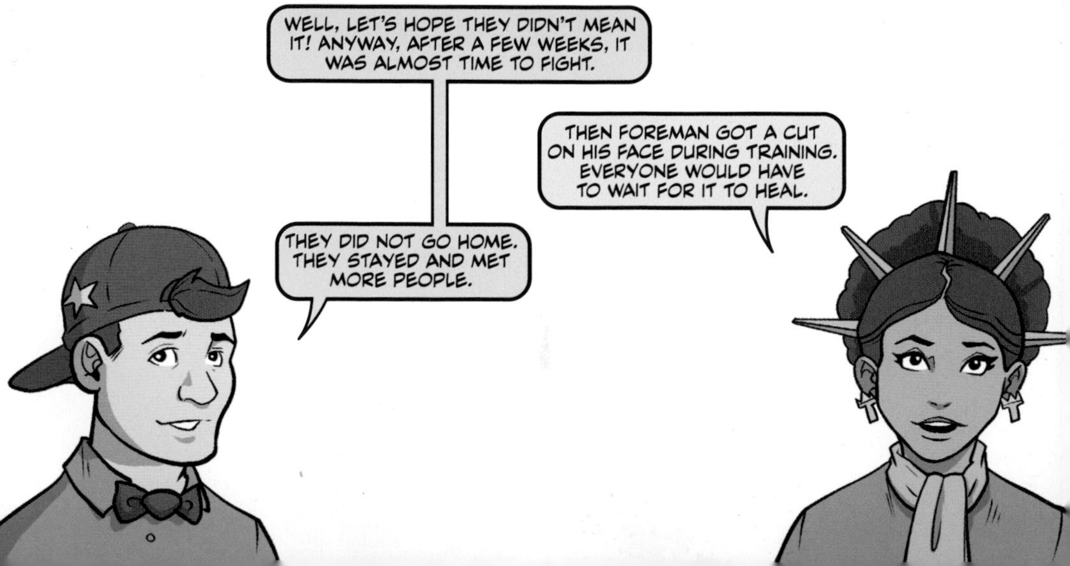
WELL, LET'S HOPE THEY DIDN'T MEAN IT! ANYWAY, AFTER A FEW WEEKS, IT WAS ALMOST TIME TO FIGHT.
THEY DID NOT GO HOME. THEY STAYED AND MET MORE PEOPLE.
THEN FOREMAN GOT A CUT ON HIS FACE DURING TRAINING. EVERYONE WOULD HAVE TO WAIT FOR IT TO HEAL.

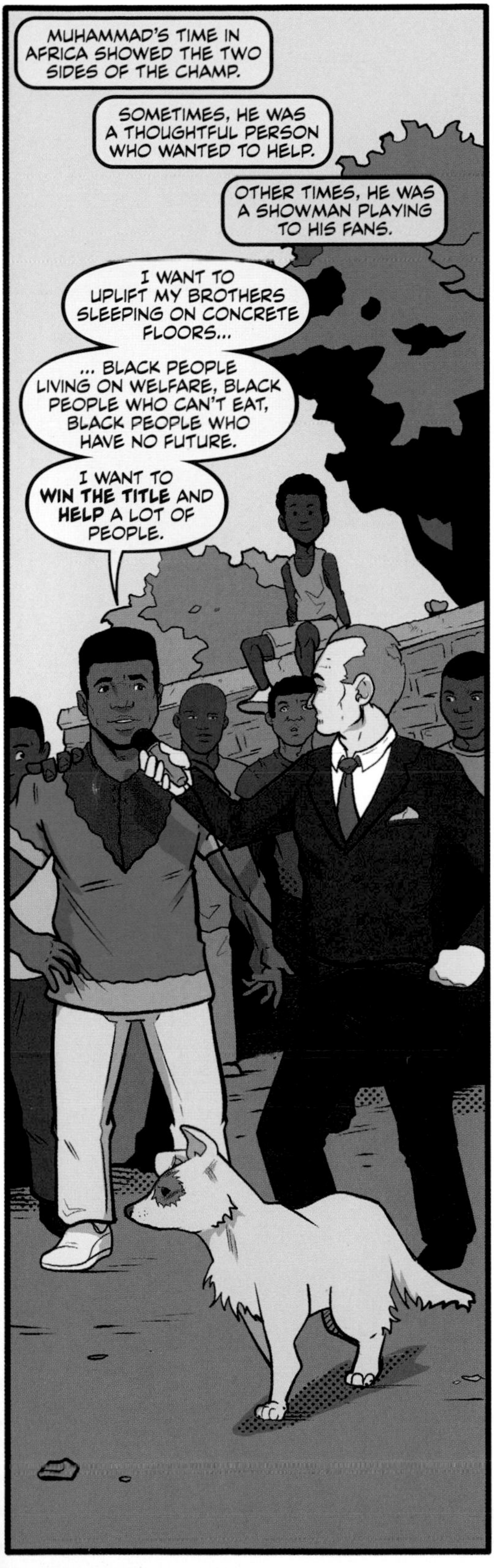
MUHAMMAD'S TIME IN AFRICA SHOWED THE TWO SIDES OF THE CHAMP.
SOMETIMES, HE WAS A THOUGHTFUL PERSON WHO WANTED TO HELP.
OTHER TIMES, HE WAS A SHOWMAN PLAYING TO HIS FANS.
I WANT TO UPLIFT MY BROTHERS SLEEPING ON CONCRETE FLOORS...
... BLACK PEOPLE LIVING ON WELFARE, BLACK PEOPLE WHO CAN'T EAT, BLACK PEOPLE WHO HAVE NO FUTURE.
I WANT TO **WIN THE TITLE** AND **HELP** A LOT OF PEOPLE.

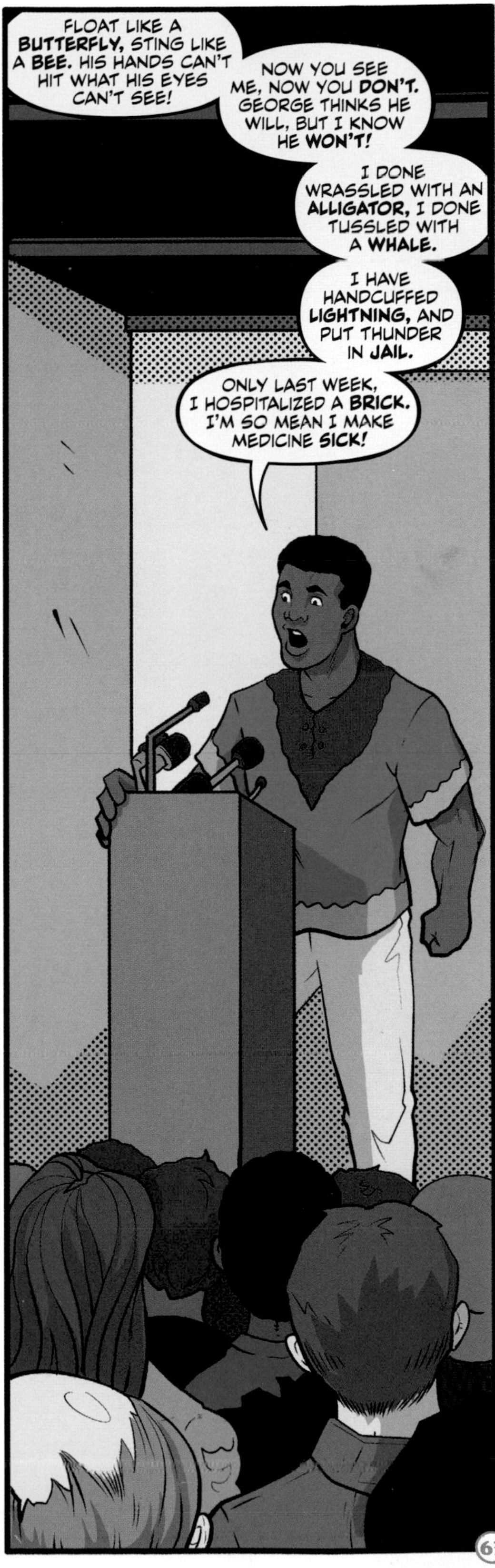
FLOAT LIKE A **BUTTERFLY,** STING LIKE A **BEE.** HIS HANDS CAN'T HIT WHAT HIS EYES CAN'T SEE!
NOW YOU SEE ME, NOW YOU **DON'T.** GEORGE THINKS HE WILL, BUT I KNOW HE **WON'T!**
I DONE WRASSLED WITH AN **ALLIGATOR,** I DONE TUSSLED WITH A **WHALE.**
I HAVE HANDCUFFED **LIGHTNING,** AND PUT THUNDER IN **JAIL.**
ONLY LAST WEEK, I HOSPITALIZED A **BRICK.** I'M SO MEAN I MAKE MEDICINE **SICK!**

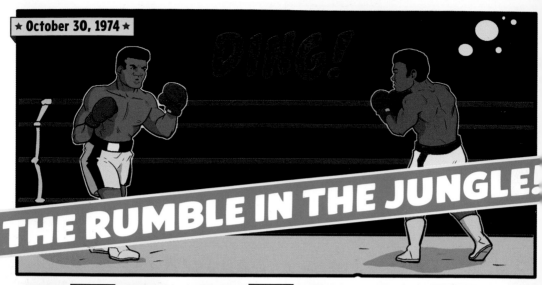

★ October 30, 1974 ★

DING!

THE RUMBLE IN THE JUNGLE!

ROUND
2

IN THE FIGHT, ALI HAD A SURPRISE FOR FOREMAN.

ROUND
4

ROUND
6

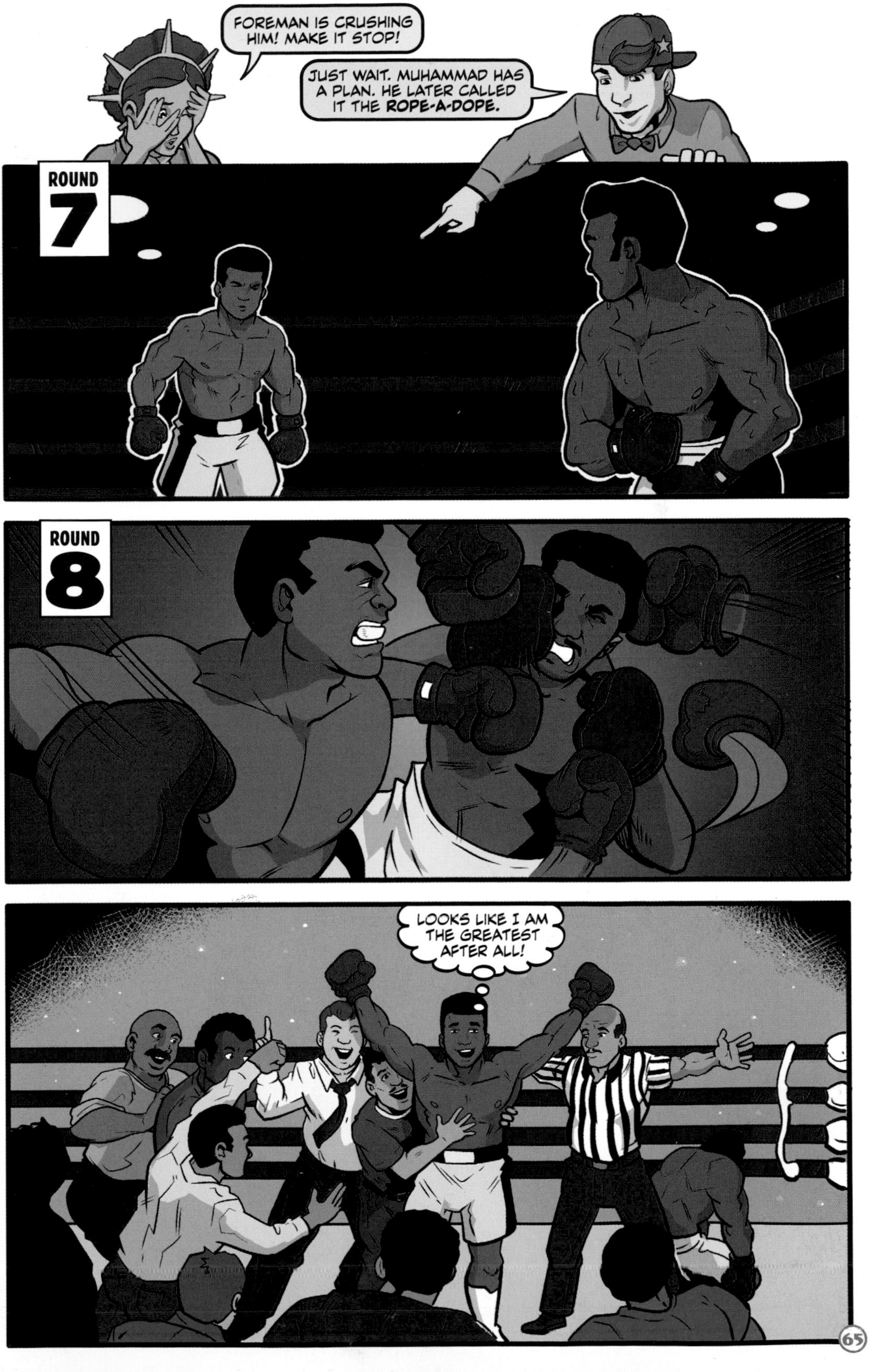
FOREMAN IS CRUSHING HIM! MAKE IT STOP!
JUST WAIT. MUHAMMAD HAS A PLAN. HE LATER CALLED IT THE **ROPE-A-DOPE.**
ROUND 7
ROUND 8
LOOKS LIKE I AM THE GREATEST AFTER ALL!

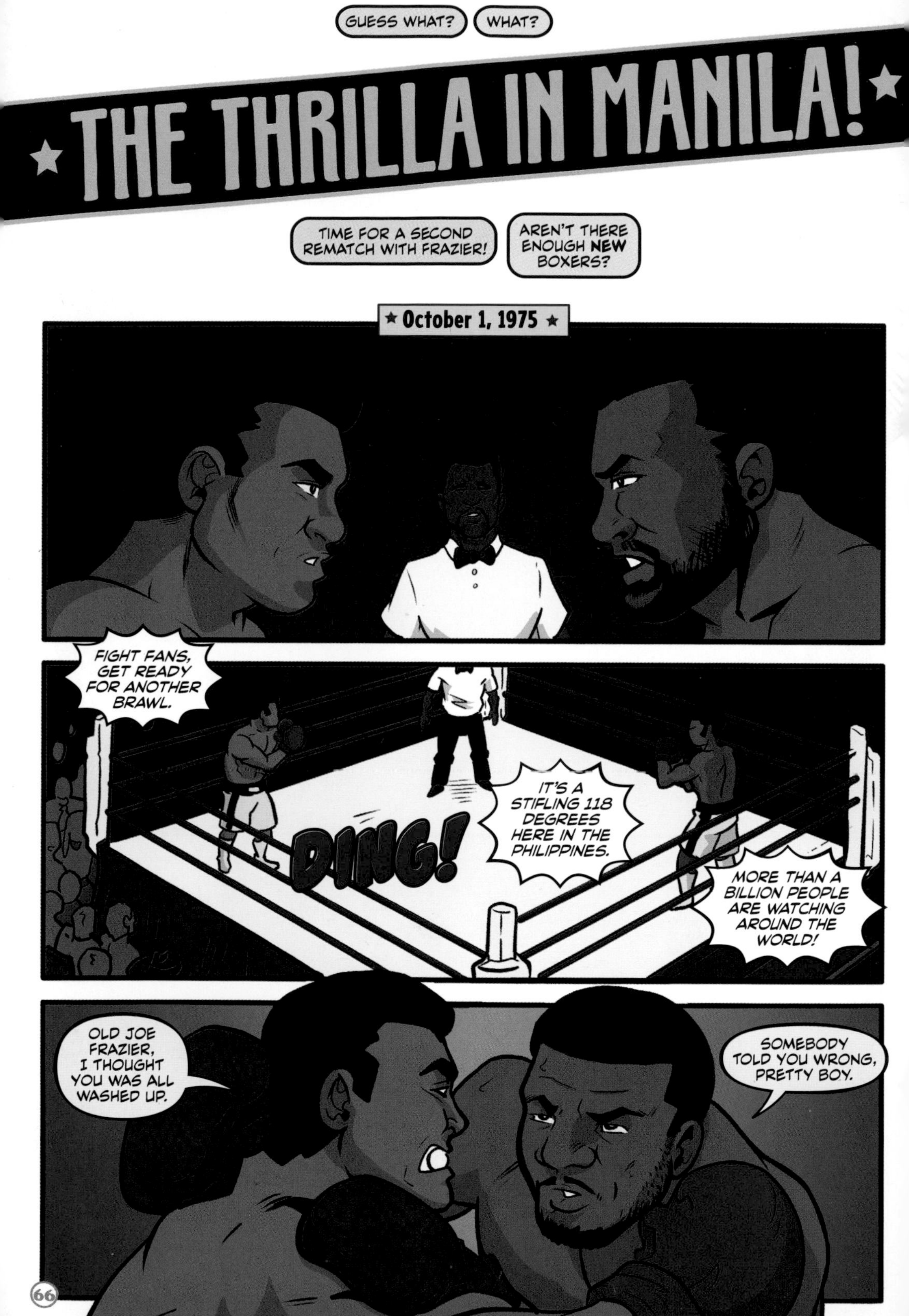
GUESS WHAT?
WHAT?
THE THRILLA IN MANILA!
TIME FOR A SECOND REMATCH WITH FRAZIER!
AREN'T THERE ENOUGH NEW BOXERS?
October 1, 1975
FIGHT FANS, GET READY FOR ANOTHER BRAWL.
DING!
IT'S A STIFLING 118 DEGREES HERE IN THE PHILIPPINES.
MORE THAN A BILLION PEOPLE ARE WATCHING AROUND THE WORLD!
OLD JOE FRAZIER, I THOUGHT YOU WAS ALL WASHED UP.
SOMEBODY TOLD YOU WRONG, PRETTY BOY.

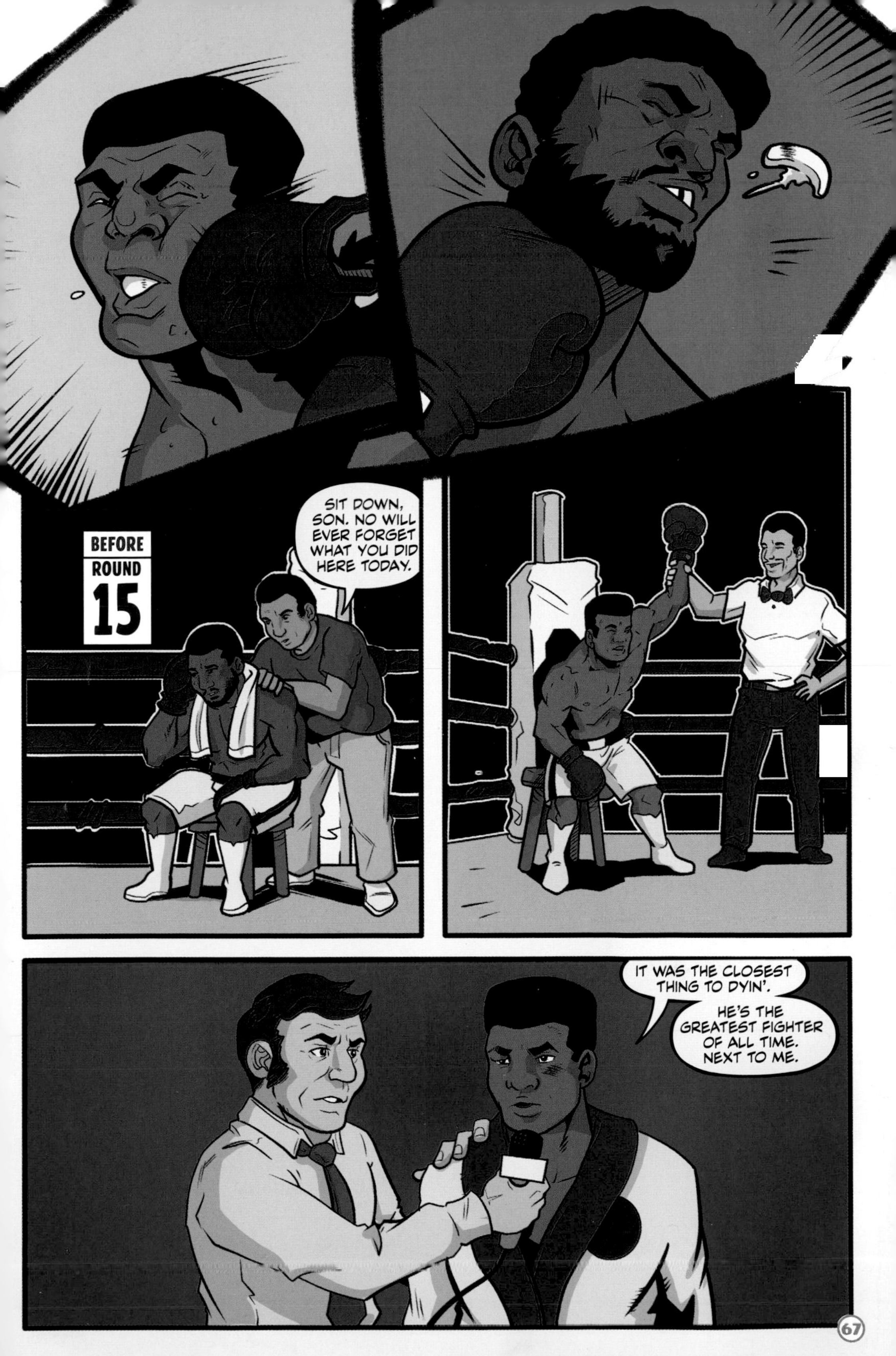
BEFORE ROUND 15
SIT DOWN, SON. NO WILL EVER FORGET WHAT YOU DID HERE TODAY.
IT WAS THE CLOSEST THING TO DYIN'.
HE'S THE GREATEST FIGHTER OF ALL TIME. NEXT TO ME.

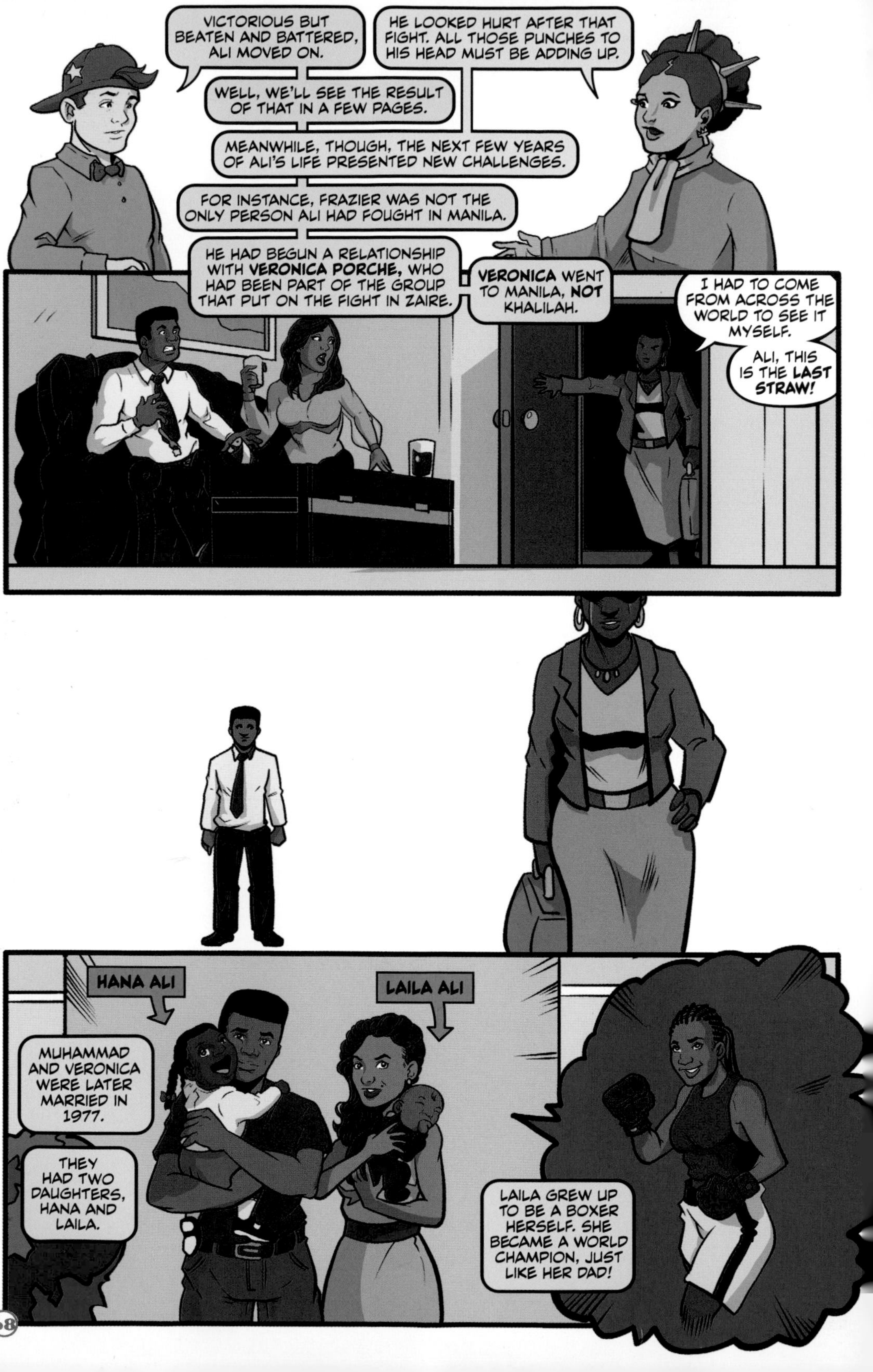
VICTORIOUS BUT BEATEN AND BATTERED, ALI MOVED ON.
HE LOOKED HURT AFTER THAT FIGHT. ALL THOSE PUNCHES TO HIS HEAD MUST BE ADDING UP.
WELL, WE'LL SEE THE RESULT OF THAT IN A FEW PAGES.
MEANWHILE, THOUGH, THE NEXT FEW YEARS OF ALI'S LIFE PRESENTED NEW CHALLENGES.
FOR INSTANCE, FRAZIER WAS NOT THE ONLY PERSON ALI HAD FOUGHT IN MANILA.
HE HAD BEGUN A RELATIONSHIP WITH **VERONICA PORCHE,** WHO HAD BEEN PART OF THE GROUP THAT PUT ON THE FIGHT IN ZAIRE.
VERONICA WENT TO MANILA, **NOT** KHALILAH.
I HAD TO COME FROM ACROSS THE WORLD TO SEE IT MYSELF.
ALI, THIS IS THE **LAST STRAW!**
HANA ALI
LAILA ALI
MUHAMMAD AND VERONICA WERE LATER MARRIED IN 1977.
THEY HAD TWO DAUGHTERS, HANA AND LAILA.
LAILA GREW UP TO BE A BOXER HERSELF. SHE BECAME A WORLD CHAMPION, JUST LIKE HER DAD!

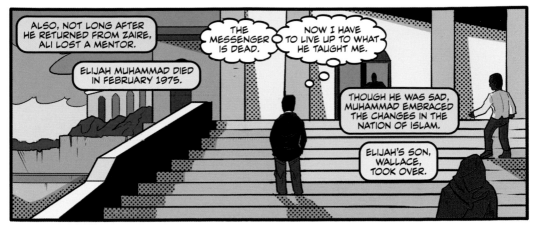

ALSO, NOT LONG AFTER HE RETURNED FROM ZAIRE, ALI LOST A MENTOR.

ELIJAH MUHAMMAD DIED IN FEBRUARY 1975.

THE MESSENGER IS DEAD.

NOW I HAVE TO LIVE UP TO WHAT HE TAUGHT ME.

THOUGH HE WAS SAD, MUHAMMAD EMBRACED THE CHANGES IN THE NATION OF ISLAM.

ELIJAH'S SON, WALLACE, TOOK OVER.

WE ARE NOT GOING TO FOLLOW THE PATH OF SEPARATION OF BLACK AND WHITE.

THE WHITE MAN IS NOT THE BLUE-EYED DEVIL.

WE ARE STOPPING THE DRESS CODE FOR MEMBERS.

WE ARE FOCUSING OUR LIVES IN ISLAM, PRAYING AT MOSQUES.

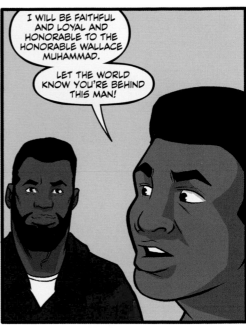

I WILL BE FAITHFUL AND LOYAL AND HONORABLE TO THE HONORABLE WALLACE MUHAMMAD.

LET THE WORLD KNOW YOU'RE BEHIND THIS MAN!

69

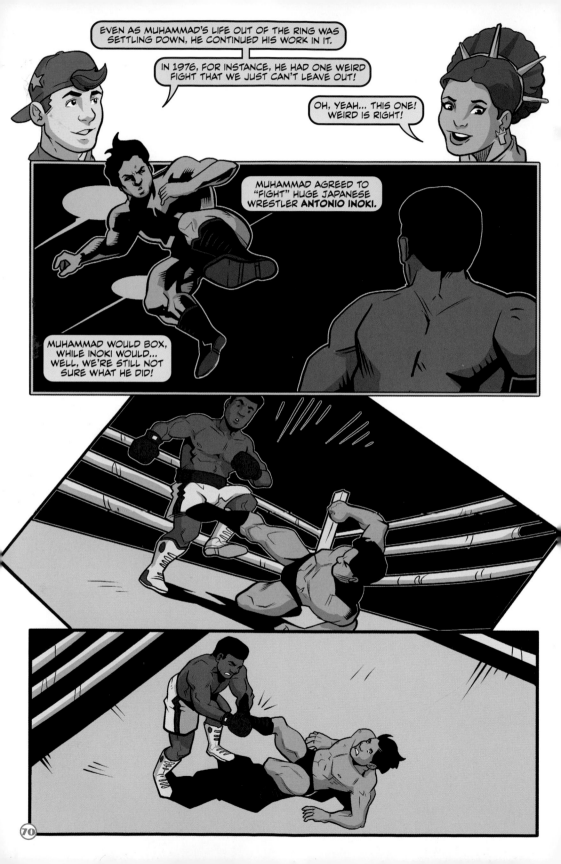

EVEN AS MUHAMMAD'S LIFE OUT OF THE RING WAS SETTLING DOWN, HE CONTINUED HIS WORK IN IT.

IN 1976, FOR INSTANCE, HE HAD ONE WEIRD FIGHT THAT WE JUST CAN'T LEAVE OUT!

OH, YEAH... THIS ONE! WEIRD IS RIGHT!

MUHAMMAD AGREED TO "FIGHT" HUGE JAPANESE WRESTLER ANTONIO INOKI.

MUHAMMAD WOULD BOX, WHILE INOKI WOULD... WELL, WE'RE STILL NOT SURE WHAT HE DID!

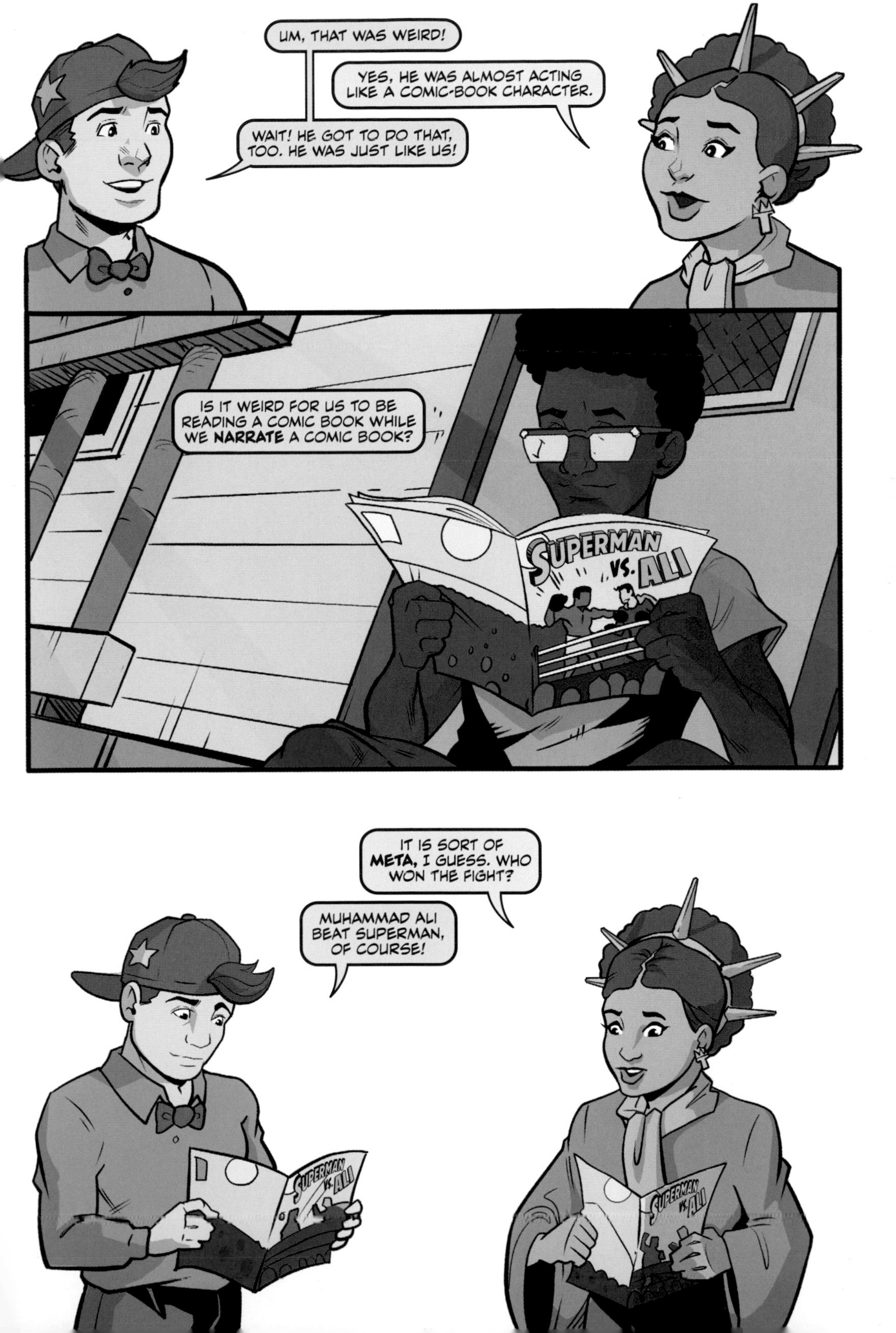

UM, THAT WAS WEIRD!
YES, HE WAS ALMOST ACTING LIKE A COMIC-BOOK CHARACTER.
WAIT! HE GOT TO DO THAT, TOO. HE WAS JUST LIKE US!
IS IT WEIRD FOR US TO BE READING A COMIC BOOK WHILE WE **NARRATE** A COMIC BOOK?
SUPERMAN VS. ALI
IT IS SORT OF **META,** I GUESS. WHO WON THE FIGHT?
MUHAMMAD ALI BEAT SUPERMAN, OF COURSE!

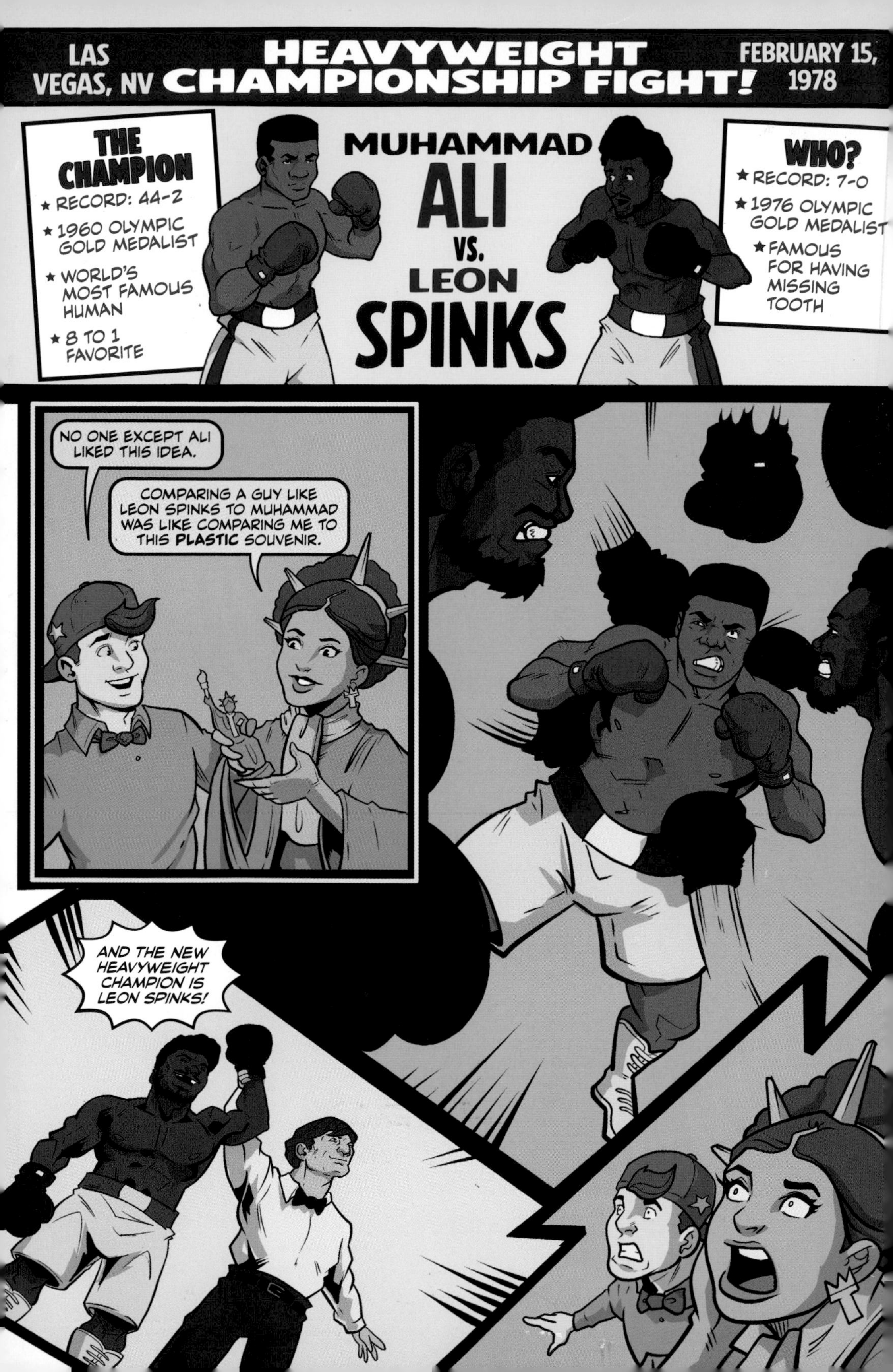
LAS VEGAS, NV
HEAVYWEIGHT CHAMPIONSHIP FIGHT!
FEBRUARY 15, 1978
THE CHAMPION
★ RECORD: 44-2
★ 1960 OLYMPIC GOLD MEDALIST
★ WORLD'S MOST FAMOUS HUMAN
★ 8 TO 1 FAVORITE
MUHAMMAD ALI VS. LEON SPINKS
WHO?
★ RECORD: 7-0
★ 1976 OLYMPIC GOLD MEDALIST
★ FAMOUS FOR HAVING MISSING TOOTH
NO ONE EXCEPT ALI LIKED THIS IDEA.
COMPARING A GUY LIKE LEON SPINKS TO MUHAMMAD WAS LIKE COMPARING ME TO THIS **PLASTIC** SOUVENIR.
AND THE NEW HEAVYWEIGHT CHAMPION IS LEON SPINKS!

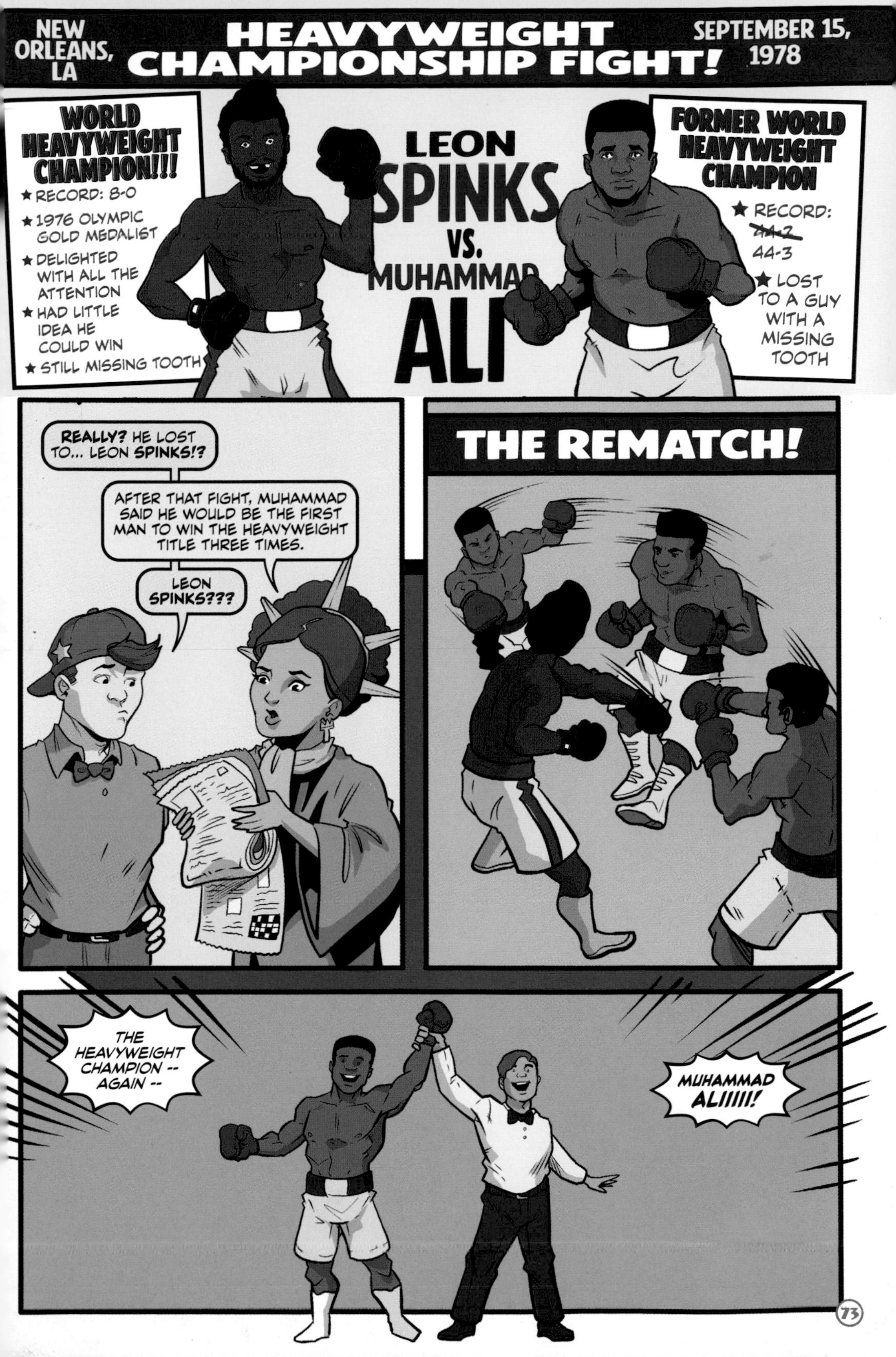

NEW ORLEANS, LA
HEAVYWEIGHT CHAMPIONSHIP FIGHT!
SEPTEMBER 15, 1978
WORLD HEAVYWEIGHT CHAMPION!!!
★ RECORD: 8-0
★ 1976 OLYMPIC GOLD MEDALIST
★ DELIGHTED WITH ALL THE ATTENTION
★ HAD LITTLE IDEA HE COULD WIN
★ STILL MISSING TOOTH
LEON SPINKS VS. MUHAMMAD ALI
FORMER WORLD HEAVYWEIGHT CHAMPION
★ RECORD: ~~44-2~~ 44-3
★ LOST TO A GUY WITH A MISSING TOOTH
REALLY? HE LOST TO... LEON SPINKS!?
AFTER THAT FIGHT, MUHAMMAD SAID HE WOULD BE THE FIRST MAN TO WIN THE HEAVYWEIGHT TITLE THREE TIMES.
LEON SPINKS???
THE REMATCH!
THE HEAVYWEIGHT CHAMPION -- AGAIN --
MUHAMMAD ALIIIII!

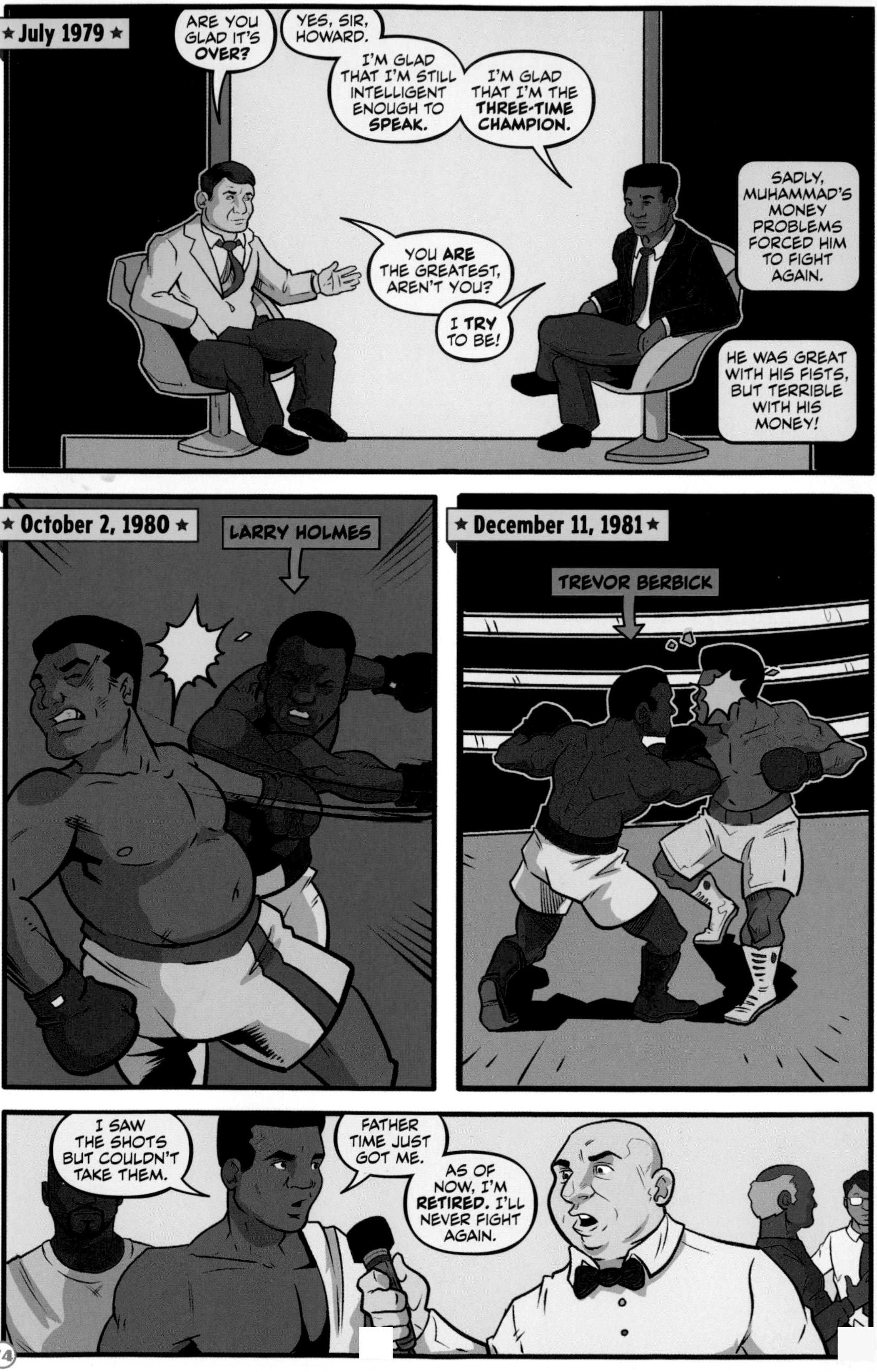
July 1979
ARE YOU GLAD IT'S OVER?
YES, SIR, HOWARD.
I'M GLAD THAT I'M STILL INTELLIGENT ENOUGH TO SPEAK.
I'M GLAD THAT I'M THE THREE-TIME CHAMPION.
YOU ARE THE GREATEST, AREN'T YOU?
I TRY TO BE!
SADLY, MUHAMMAD'S MONEY PROBLEMS FORCED HIM TO FIGHT AGAIN.
HE WAS GREAT WITH HIS FISTS, BUT TERRIBLE WITH HIS MONEY!
October 2, 1980
LARRY HOLMES
December 11, 1981
TREVOR BERBICK
I SAW THE SHOTS BUT COULDN'T TAKE THEM.
FATHER TIME JUST GOT ME.
AS OF NOW, I'M RETIRED. I'LL NEVER FIGHT AGAIN.

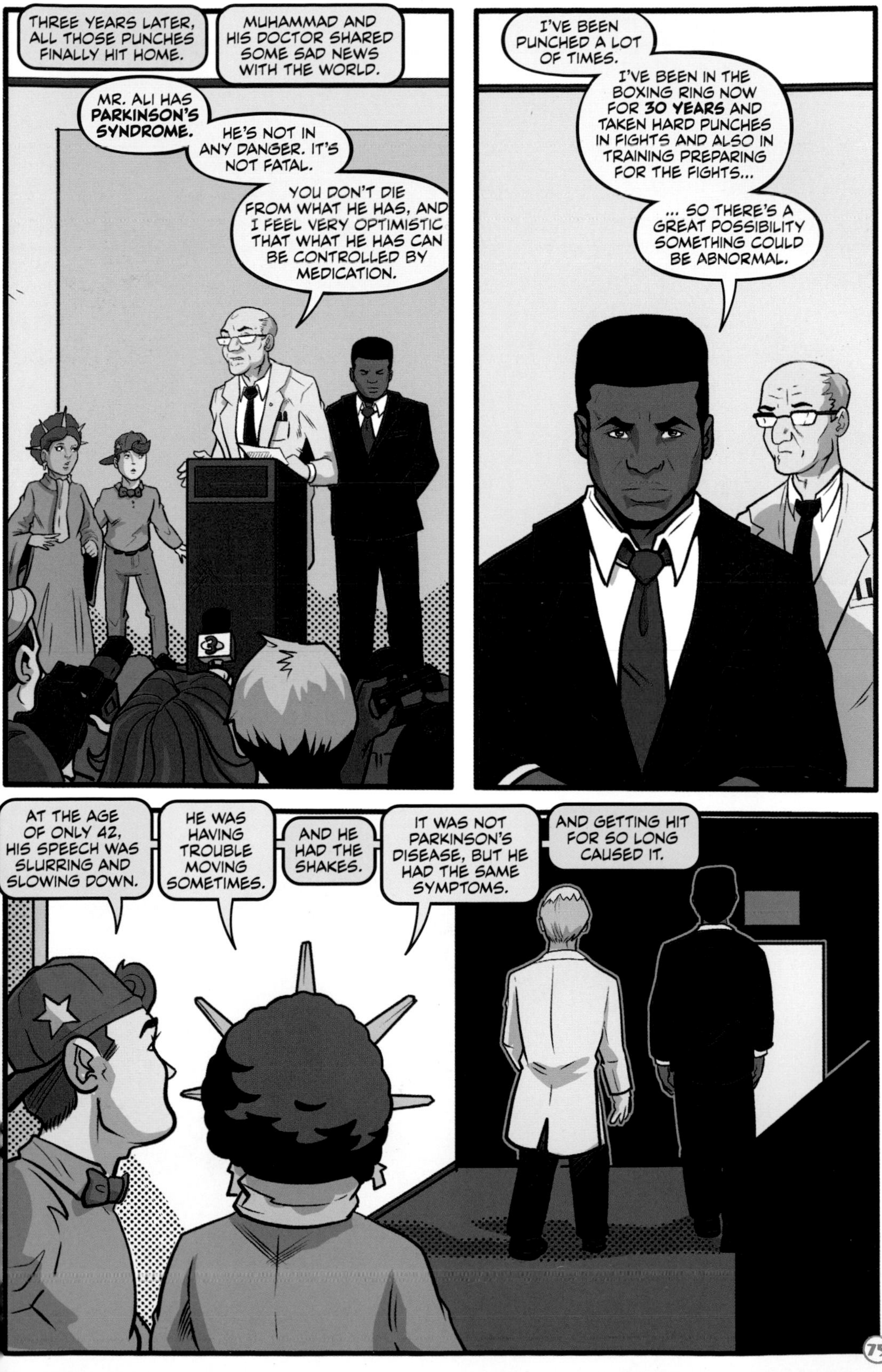
THREE YEARS LATER, ALL THOSE PUNCHES FINALLY HIT HOME.
MUHAMMAD AND HIS DOCTOR SHARED SOME SAD NEWS WITH THE WORLD.
MR. ALI HAS **PARKINSON'S SYNDROME.**
HE'S NOT IN ANY DANGER. IT'S NOT FATAL.
YOU DON'T DIE FROM WHAT HE HAS, AND I FEEL VERY OPTIMISTIC THAT WHAT HE HAS CAN BE CONTROLLED BY MEDICATION.
I'VE BEEN PUNCHED A LOT OF TIMES.
I'VE BEEN IN THE BOXING RING NOW FOR **30 YEARS** AND TAKEN HARD PUNCHES IN FIGHTS AND ALSO IN TRAINING PREPARING FOR THE FIGHTS...
... SO THERE'S A GREAT POSSIBILITY SOMETHING COULD BE ABNORMAL.
AT THE AGE OF ONLY 42, HIS SPEECH WAS SLURRING AND SLOWING DOWN.
HE WAS HAVING TROUBLE MOVING SOMETIMES.
AND HE HAD THE SHAKES.
IT WAS NOT PARKINSON'S DISEASE, BUT HE HAD THE SAME SYMPTOMS.
AND GETTING HIT FOR SO LONG CAUSED IT.

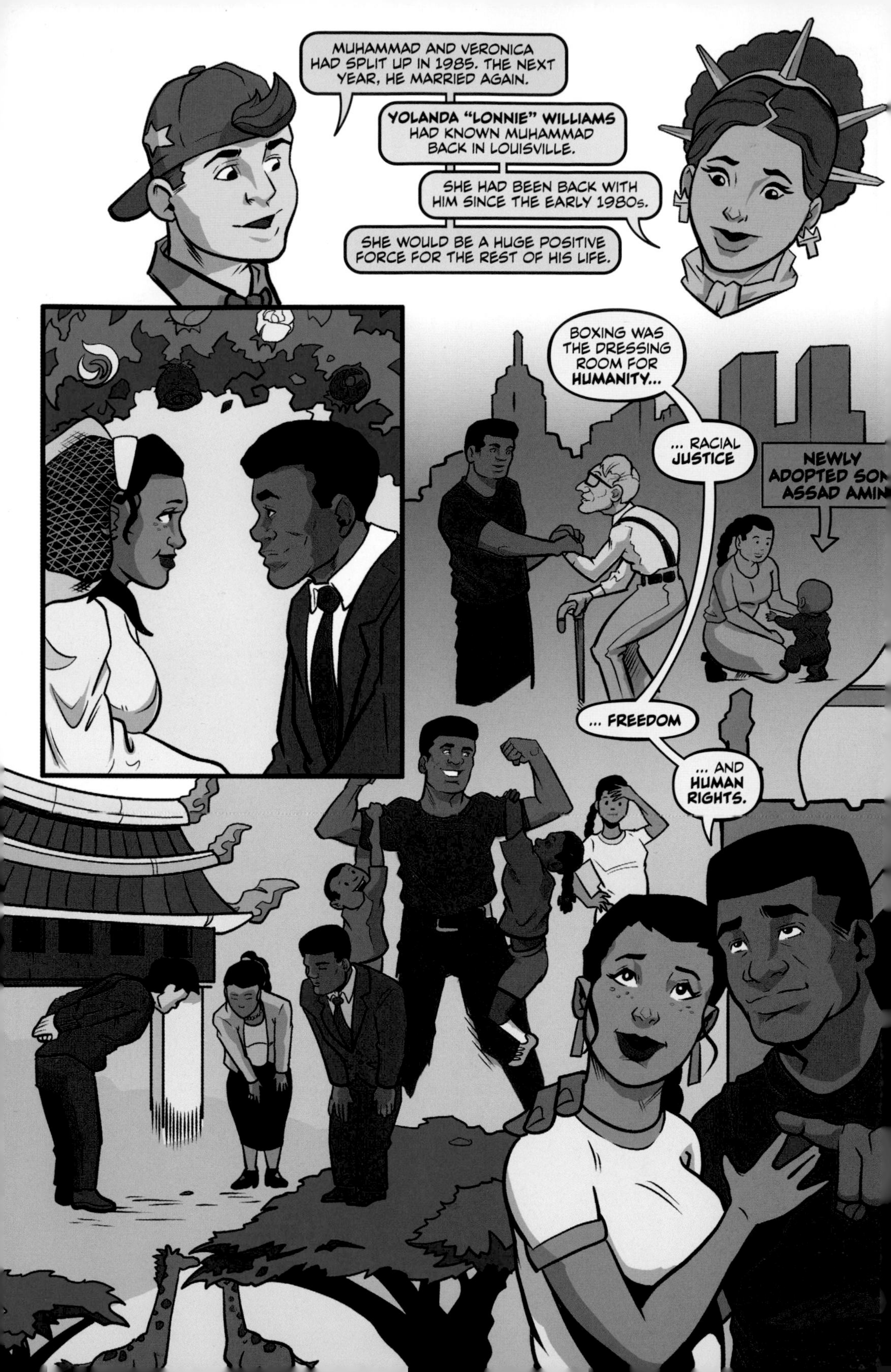

MUHAMMAD AND VERONICA HAD SPLIT UP IN 1985. THE NEXT YEAR, HE MARRIED AGAIN.
YOLANDA "LONNIE" WILLIAMS HAD KNOWN MUHAMMAD BACK IN LOUISVILLE.
SHE HAD BEEN BACK WITH HIM SINCE THE EARLY 1980s.
SHE WOULD BE A HUGE POSITIVE FORCE FOR THE REST OF HIS LIFE.
BOXING WAS THE DRESSING ROOM FOR HUMANITY...
... RACIAL JUSTICE
NEWLY ADOPTED SON ASSAD AMIN
... FREEDOM
... AND HUMAN RIGHTS.

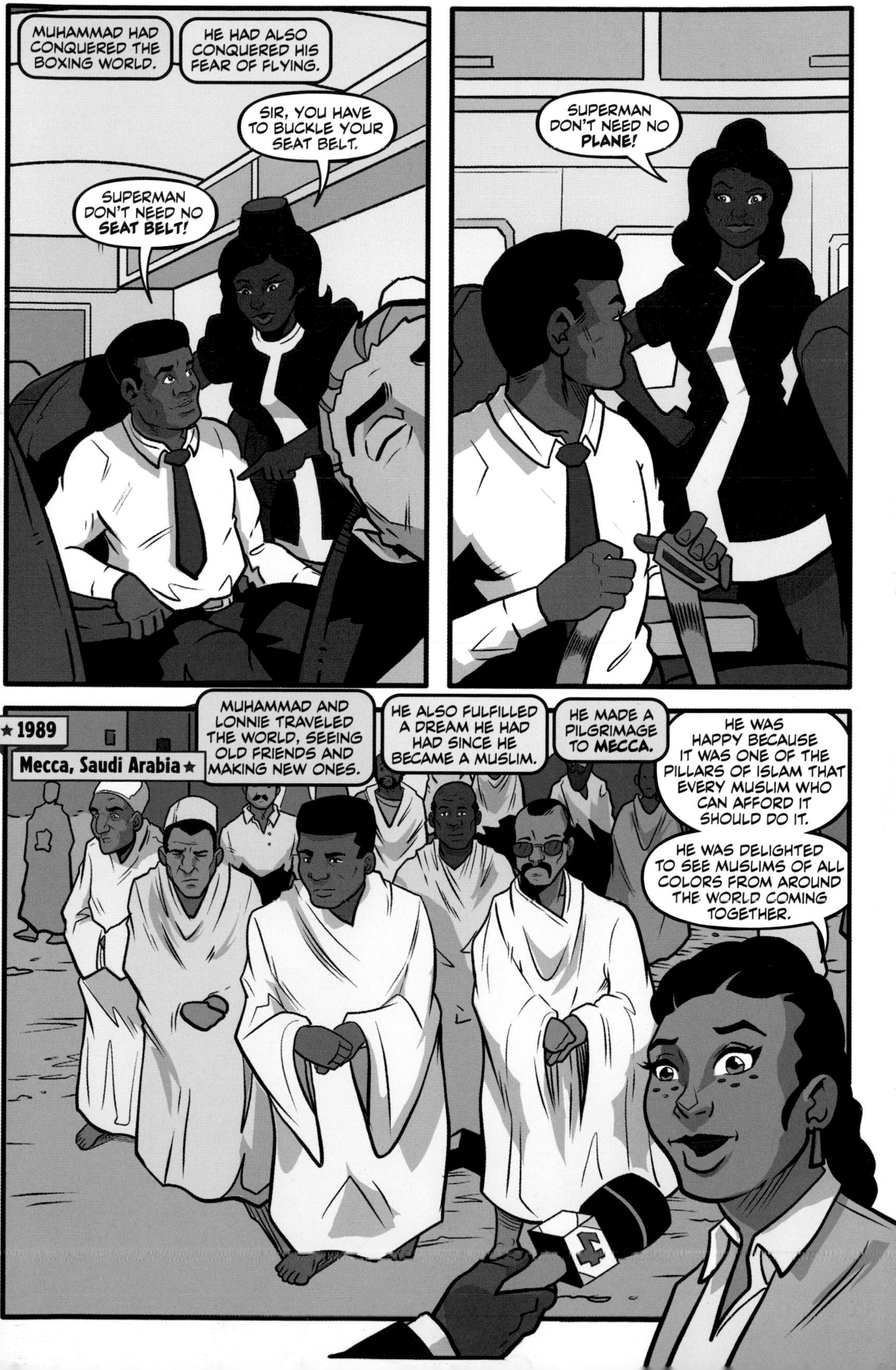
MUHAMMAD HAD CONQUERED THE BOXING WORLD.
HE HAD ALSO CONQUERED HIS FEAR OF FLYING.
SIR, YOU HAVE TO BUCKLE YOUR SEAT BELT.
SUPERMAN DON'T NEED NO SEAT BELT!
SUPERMAN DON'T NEED NO PLANE!
1989
Mecca, Saudi Arabia
MUHAMMAD AND LONNIE TRAVELED THE WORLD, SEEING OLD FRIENDS AND MAKING NEW ONES.
HE ALSO FULFILLED A DREAM HE HAD HAD SINCE HE BECAME A MUSLIM.
HE MADE A PILGRIMAGE TO MECCA.
HE WAS HAPPY BECAUSE IT WAS ONE OF THE PILLARS OF ISLAM THAT EVERY MUSLIM WHO CAN AFFORD IT SHOULD DO IT.
HE WAS DELIGHTED TO SEE MUSLIMS OF ALL COLORS FROM AROUND THE WORLD COMING TOGETHER.

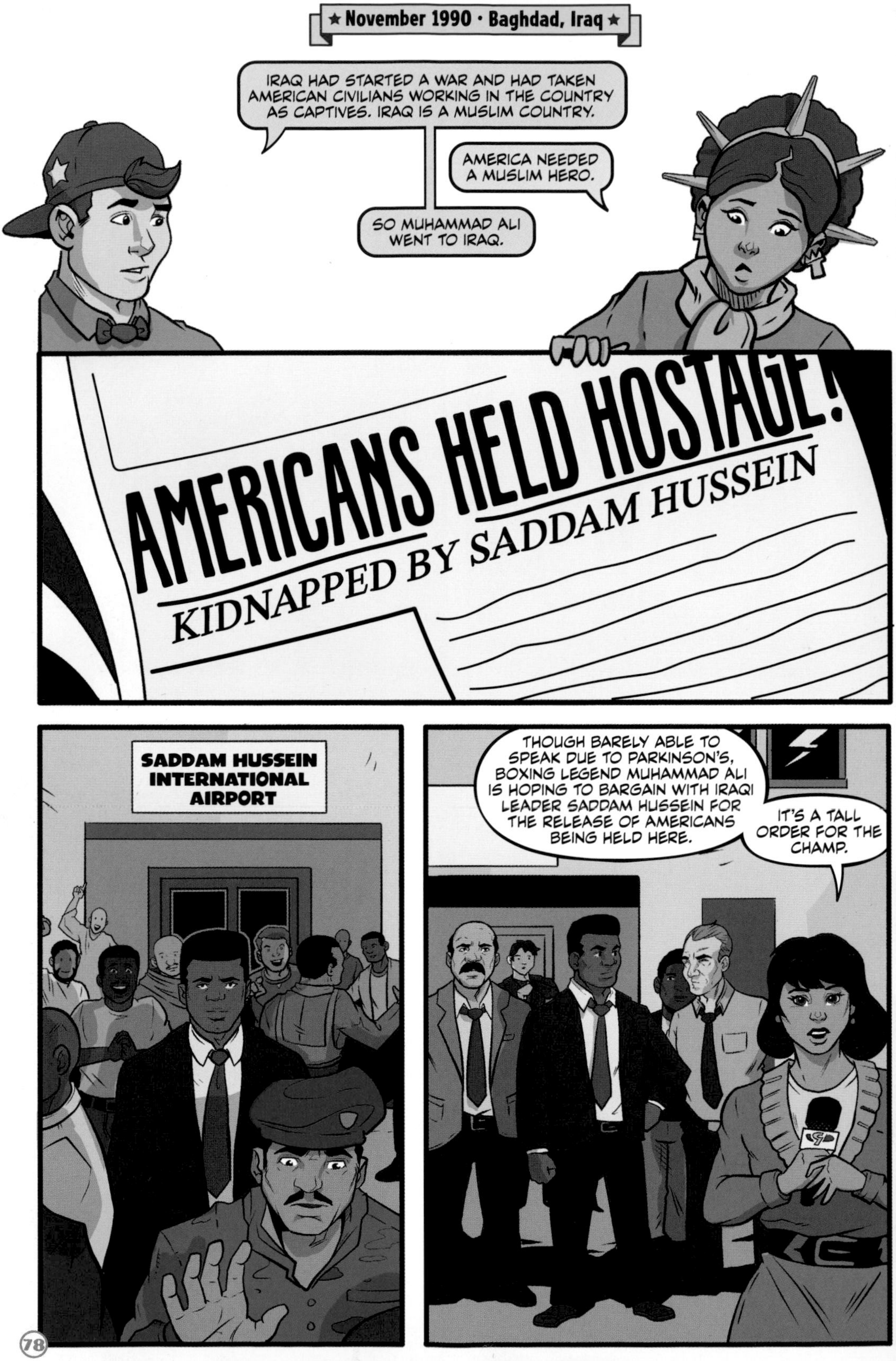
★ November 1990 · Baghdad, Iraq ★
IRAQ HAD STARTED A WAR AND HAD TAKEN AMERICAN CIVILIANS WORKING IN THE COUNTRY AS CAPTIVES. IRAQ IS A MUSLIM COUNTRY.
AMERICA NEEDED A MUSLIM HERO.
SO MUHAMMAD ALI WENT TO IRAQ.
AMERICANS HELD HOSTAGE!
KIDNAPPED BY SADDAM HUSSEIN
SADDAM HUSSEIN INTERNATIONAL AIRPORT
THOUGH BARELY ABLE TO SPEAK DUE TO PARKINSON'S, BOXING LEGEND MUHAMMAD ALI IS HOPING TO BARGAIN WITH IRAQI LEADER SADDAM HUSSEIN FOR THE RELEASE OF AMERICANS BEING HELD HERE.
IT'S A TALL ORDER FOR THE CHAMP.

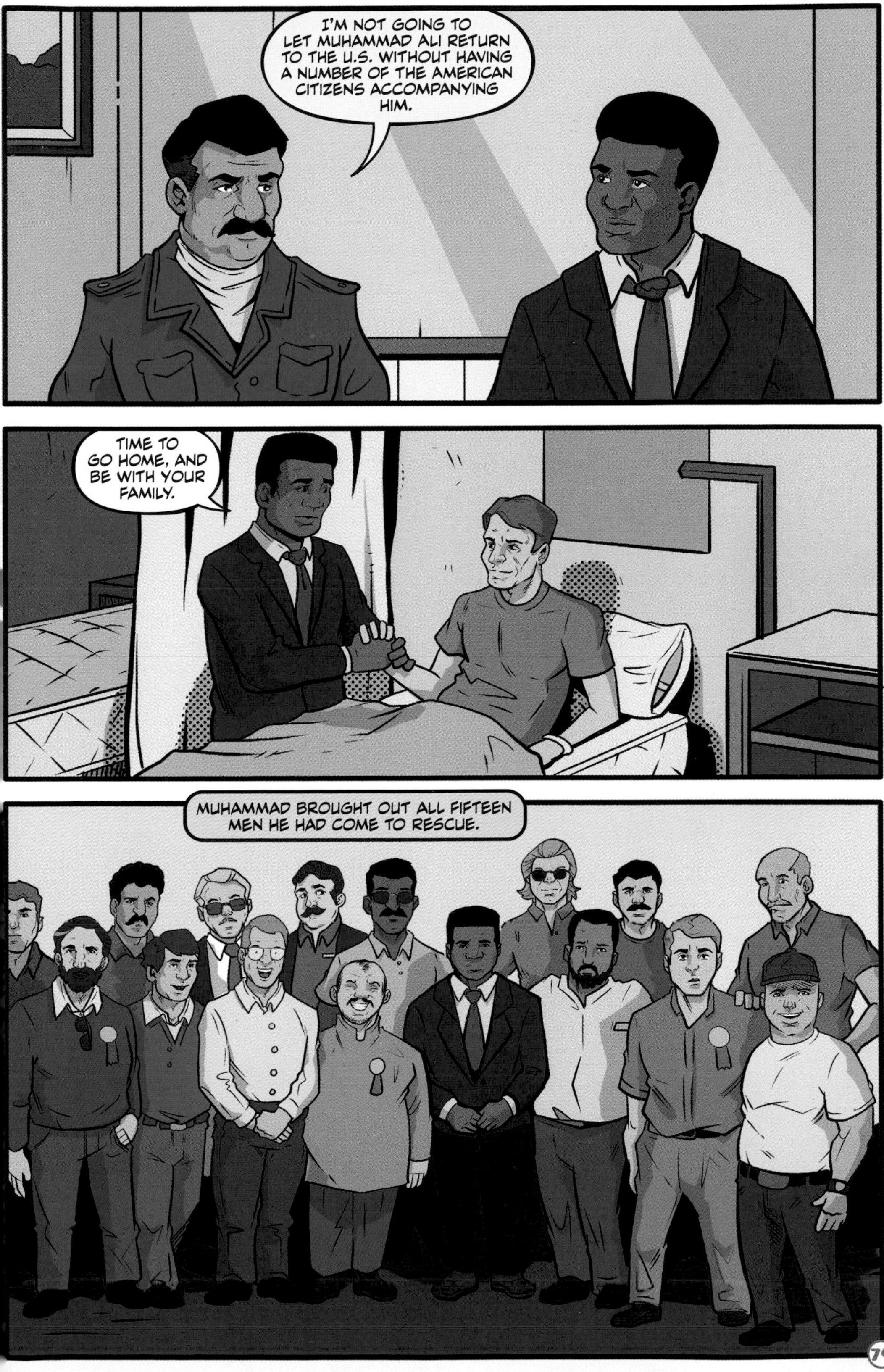
I'M NOT GOING TO LET MUHAMMAD ALI RETURN TO THE U.S. WITHOUT HAVING A NUMBER OF THE AMERICAN CITIZENS ACCOMPANYING HIM.
TIME TO GO HOME, AND BE WITH YOUR FAMILY.
MUHAMMAD BROUGHT OUT ALL FIFTEEN MEN HE HAD COME TO RESCUE.

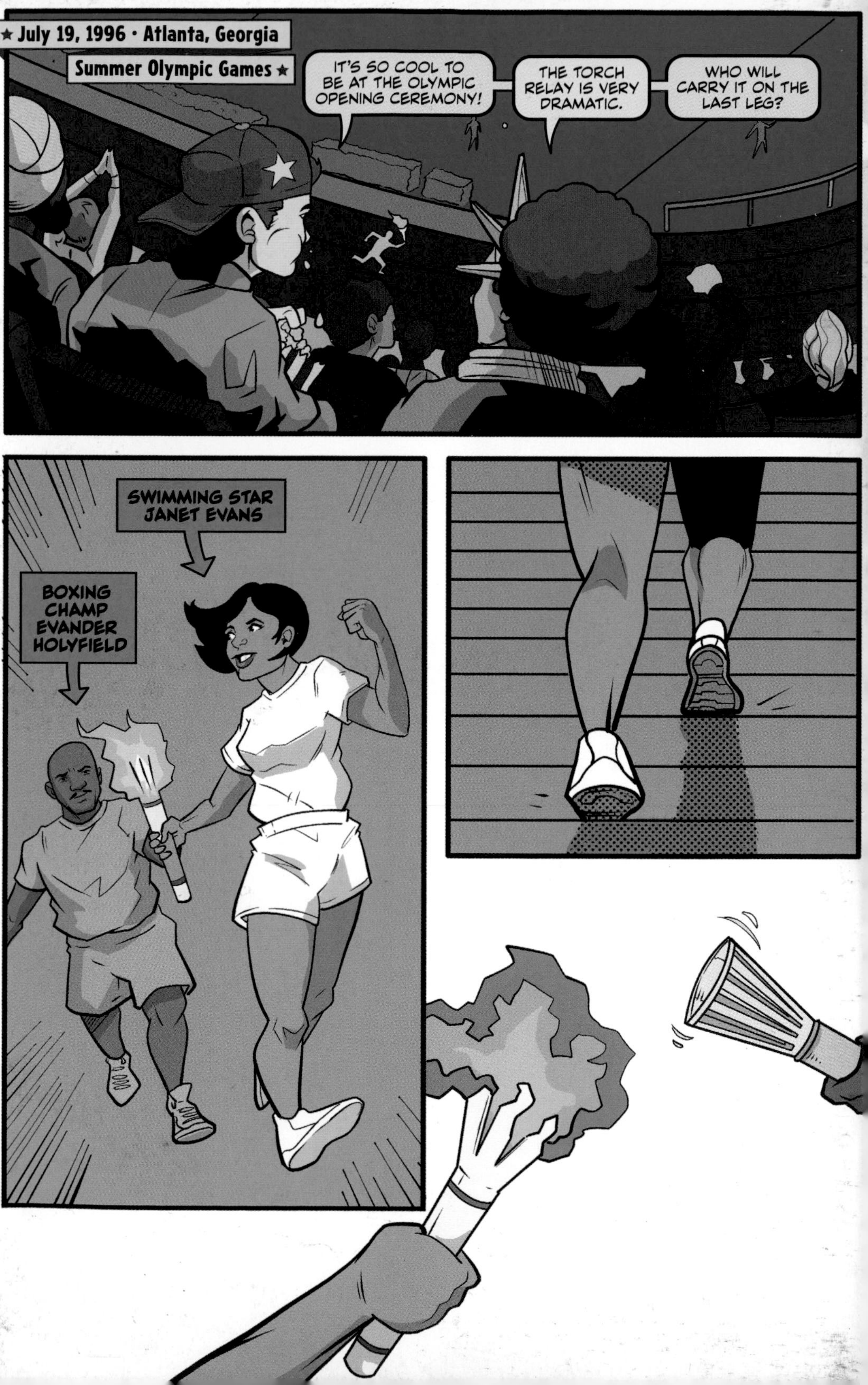
★ July 19, 1996 • Atlanta, Georgia
Summer Olympic Games ★
IT'S SO COOL TO BE AT THE OLYMPIC OPENING CEREMONY!
THE TORCH RELAY IS VERY DRAMATIC.
WHO WILL CARRY IT ON THE LAST LEG?
SWIMMING STAR JANET EVANS
BOXING CHAMP EVANDER HOLYFIELD

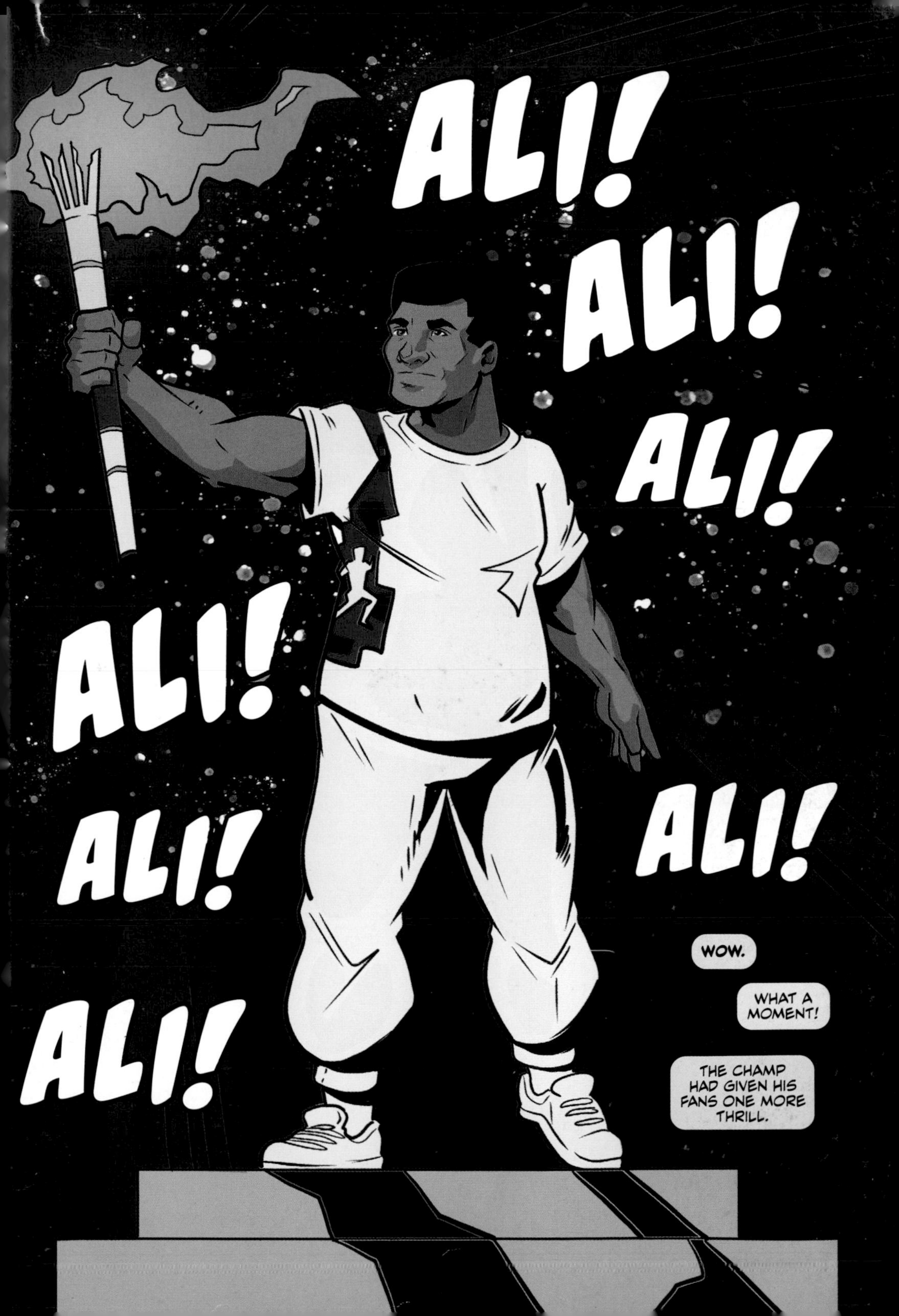
ALI!
ALI!
ALI!
ALI!
ALI!
ALI!
ALI!
WOW.
WHAT A MOMENT!
THE CHAMP HAD GIVEN HIS FANS ONE MORE THRILL.

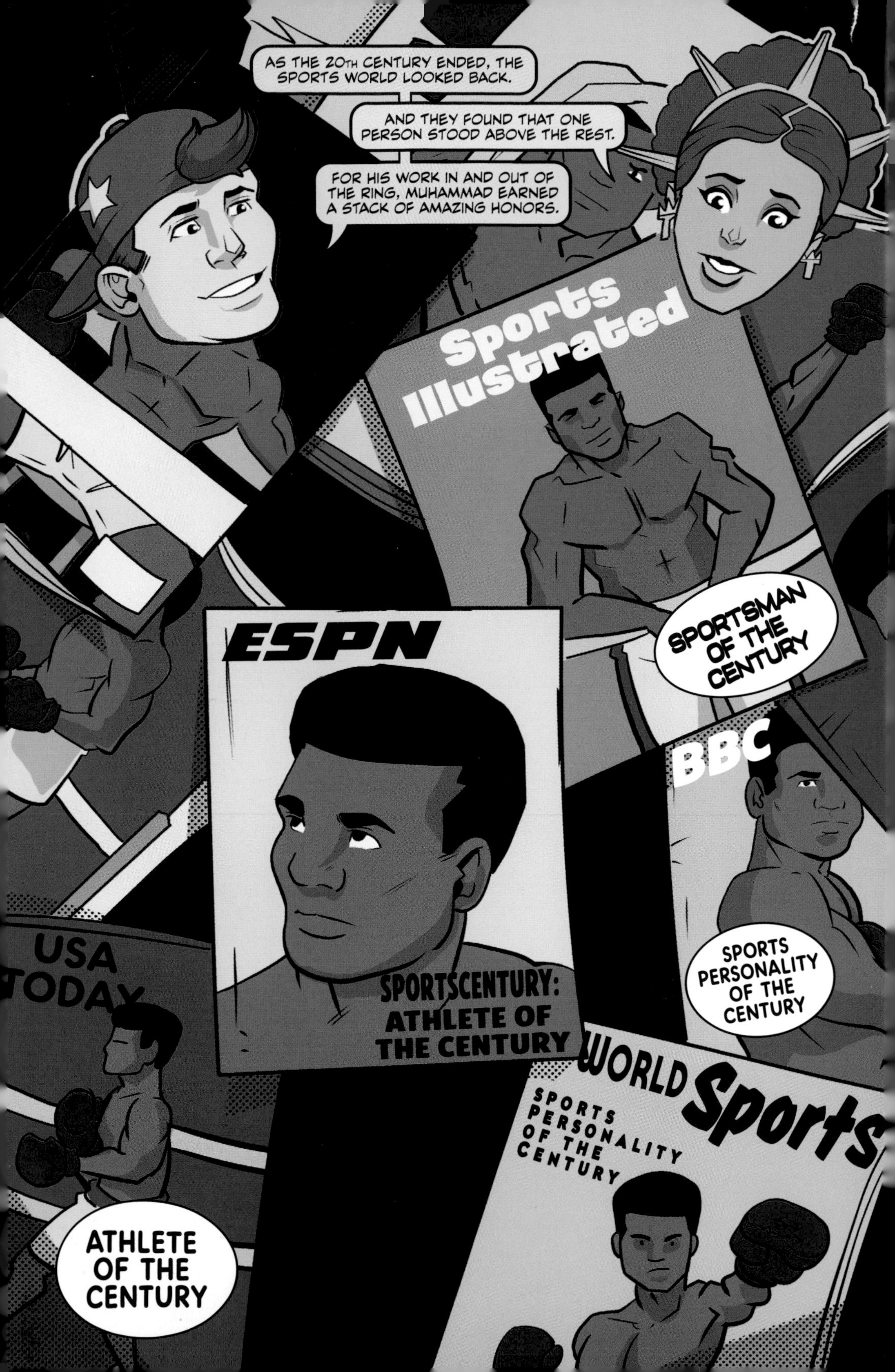
AS THE 20TH CENTURY ENDED, THE SPORTS WORLD LOOKED BACK.
AND THEY FOUND THAT ONE PERSON STOOD ABOVE THE REST.
FOR HIS WORK IN AND OUT OF THE RING, MUHAMMAD EARNED A STACK OF AMAZING HONORS.
Sports Illustrated
SPORTSMAN OF THE CENTURY
ESPN
SPORTSCENTURY: ATHLETE OF THE CENTURY
BBC
SPORTS PERSONALITY OF THE CENTURY
USA TODAY
ATHLETE OF THE CENTURY
WORLD Sports
SPORTS PERSONALITY OF THE CENTURY

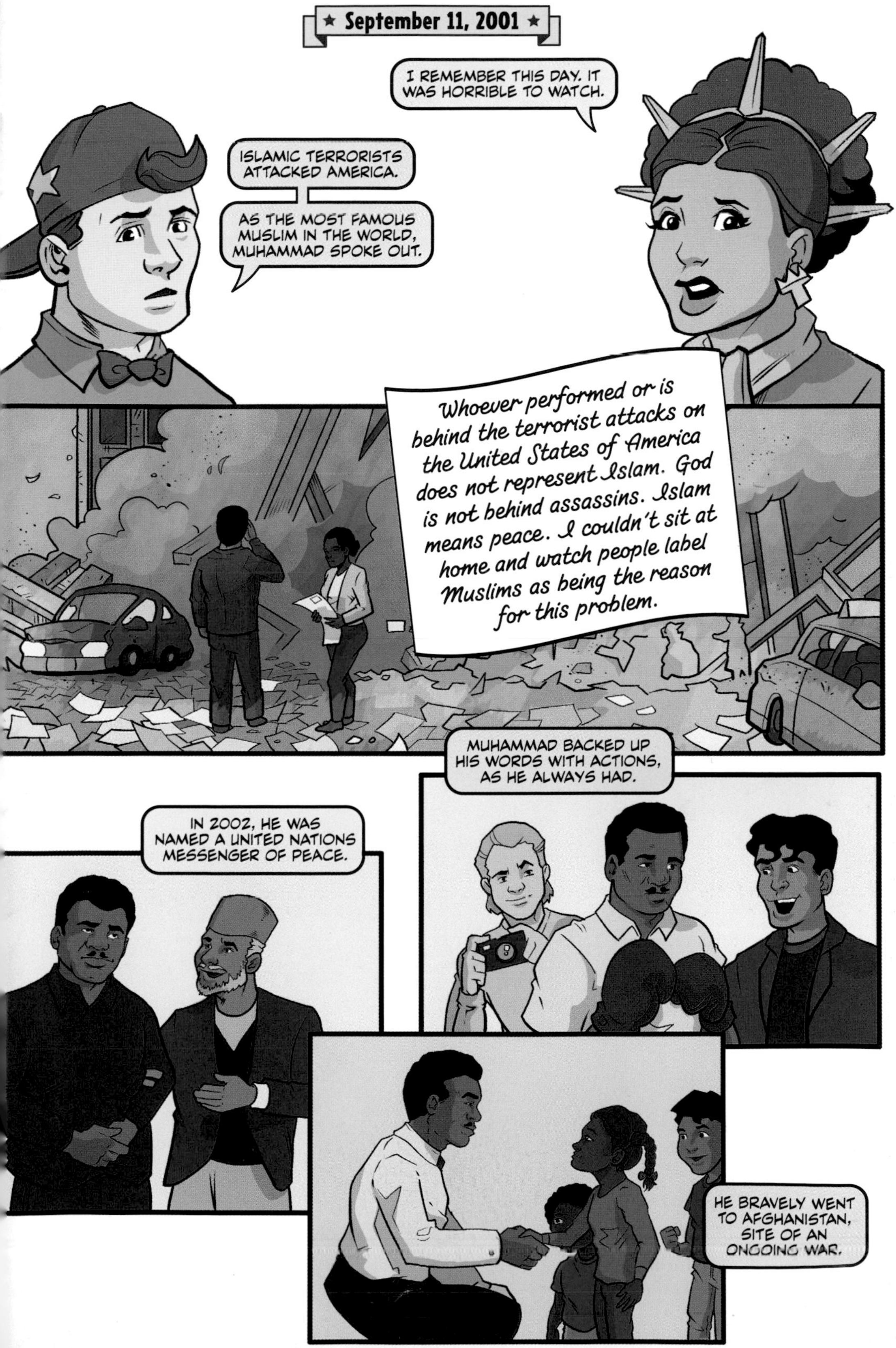
September 11, 2001
I REMEMBER THIS DAY. IT WAS HORRIBLE TO WATCH.
ISLAMIC TERRORISTS ATTACKED AMERICA.
AS THE MOST FAMOUS MUSLIM IN THE WORLD, MUHAMMAD SPOKE OUT.
Whoever performed or is behind the terrorist attacks on the United States of America does not represent Islam. God is not behind assassins. Islam means peace. I couldn't sit at home and watch people label Muslims as being the reason for this problem.
MUHAMMAD BACKED UP HIS WORDS WITH ACTIONS, AS HE ALWAYS HAD.
IN 2002, HE WAS NAMED A UNITED NATIONS MESSENGER OF PEACE.
HE BRAVELY WENT TO AFGHANISTAN, SITE OF AN ONGOING WAR.

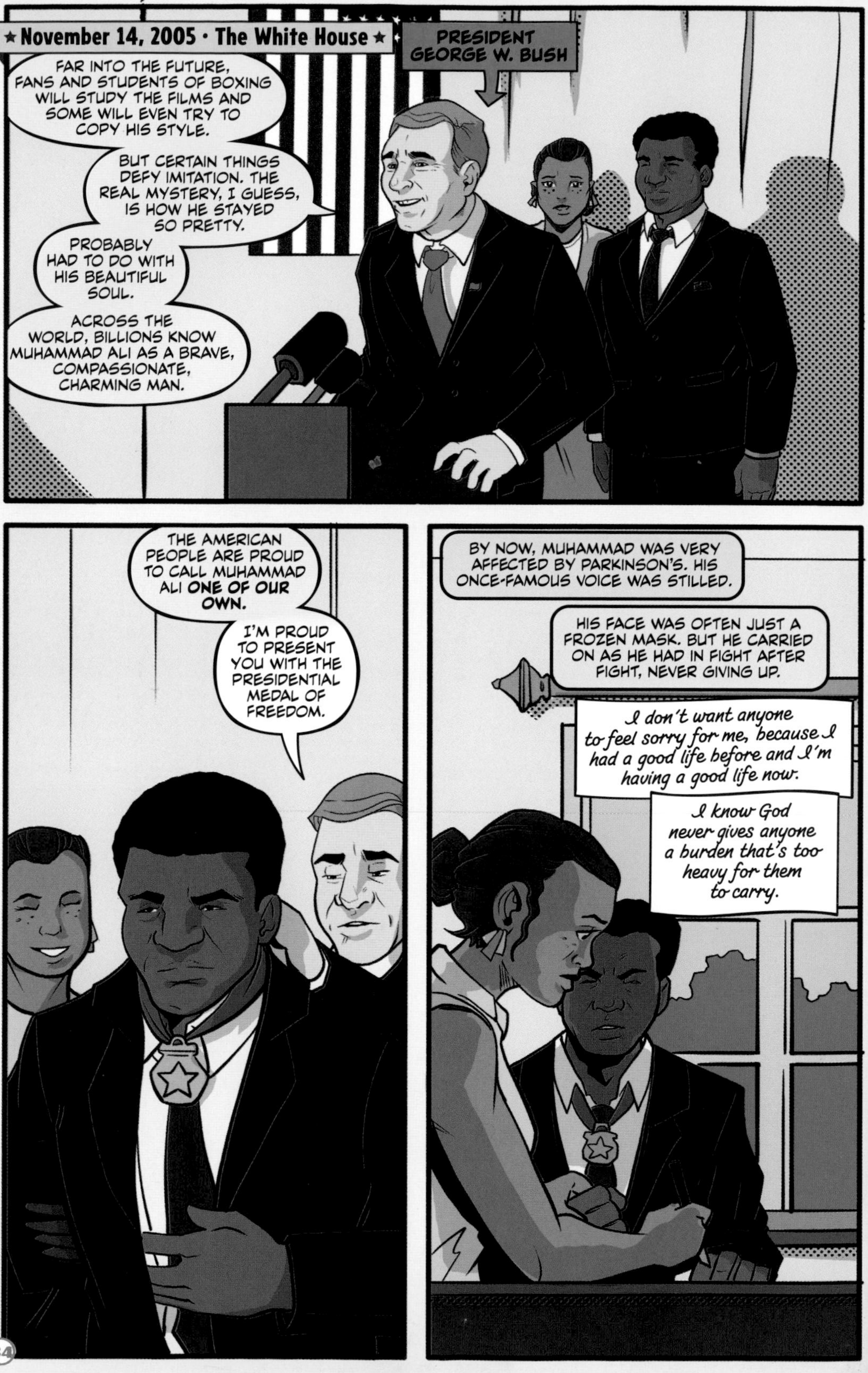
November 14, 2005 · The White House
PRESIDENT GEORGE W. BUSH
FAR INTO THE FUTURE, FANS AND STUDENTS OF BOXING WILL STUDY THE FILMS AND SOME WILL EVEN TRY TO COPY HIS STYLE.
BUT CERTAIN THINGS DEFY IMITATION. THE REAL MYSTERY, I GUESS, IS HOW HE STAYED SO PRETTY.
PROBABLY HAD TO DO WITH HIS BEAUTIFUL SOUL.
ACROSS THE WORLD, BILLIONS KNOW MUHAMMAD ALI AS A BRAVE, COMPASSIONATE, CHARMING MAN.
THE AMERICAN PEOPLE ARE PROUD TO CALL MUHAMMAD ALI ONE OF OUR OWN.
I'M PROUD TO PRESENT YOU WITH THE PRESIDENTIAL MEDAL OF FREEDOM.
BY NOW, MUHAMMAD WAS VERY AFFECTED BY PARKINSON'S. HIS ONCE-FAMOUS VOICE WAS STILLED.
HIS FACE WAS OFTEN JUST A FROZEN MASK. BUT HE CARRIED ON AS HE HAD IN FIGHT AFTER FIGHT, NEVER GIVING UP.
I don't want anyone to feel sorry for me, because I had a good life before and I'm having a good life now.
I know God never gives anyone a burden that's too heavy for them to carry.

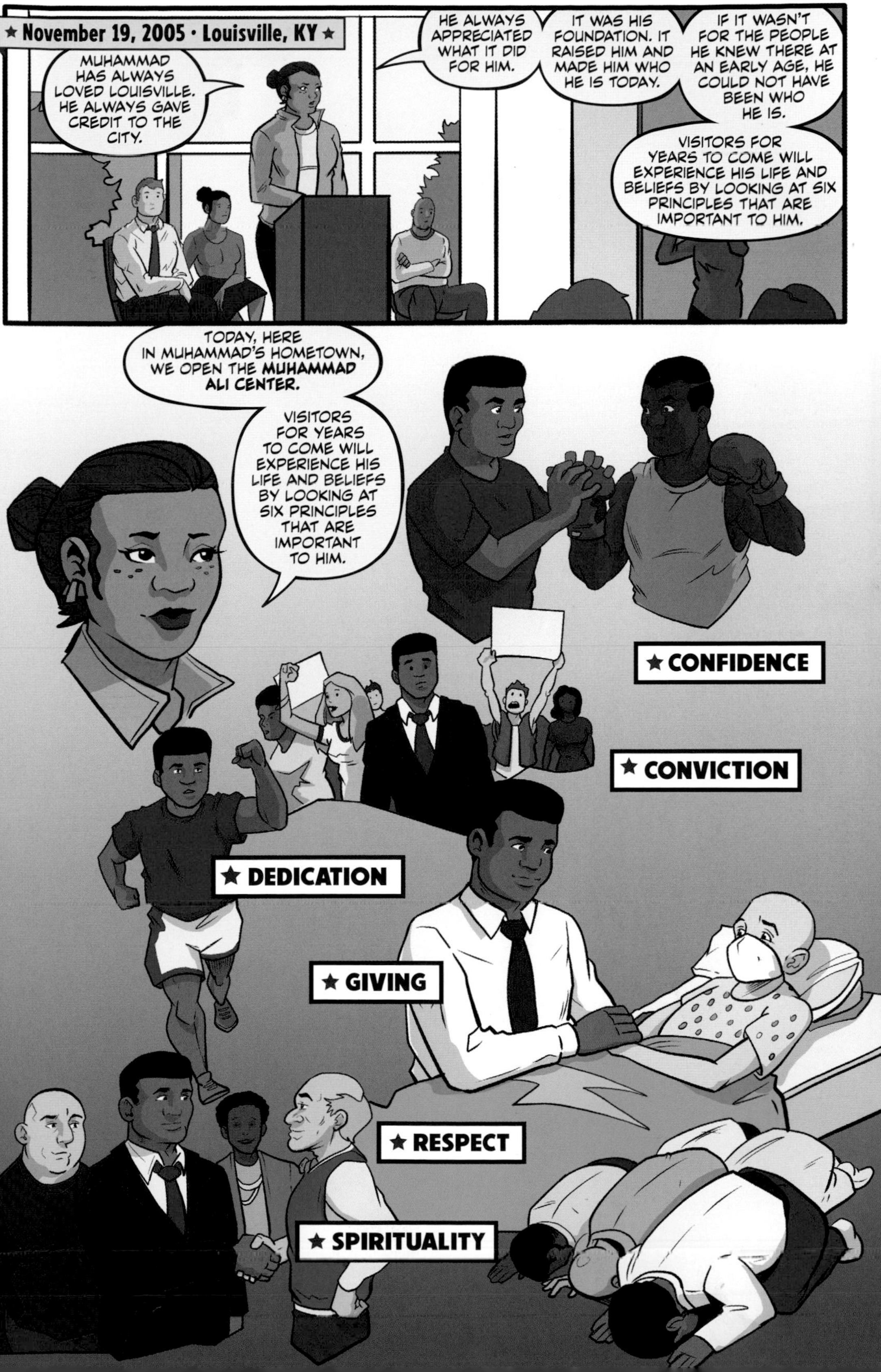
★ November 19, 2005 · Louisville, KY ★
MUHAMMAD HAS ALWAYS LOVED LOUISVILLE. HE ALWAYS GAVE CREDIT TO THE CITY.
HE ALWAYS APPRECIATED WHAT IT DID FOR HIM.
IT WAS HIS FOUNDATION. IT RAISED HIM AND MADE HIM WHO HE IS TODAY.
IF IT WASN'T FOR THE PEOPLE HE KNEW THERE AT AN EARLY AGE, HE COULD NOT HAVE BEEN WHO HE IS.
VISITORS FOR YEARS TO COME WILL EXPERIENCE HIS LIFE AND BELIEFS BY LOOKING AT SIX PRINCIPLES THAT ARE IMPORTANT TO HIM.
TODAY, HERE IN MUHAMMAD'S HOMETOWN, WE OPEN THE **MUHAMMAD ALI CENTER.**
VISITORS FOR YEARS TO COME WILL EXPERIENCE HIS LIFE AND BELIEFS BY LOOKING AT SIX PRINCIPLES THAT ARE IMPORTANT TO HIM.
★ CONFIDENCE
★ CONVICTION
★ DEDICATION
★ GIVING
★ RESPECT
★ SPIRITUALITY

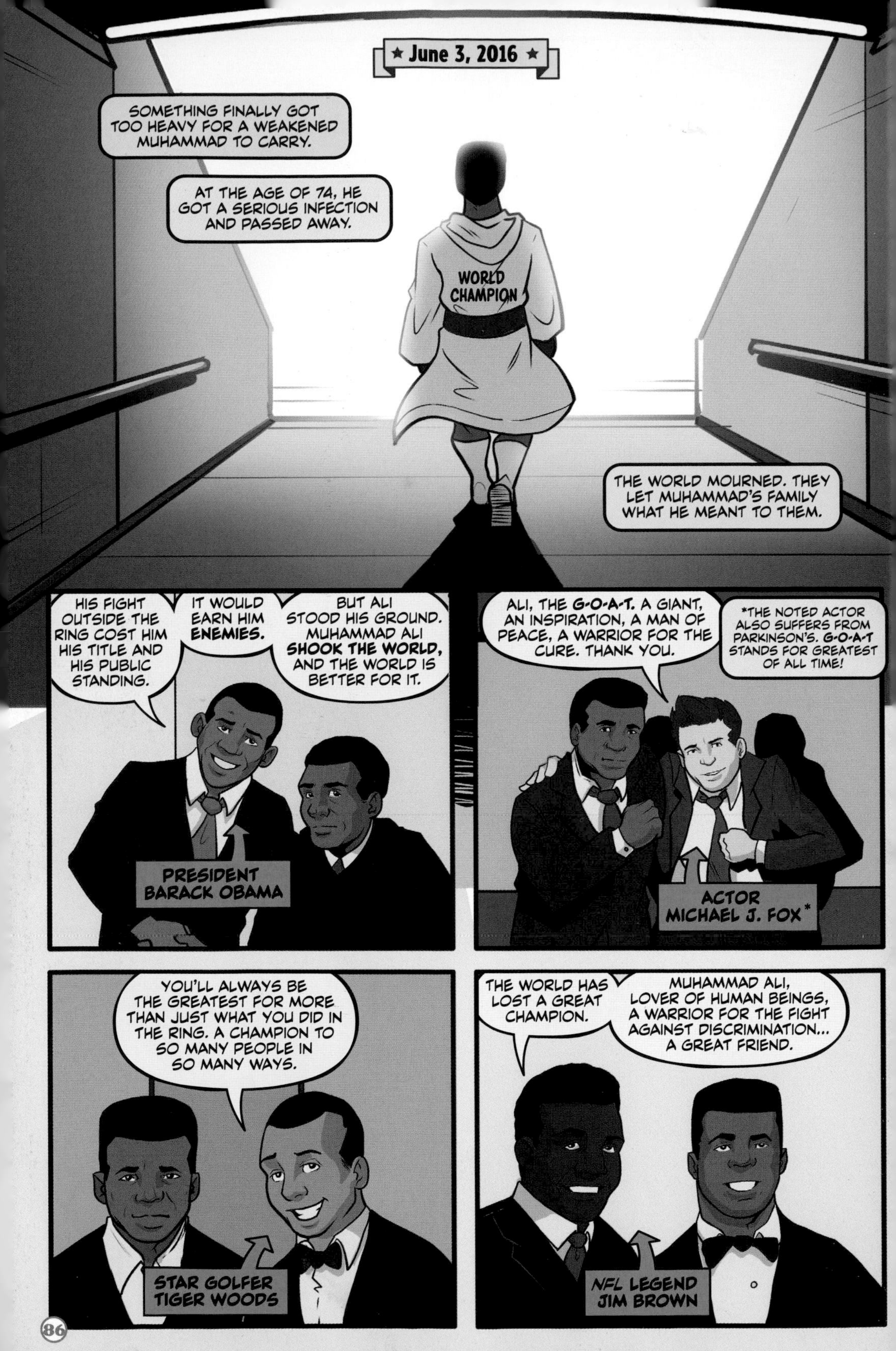
★ June 3, 2016 ★
SOMETHING FINALLY GOT TOO HEAVY FOR A WEAKENED MUHAMMAD TO CARRY.
AT THE AGE OF 74, HE GOT A SERIOUS INFECTION AND PASSED AWAY.
WORLD CHAMPION
THE WORLD MOURNED. THEY LET MUHAMMAD'S FAMILY WHAT HE MEANT TO THEM.
HIS FIGHT OUTSIDE THE RING COST HIM HIS TITLE AND HIS PUBLIC STANDING.
IT WOULD EARN HIM ENEMIES.
BUT ALI STOOD HIS GROUND. MUHAMMAD ALI SHOOK THE WORLD, AND THE WORLD IS BETTER FOR IT.
PRESIDENT BARACK OBAMA
ALI, THE G-O-A-T. A GIANT, AN INSPIRATION, A MAN OF PEACE, A WARRIOR FOR THE CURE. THANK YOU.
*THE NOTED ACTOR ALSO SUFFERS FROM PARKINSON'S. G-O-A-T STANDS FOR GREATEST OF ALL TIME!
ACTOR MICHAEL J. FOX*
YOU'LL ALWAYS BE THE GREATEST FOR MORE THAN JUST WHAT YOU DID IN THE RING. A CHAMPION TO SO MANY PEOPLE IN SO MANY WAYS.
STAR GOLFER TIGER WOODS
THE WORLD HAS LOST A GREAT CHAMPION.
MUHAMMAD ALI, LOVER OF HUMAN BEINGS, A WARRIOR FOR THE FIGHT AGAINST DISCRIMINATION... A GREAT FRIEND.
NFL LEGEND JIM BROWN

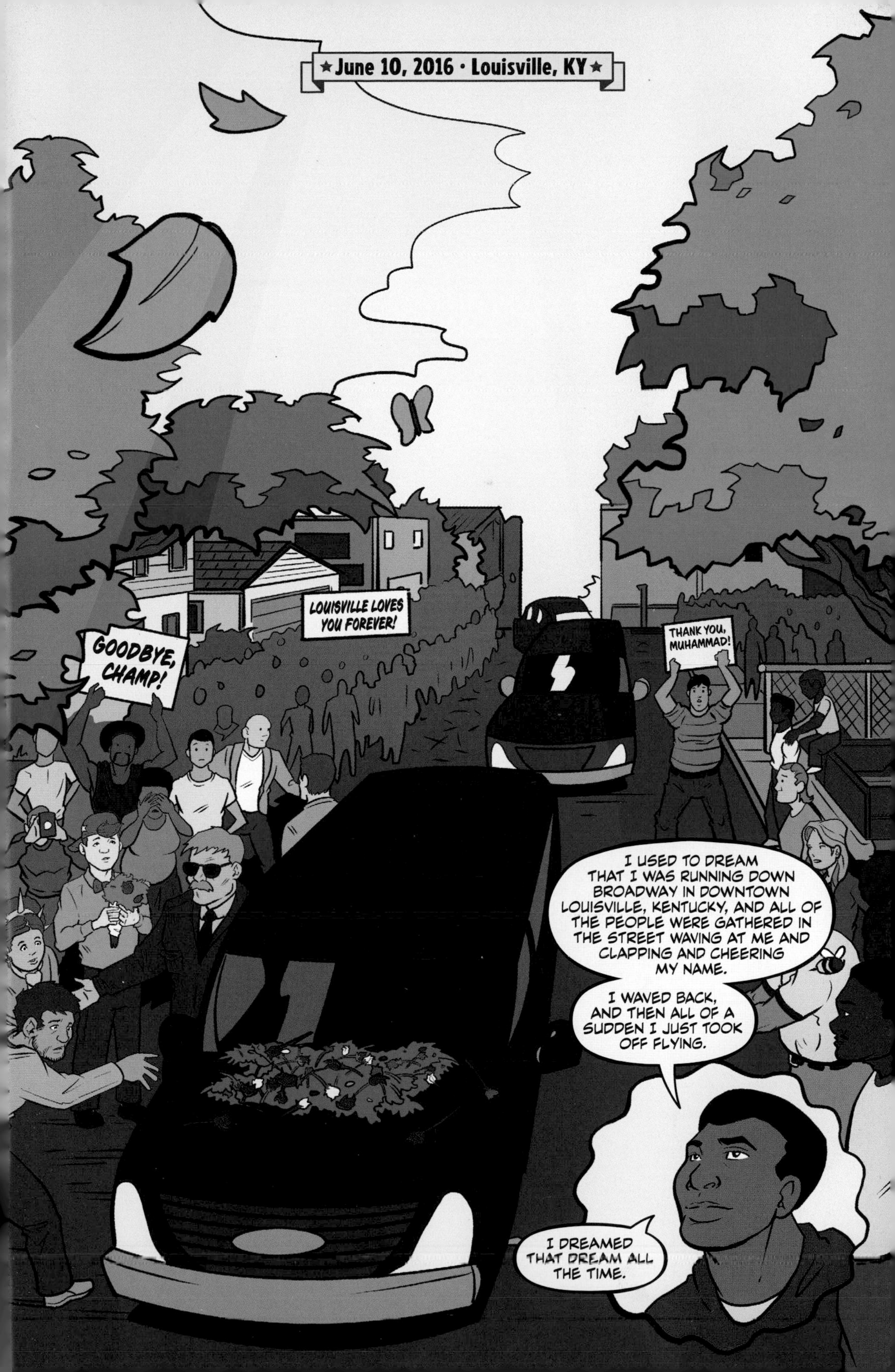
★June 10, 2016 • Louisville, KY★
GOODBYE, CHAMP!
LOUISVILLE LOVES YOU FOREVER!
THANK YOU, MUHAMMAD!
I USED TO DREAM THAT I WAS RUNNING DOWN BROADWAY IN DOWNTOWN LOUISVILLE, KENTUCKY, AND ALL OF THE PEOPLE WERE GATHERED IN THE STREET WAVING AT ME AND CLAPPING AND CHEERING MY NAME.
I WAVED BACK, AND THEN ALL OF A SUDDEN I JUST TOOK OFF FLYING.
I DREAMED THAT DREAM ALL THE TIME.

 IN 2016, ESPN CREATED THE **MUHAMMAD ALI SPORTS HUMANITARIAN AWARD** TO HONOR PEOPLE WHO CARRIED ON THE CHAMP'S SPIRIT.

SPORTS ILLUSTRATED ALSO RENAMED ITS LEGACY AWARD AFTER ALI IN 2016. AND THE **MUHAMMAD ALI CENTER** NAMES HUMANITARIANS OF THE YEAR IN DIFFERENT FIELDS.

HERE ARE JUST A FEW OF THE WINNERS OF THESE IMPORTANT AWARDS...

MICHAEL J. FOX 2019 ALI CENTER

★ ACTOR WHO LED FIGHT FOR PARKINSON'S CURE

JOHN CENA (*WWE*) 2018 *SPORTS ILLUSTRATED*

★ CAREER-LONG SUPPORT OF MAKE-A-WISH FOUNDATION

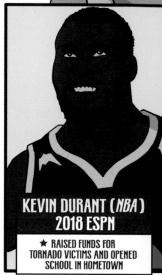

KEVIN DURANT (*NBA*) 2018 ESPN

★ RAISED FUNDS FOR TORNADO VICTIMS AND OPENED SCHOOL IN HOMETOWN

JON SECADA (SINGER) 2017 ALI CENTER

★ SUPPORTED AIDS RESEARCH CHARITIES AND HELPED HISPANIC YOUTH

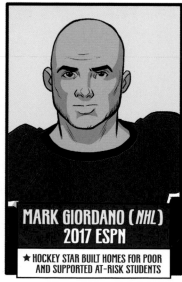

MARK GIORDANO (*NHL*) 2017 ESPN

★ HOCKEY STAR BUILT HOMES FOR POOR AND SUPPORTED AT-RISK STUDENTS

TAMIKA CATCHINGS (*WNBA*), 2015 ESPN

★ OVERCAME HEARING DIFFICULTIES TO BECOME A STAR AND AN INSPIRATION

NEWS FLASH! IN 2019, LOUISVILLE RENAMED ITS CITY AIRPORT AFTER **MUHAMMAD ALI!**

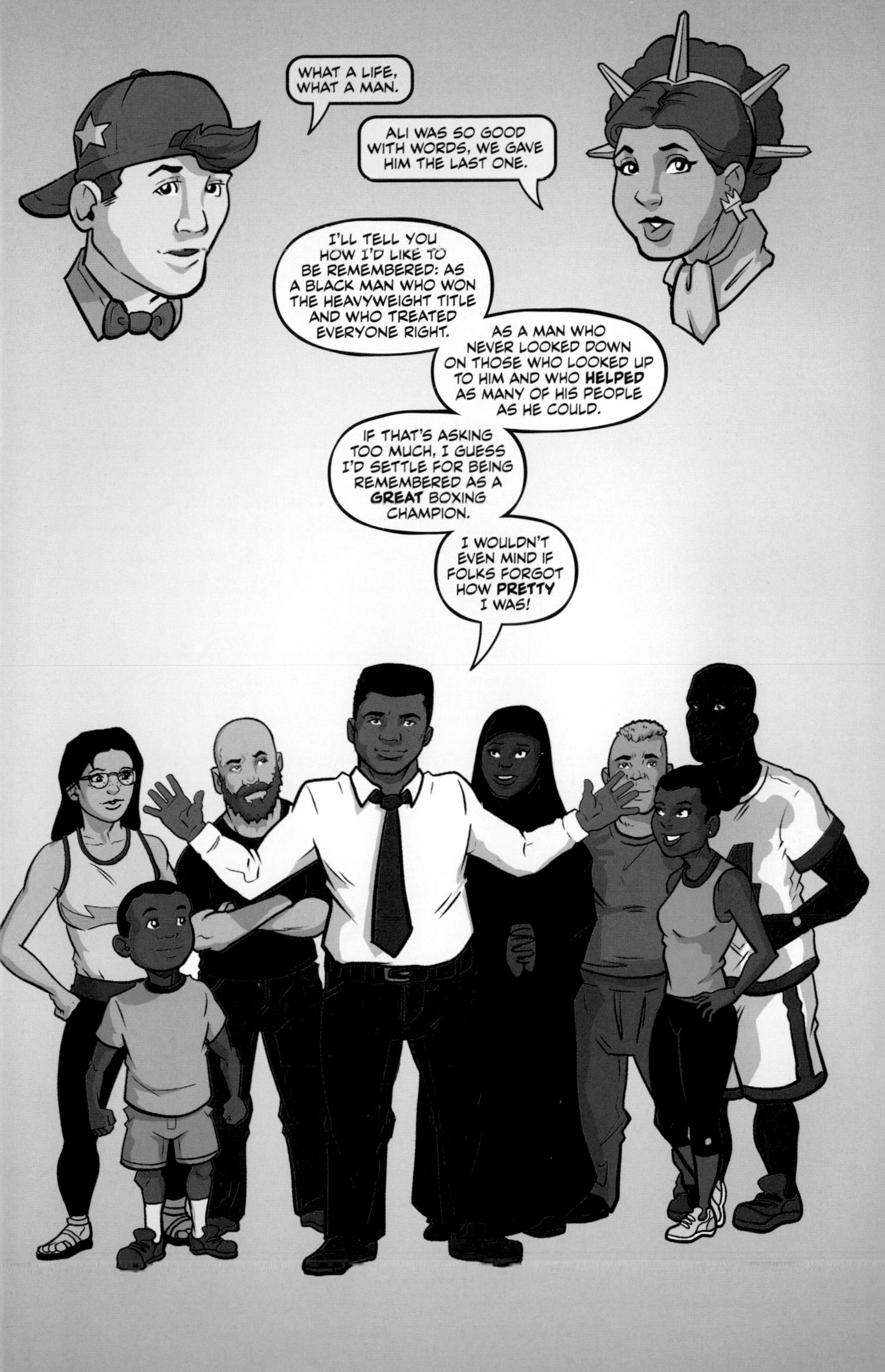
WHAT A LIFE, WHAT A MAN.
ALI WAS SO GOOD WITH WORDS, WE GAVE HIM THE LAST ONE.
I'LL TELL YOU HOW I'D LIKE TO BE REMEMBERED: AS A BLACK MAN WHO WON THE HEAVYWEIGHT TITLE AND WHO TREATED EVERYONE RIGHT.
AS A MAN WHO NEVER LOOKED DOWN ON THOSE WHO LOOKED UP TO HIM AND WHO **HELPED** AS MANY OF HIS PEOPLE AS HE COULD.
IF THAT'S ASKING TOO MUCH, I GUESS I'D SETTLE FOR BEING REMEMBERED AS A **GREAT** BOXING CHAMPION.
I WOULDN'T EVEN MIND IF FOLKS FORGOT HOW **PRETTY** I WAS!

SPORTS PIONEERS

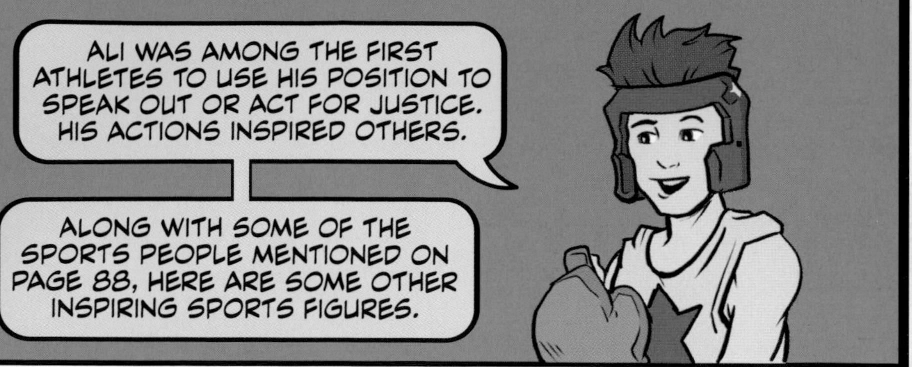
ALI WAS AMONG THE FIRST ATHLETES TO USE HIS POSITION TO SPEAK OUT OR ACT FOR JUSTICE. HIS ACTIONS INSPIRED OTHERS.
ALONG WITH SOME OF THE SPORTS PEOPLE MENTIONED ON PAGE 88, HERE ARE SOME OTHER INSPIRING SPORTS FIGURES.

KAREEM ABDUL-JABBAR is a seven-time *NBA* MVP and the league's all-time leading scorer. He used his fame and celebrity to promote African American stories and causes and was named Global Cultural Ambassador by the U.S. government.

ARTHUR ASHE was the first African American man to win major tennis tournaments, and was later an activist for AIDS, the disease that took his life in 1993.

BILLIE JEAN KING was a tennis star who continues to lead fights for the rights of women and members of the LGBTQ community.

MEGAN RAPINOE helped the U.S. Women's National Team win the World Cup in 2015 and 2019 and used her visibility to call for equal pay for women athletes.

The first African American player in *Major League Baseball* in 1947, **JACKIE ROBINSON** courageously fought racism on and off the field.

Though a solid *NFL* star, **PAT TILLMAN** gave up his career to join the U.S. Army in 2002 following the 9-11 attacks; he was killed in combat in 2004.

VENUS WILLIAMS is a superstar tennis player who fought for equal pay for women at important tournaments, such as Wimbledon in England.

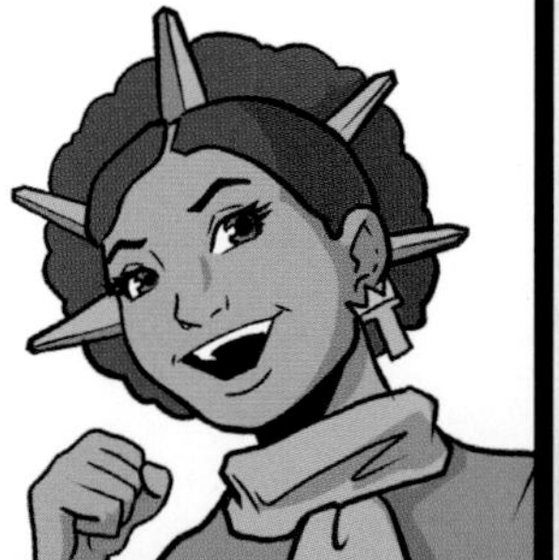

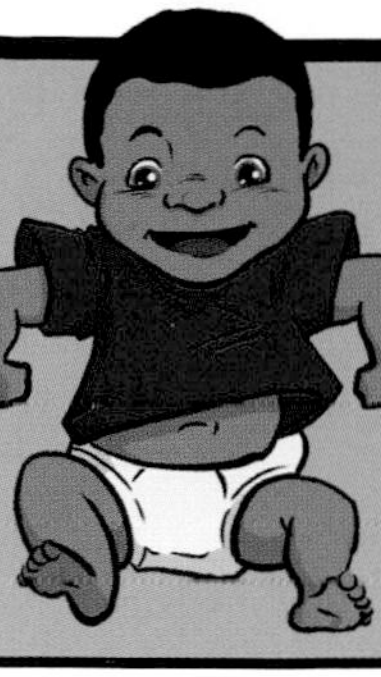

MUHAMMAD ALI TIMELINE

1942	Cassius Clay is born in Louisville, Kentucky.
1954	Clay boxes for the first time.
1960	He wins the Olympic light-heavyweight gold medal in Rome.
1964	He wins world heavyweight championship by beating Sonny Liston and changes his name to Muhammad Ali.
1967	After refusing to enlist in the Army, Ali is arrested and banned from boxing.
1970	He returns to boxing; his arrest is later overturned by the Supreme Court.
1971	Ali loses the "Fight of the Century" to Joe Frazier.
1974	In Zaire, Ali gets his heavyweight title back by beating George Foreman.
1978	Ali loses to and then defeats Leon Spinks to regain title for third time.
1981	Ali retires from boxing.
1984	The retired champ is diagnosed with Parkinson's syndrome.
1996	Shocking the world again, he lights the torch to open Summer Olympics in Atlanta.
2005	Ali is awarded the Presidential Medal of Freedom.
2016	Muhammad Ali dies.

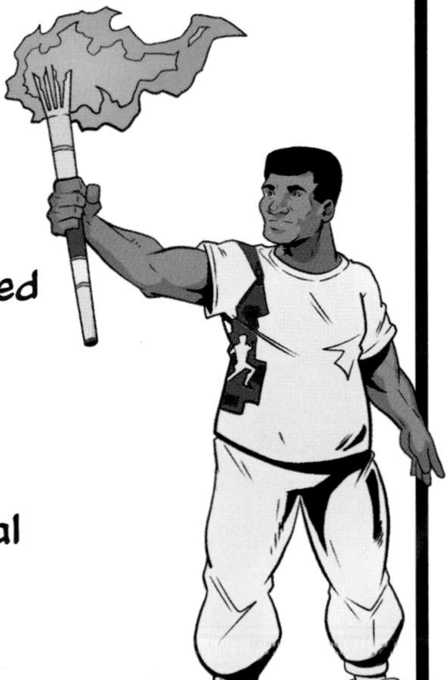

GLOSSARY

ALLAH: The name of God in Islam.

AMATEUR: An athlete who takes part without earning money.

APPEALED: Asked a court to reconsider an earlier judgment.

CONSCIENTIOUS OBJECTOR: A person who refused to take part in the military due to their religious beliefs.

CONVICTION: In this meaning, the process of being found guilty of a crime.

EVASION: The avoiding of something.

EXPENSES: Money that is needed to live on.

INDUCTED: In this meaning, called by law to join the armed forces.

PILGRIMAGE: A journey with a religious purpose.

SEGREGATED: Separated based on race or ethnicity.

SYNDROME: A physical condition that resembles a disease.

UNANIMOUS: Agreed to by all voting parties.

VIETCONG: The name of the Communist rebels that fought in the Vietnam War.

FIND OUT MORE

BOOKS

Buckley, James, Jr. *Muhammad Ali.* Trailblazers of the Modern World. New York: World Almanac, 2004.

Buckley, James, Jr. *Who Was Muhammad Ali?* Who Was series. New York: Penguin Workshop, 2016.

Myers, Walter Dean. *The Greatest: Muhammad Ali.* New York: Scholastic, 2016.

Smith, Charles R., Jr. *12 Rounds to Glory: The Story of Muhammad Ali.* Boston: Candlewick, 2010.

Timblin, Stephen. *Muhammad Ali: King of the Ring.* New York: Sterling Publishing, 2010.

WEBSITES

ESPN *SportsCentury* Project: The Greatest
http://www.espn.com/classic/alimuhammad.html

International Boxing Hall of Fame
www.ibhof.com

Muhammad Ali Center in Louisville, KY
https://alicenter.org/

VIDEOS

Fuqua, Antoine, dir.
What's My Name: Muhammad Ali.
New York: HBO, 2016.

Lewins, Clare, dir. *I Am Ali.*
Universal City, CA:
Universal Studios, 2014.

SHOW ME HISTORY!

COLLECT EVERY BOOK IN THE SERIES AND FIND THE *STORY* IN HISTORY!